Praise for the work of Verna Mae Weeks:

'The diminutive writer epitomizes history, having lived through a good portion of it and researched and written about considerably more.
    'Her diligence in scouring dust-laden government documents that haven't seen the light of day in up to 250 years, or more, is legendary. Weeks' rummaging of old newspapers, diaries, circulars and even university theses has given her a unique perspective on history – a perspective virtually unknown among many historians.'

    – Mark Holmes, *The Mississauga News*, February 15, 1995

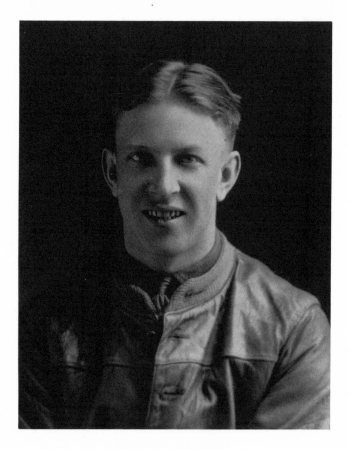

C. A. (Duke) Schiller

A descendant of John Schiller who established Canada's first commercial winery at Cooksville, Ontario, Duke Schiller became a famous bush pilot who helped to map the northlands, carried the early mining prospectors, and completed many rescue missions.

Upon the inauguration of Canada's Air Mail service in May, 1928, he was the pilot of the Transcontinental Airways plane which carried the mail from the Steamship 'Empress of Scotland', on the first leg of the new route, from Rimouski to Montreal. (Photo: National Archives of Canada, Neg. No. C49323)

Cooksville
Village of the Past

Verna Mae Weeks

I wish to thank my husband, Roy Weeks, who researched so many of the local newspapers.

He and I together thank the Librarians in the History Department on the Third Floor of the Mississauga Central Library, the Archivists at the Region of Peel Archives in Brampton, and the Archivist at the Bush Plane Heritage Museum in Sault Ste. Marie for helping us with our project.

To Mary Anne Kelly, Mildred Bonhomme, Barb Tindall and the Cooksville people who helped with information and pictures, we express our appreciation.

Published by Verna Mae Weeks, 6509 Glen Erin Drive, Apt. 910, Mississauga, Ontario L5N 2X9.

Cover photo of the Cooksville House, from a painting by Roxann Vivian Smith. Back cover illustration courtesy of the Mississauga News.

Typeset in Ehrhardt, printed on Zephyr Antique Laid, sewn into signatures and bound by the The Porcupine's Quill (Erin, Ontario).

ISBN 0-9691301-7-1

Contents

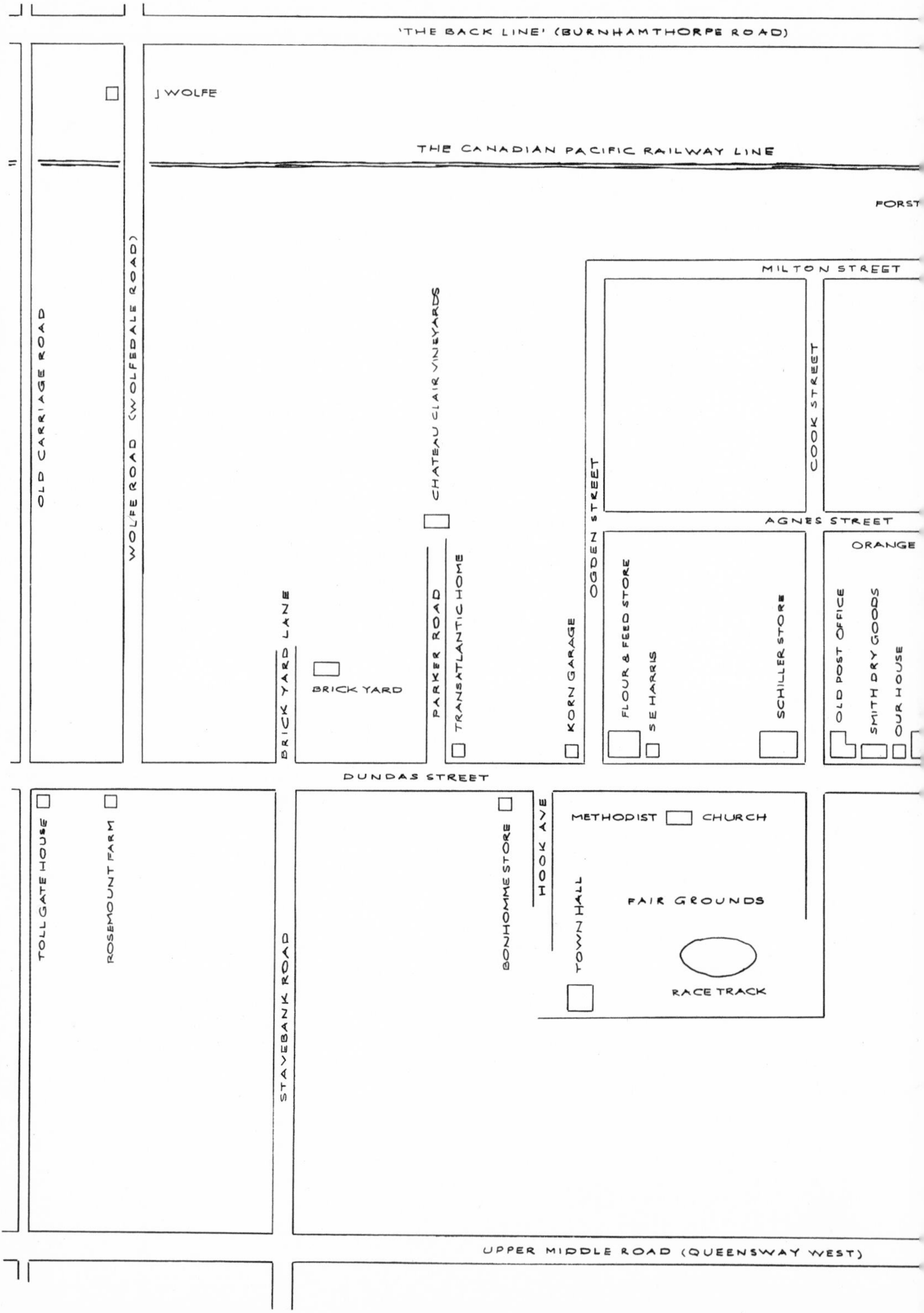

'THE BACK LINE' (BURNHAMTHORPE ROAD)

J WOLFE

THE CANADIAN PACIFIC RAILWAY LINE

FORST

MILTON STREET

COOK STREET

OLD CARRIAGE ROAD

WOLFE ROAD (WOLFEDALE ROAD)

CHATEAU CLAIR VINEYARDS

AGNES STREET

ORANGE

OGDEN STREET

BRICK YARD LANE

PARKER ROAD

TRANSATLANTIC HOME

KORN GARAGE

FLOUR & FEED STORE

S E HARRIS

SCHILLER STORE

OLD POST OFFICE

SMITH DRY GOODS

OUR HOUSE

BRICK YARD

DUNDAS STREET

TOLL GATE HOUSE

ROSEMOUNT FARM

STAVEBANK ROAD

BONHOMME STORE

HOOK AVE

METHODIST CHURCH

TOWN HALL

FAIR GROUNDS

RACE TRACK

UPPER MIDDLE ROAD (QUEENSWAY WEST)

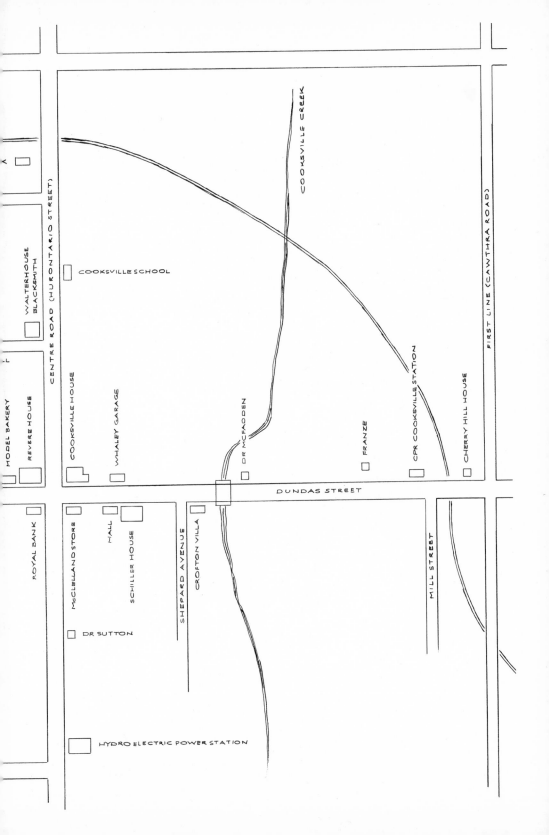

Dedicated to Duke Schiller –

'Since the dawn of commercial aviation in this country his name has been a legend among the airmen of North America.'
— *The Port Credit Weekly*, March 18, 1943

Introduction

IT WAS AT THE BEGINNING of October of 1928, when I was eight years old, that I moved with my father, mother, and little brother to what was then called a 'small dwelling,' situated west of the four corners of Cooksville, near Cook Street. This house, which was even then, to my eyes, tiny, was of roughcast, grey in colour, and showed more than a few cracks from age and the hard knocks of years past.

It possessed four rooms which, on my first sight of them, astonished me as no other rooms had ever done before, due to the fact of their walls being constructed of wide wooden boards painted with shiny, cream-coloured enamel, on which I could notice little movements made by myself as I walked about the room. These reflections were somewhat similar to those noticed on the smooth surface of Lake Aquitaine in Mississauga, on a particularly calm day in summer.

Inside the house was a large room on the right, which was living room, dining room and kitchen combined, for us; and a large cook stove stood off to the side, its long pipes going upward and stretching like arms about the room to keep us warm. There were two small bedrooms on the left, one behind the other, and another small, extra room behind the large one, for pantry, storage, or laundry room, whichever my mother happened to be using it for at the time.

You had to be careful never to be caught by surprise upon entering this extra room, since it had in the centre of the floor a trapdoor which might be opened at any time for the purpose of going 'down cellar' into the darkened space below, to bring up such needs as potatoes or carrots, or coal in a bucket for the stove.

There were two windows at the front of our house, and a door in the middle, with a recessed porch. When you stepped down three steps from our front door, off this porch, your foot landed on the pavement of a cement sidewalk and you found yourself standing on the main street of the village, with people walking by around you, going about their daily business, and with cars, trucks, or perhaps a farm wagon, driving along Dundas.

Today, this street is called Dundas Street West, but in those far-off times we called it simply Dundas Street, with a definite accent on the 'das' part. Can you say it that way? That way, we could always tell a visitor from a home town person; because we always said we lived on Dun-das Street.

Evenings, in this little house, we played games – Lotto, Parcheesi, Euchre, Snakes and Ladders, Old Maid, Snap!, Checkers, Rummy, and Poker (with wooden matches). People came in, evenings, before the days of radio and television, and played cards; among them were people from the brick yard, people who ran the fruit and vegetable market, and a man who had a garage. Although, today, I could not tell you how to play the games of 'poker,' or 'rummy,' I can assure you that, then, little kids of eight years became experts at 'raking in the matches,' on those old winter evenings.

Other times, I read *True Story* magazines which my father brought home, and still recall a name from one of the stories – 'Samuella Tancred Mays.' My mother called such books trash, and threw them out, but I don't believe, today, that Samuella ever did me any harm, that I can think of.

Summertimes I played with school friends, a game of jacks, with a small ball and a handful of metal pieces, on our front porch. Outside, on the back porch, my daily tasks were peeling potatoes or shelling peas, for supper. After supper, my little brother (then six years old) and I took turns washing the dishes; one evening I would wash and he would dry, and the next evening he stood on a box and washed while I dried. Once in a while I think of those times and wonder just how clean the two of us got those dishes, in the water pumped from the well in our backyard, heated in the kettle on our cook stove, and turned into suds with a bar of laundry soap.

As I drive along Dundas Street West today, I always glance over at where the little roughcast house used to stand. Once, my husband and I went for a sandwich and coffee at the restaurant which stands there today at 35 Dundas Street West, and I sat looking about, wondering just where our bedrooms used to be, and where our old oak buffet used to stand. I look at the parking lot and recall Mr Pardy, our neighbour, sitting at his work bench by the window of the red brick building with the name P. PARDY painted on the wall, making harnesses for horses throughout the whole area. I didn't know, on that day when he mended the strap on my sandal, that Mr Pardy had been, as a young man, a bobby on the streets of London, England.

My brother Lloyd and myself, with our mother Mary Denison, and our dog Bud, 1928. (Photo: Milford Denison)

As the research, by my husband and myself, has uncovered the earliest days of Cooksville, it has given me a wonderful sense of satisfaction in knowing that, apart from my own memories of this village of the past where my brother and I once spent such happy days while we were growing up, I was not mistaken – Cooksville really was a special kind of place, more than we ourselves ever knew.

Uniforms, 1814-15, Captain and Private, Canada, 29th
(Worcestershire) Regiment of Foot. (Photo: Metropolitan Toronto
Reference Library, J. Ross Robertson Collection, T 15415)

Chapter 1: The Soldier Settler

AFTER THE AMERICAN REVOLUTIONARY WAR ended, John Butler's Rangers, soldiers of his provincial regiment who had remained loyal to the British King George III, settled the Niagara district of Upper Canada. Besides these provincial men, in 1783, when the British regulars were about to return to England their ranks were reduced in numbers and soldiers who had served the whole three years for which they had signed up, and who now wished to remain in Canada, were allowed to do so. Corporals discharged under these circumstances were given the designation of 'reduced' corporals.

The land was later surveyed to form townships and, under the command of Colonel John Simcoe, the York Rangers put through the Dundas road, from Toronto to Hamilton. To the Cooksville area, in 1805, when lots were being awarded to ex-soldiers for their service during the War, there came one soldier who received not one, but two lots. He was not a former member of the provincial forces, but had been a corporal of the 29th (Worcestershire) Regiment of Foot, of the British regulars. He was a shoemaker, and his name was John Schiller.

This man had earlier received a Land Location Ticket for four hundred acres, but due to the hardships of conditions then existing, of surveying crews not being able to keep up with the demand by so many new settlers coming in, and of squatters taking over places they fancied, he had been unable to locate his land.

He was living in Niagara Township, in the County of Lincoln, and when he heard that lots were being granted along the new Dundas road, he submitted a new Petition, for the same amount of land, four hundred acres. At the bottom of his application was a statement signed by Colonel Allan McLean certifying his service, and noting that 'to the best of my recollection he always behaved himself as a good Soldier.'

This petition was granted by Peter Russell, President Administering the Government for Upper Canada, on July 25th, 1806. John Schiller received Lots Number 9 and 17 in the First Concession North of Dundas Street.

It was on May 31st of 1810 that he went personally to York, accompanied by James McNabb, Allan Robinet, and John Silverthorn, who verified that he had cleared the land and erected a house on Lot 9. On October 12th of 1811, he returned to York with James McNabb, after clearing and fencing another five acres, and erecting another house, on his other lot, Number 17.

GRANT to *John Schiller*

of the Townſhip of *Niagara* — 1145

In the County of *Lincoln*

In the ——— Diſtrict *of Niagara, Shoemaker*

late a ſoldier in the 29th Regiment — all that parcel of Land —

In the Townſhip of *Toronto*

In the County of *York*

In the *Home* ——— Diſtrict being

Lot Number *17* ———

In the *1* Conceſſion

North of Dundas Street That is to ſay

commencing in front of the ſaid *1st* Conceſſion

At the South-~~Eaſt~~ *~erly* Angle of ——— the ſaid Lot *No. 17.*

Then North *45* Degrees ~~Minutes~~ Weſt *100* Chains ——— ~~Links~~

more or leſs to the allowance for Road in the Rear of the ſaid Conceſſion ———

Then ~~South~~ *North* *38* Degrees *Eaſt* ~~Minutes Weſt~~ *20* Chains ——— ~~Links~~

more or leſs to the limit between Lots No. *17 & 16* ———

Then South *45* Degrees ~~Minutes~~ Eaſt *100* Chains ——— ~~Links~~

more or leſs to the allowance for Road in front of the ſaid Conceſſion ———

Then ~~North~~ *South* *38* Degrees *Weſt* ~~Minutes Eaſt~~ *20* Chains ——— ~~Links~~

. more or leſs to the place of beginning

containing *200* ——— Acres ——— more or leſs *also*

For which an allotment of *28* ——— Acres and *4* ſevenths

is made for a Proteſtant Clergy, in Lot No. *6* ——— in the *2d Conceſſion*

South of Dundas Street in ~~Conceſſion~~ of the ſaid Townſhip of *Toronto* —

Order in Council *22d July 1806 under* *Thos. Ridout*

the Adminiſtration of Mr. Preſident Grant for 400 Acres *Surveyr Genl*

including former grants as a Reduced Corporal S. G. O. fiat No. *604*

~~Warrant No.~~ *Regl acted upon* Deſcription Number *1444*.

~~C. O. No.~~ *22d December 1797* *Jo. 10 Octr 1811*

~~R. G. O. No.~~

A. G. O. No. *6483* *Privileged by the*

23d July 1806. *Inspector General*

The Settlement duty performed

Copy of Land Grant, Lot 17 NDS, to John Schiller, #1145 – Archives
of Ontario, RG 1, C-IV, Township of Toronto.

also

GRANT to *John Schiller*

of the Township of *Niagara*

In the County of *Lincoln*

In the _____ Diſtrict *of Niagara, Shoemaker*

late a Soldier in the 29ᵗʰ Regiment / all that parcel of Land

In the Townſhip of *Toronto*

In the County of *York*

In the *Home* _____ Diſtrict · · · · · · · · being

Lot Number *9* _____

In the ___*1*___ Conceſſion · · · · · That is to ſay

North of Dundas Street

also

commencing in front of the ſaid _____ *1ˢᵗ* Conceſſion

easterly

At the South ~~Eaſt~~ Angle of _____ the ſaid Lot *N.° 9*

Then North *45* Degrees ~~Minutes~~ Weſt *100* Chains ~~Links~~

more or leſs to the allowance for Road in the Rear of the ſaid Conceſſion _____

North

Then ~~South~~ *38* Degrees *East* ~~Minutes Weſt~~ *20* · Chains ~~Links~~

more or leſs to the limit between Lots No. *9 & 8* _____

Then South *45* Degrees ~~Minutes~~ Eaſt *100* Chains ~~Links~~

more or leſs to the allowance for Road in front of the ſaid Conceſſion _____

South

Then ~~North~~ *38* Degrees *West* ~~Minutes Eaſt~~ *20* Chains ~~Links~~

more or leſs to the place of beginning

containing *200* _____ Acres _____ more or leſs

For which an allotment of *28* _____ Acres and *4* _____ ſevenths

is made for a Proteſtant Clergy, in Lot No. *35* _____ in the *2ᵈ* Conceſſion

South of Dundas Street ~~in _____ Conceſſion~~ of the ſaid Townſhip of *Toronto*

Order in Council *22ᵈ July 1806 under the*
administ: of Mr. President Grant for 400 acy
including former grants as a reduced Disposal

~~Warrant No.~~

~~G.O. No.~~

~~R.C.O. No.~~

A. G. O. No. *6483*
23. July 1806.

Thoˢ Ridout
Survy.ʳ Genˡ

S. G. O. fiat No. *604*

Deſcription Number *1445*

Regˢ acted upon
22ᵈ Decemᵗ 1797.
Privileged by the Inspector
General.

Ẏo. 10. Octʳ
1811

The Settlement Duty performed.

Copy of Land Grant, Lot 9 NDS, to John Schiller, #1115 – Archives
of Ontario, RG 1, C-IV, Township of Toronto.

Thus he had fulfilled his duties, over this long period, from when his first Grant had been registered in 1797, passed in 1806, and finally a Patent issued to him, on October 12th, 1811. He had been a good soldier, and was now a good settler. From wild grapes he found growing near his own land, near the Credit River, John Schiller cultivated new domestic vines and by 1811, he and his sons were operating a small winery business, which was the earliest beginnings of the great wine industry carried out in Cooksville over many years.

On April 17, 1812, John Schiller sold the whole two hundred acres of Lot 9, located east of what is now Dundas Street East and Cawthra Road, to James McNabb; but he remained on his land on Lot 17. In 1814, at the Court of Quarter Sessions, he was appointed a Pound Keeper in the Home District of Toronto. A pound keeper kept strayed or rescued animals in a fenced-off area of his property until the owners came and paid a fee for their recovery.

We have no more information regarding the soldier himself, for by now he was old, and in those early days people who grew old and died were usually buried on their own land, by their families, covered over on a hillside, surrounded perhaps by a little grove of trees. Most settlers protected their family graves with wooden fences which, over the years, gradually disappeared, knocked down by roving cattle, or by bitter storms of winter. A few were provided with granite stones, but these had to be brought in from either Kingston or Newark, and were more than most settlers could provide.

In August of 1824, Michael and William Schiller began to divide up Lot 17, located on Dundas Street West, just outside the village limits of Cooksville, subdividing and selling to Thomas Silverthorn and Stanous Daniell; by 1827, Matthew Treanor and, later, Daniel Barber owned acreages on Lot 17.

William was a cooper, who made the barrels for shipping the wine, and Stanous Daniell, who bought sixty-six acres of the Schiller land, was an innkeeper, who kept an inn farther to the west along the Dundas road, in that rough track of road between Cooksville and Springfield-on-the-Credit. By 1826, the rest of the land was being divided and sold, with Michael Schiller signing the Bargain and Sale document with 'his mark,' an X.

Shortly afterwards, Michael Schiller died and, on September 1st, 1828, he was one of the first to be buried at Springfield, in what later became known as the Cosmopolitan Cemetery on the high banks overlooking the Credit River, not so very far from his home.

The Schiller family remained in the district and, in 1840, young David Schiller, by profession a mason, married Lucinda Miller and bought back, for the sum of twelve pounds and ten shillings, thirty-three acres of the soldier's original grant on Lot 17.

On March 15th, 1852, the Widow Schiller, whose Christian name was not recorded, only her great age of ninety-six years, was also laid to rest in the cemetery at Springfield.

Chapter 2: Jacob Cook

ON JUNE 19TH, 1819, David Shannon received his Patent for all two hundred acres of Lot Number 16 on the south side of Dundas Street, and on August 30th of the same year, he sold the whole parcel of land to Jacob Cook for the sum of thirty pounds sterling of the lawful money of Upper Canada. Jacob, born in Lancaster County, Pennsylvania, was twenty-three years of age.

The War of 1812 was just over and, by 1819, settlement was really going ahead. Jacob Cook erected a homestead on his newly-bought land, and married Anna Ogden. The following year he received a contract to carry the mail from Ancaster to York (Toronto); he had lived at Ancaster since leaving Pennsylvania in 1804 and knew the terrain between the two towns, through the forest trails and over the hills.

The main communications between the settlers' new province and the British Isles were brought into the country from Liverpool, through New York, and thence to the Niagara district. Only two mails per week left Niagara for Ancaster and York. Jacob Cook, therefore, set out to improve these conditions and, in 1820, asked for and received permission to deliver the mails. His situation at the southwest corner of the new Dundas road and the Hurontario road running south to the lake, was at the point halfway between what was then known as Harrisville and Ancaster, just right for a stopover.

At first, Jacob carried the mail bags, riding horseback through the bush, through all kinds of weather, but in 1828 he bought one acre of land from Silas Fletcher, who owned Lot Number 15 on the north side of Dundas. This land was across the road from Jacob's home and, by 1829, he had built an inn on the northeast corner of Dundas and Hurontario Streets.

A Canadian Stage Coach, c.1830s. (Photo: from *A History of the Canadian People*, by Wm. Stewart Wallace, 1931)

In 1830, Harrisville was flourishing and Jacob Cook was running a stage coach line, with horses being changed at his own hotel. The hotel was a storey-and-a-half high, built of brick, and had a stable to handle two pairs of horses. Stage coaches came into the yard, not only picking up and dropping off the mails, but supplying transportation for passengers along the way.

Many years later, when she was almost a century old, Mrs Mary Langdon told of her father's exciting business – of how the great yellow coaches had come into the inn yard, horses tramping and jingling the bells on their harnesses. She had seen the passengers getting off and going into the warmth of the hotel, to eat in the dining room and learn the news of the day, which was seldom to be learned in any other way. Mrs Langdon never forgot about the times when the stage drivers blew loud blasts on their horns, warning the passengers to hurry because the horses had been exchanged and the coaches were ready to depart.

Many coaches travelled past Cook's Hotel, not only from east and west, but from north and south as well. William Harris, called 'Ginger' by everyone, had built a white frame hotel north of Streetsville, in the

Jacob Cook. (Photo: from Pictorial Atlas of Peel, 1877)

hamlet named Harris' Corners, and his stage coaches stopped regularly to exchange horses on their way to Toronto.

Jacob Cook's stage line grew. His mail stages ran to Hamilton, Niagara, Queenston, Brantford, London, Galt, Preston, Goderich, and even to Kingston. As well, he had a short line running cross-country, linking Cheltenham and Georgetown. He owned practically a monopoly on the mail and stage coach lines of Upper Canada. His brothers were interested in the business and went even further afield. Stage coaches came and went, day by day, with the stables growing ever larger, and all of these mail routes seemed to centre around Jacob Cook's Hotel, at Cooksville.

In 1836, because of his great enterprise, the name of the village was changed to Cooksville and, up until 1848, Jacob Cook carried on his business of transporting the mails, at the same time becoming involved in most of the business connected with the village. He became part of everything, from real estate deals to being the Magistrate and Justice of the Peace; he was also a Lieutenant in the Militia. He gave the ground for the building of the Rechabites Hall, and laid the cornerstone for it on May 28th, 1848.

However, in 1852, when a terrible fire swept the village, the hotel he had built was destroyed, and the following year his daughter Mary married Henry Langdon, an Englishman who had come to Canada as a

Mrs Henry Langdon, daughter of Jacob Cook, and mother-in-law of George McClelland, on steps of the McClelland house, 1926. (Photo: Mississauga Central Library, Cooksville Vol.1, F 100)

boy of thirteen. Henry was interested in the stage business and they went to live at Guelph, and then Buffalo, to look after that line.

His son, Miles Washington Cook, who had left Cooksville at the age of sixteen to be educated at Syracuse, New York, and afterwards at Toronto University, returned to look after his father's estate and received from his father, in 1869, a subdivided part of Lot 15, on the east side of Hurontario Street south of Dundas. Jacob never left his homestead house, and lived there until he died at the age of seventy-seven, in 1873.

When Henry Langdon died, in 1884, Jacob Cook's daughter returned to Cooksville to live in the homestead with her brother, Miles Washington Cook, who retained the quaint old document, the Deed to the original Lot Number 16, which had attached to it a huge seal weighing approximately ten to twelve ounces. M. W. Cook Esq. was probably one of the best known men in Toronto Township, being an active politician, Liberal in views, and becoming for a time Warden of the County. In May, 1893, he advertised in *The Streetsville Review*, for private sale, his frame barn, 'to be removed before July 1st.' As well, he offered a Gurney Reaper 'Harvest Queen' in good condition; 1 Mower, first-class; and 1 Market Wagon, 3 springs and 2 seats. Listed also were 500 bushels of Turnips, 200 bushels of Carrots, and 100 bushels of Potatoes.

Three years later, there appeared in *The Brampton Conservator* of February, 1896, an advertisement regarding the estate of the late M. W. Cook, when all of his property was offered for sale by auction, at King's Hotel. He left much land in Cooksville, but it was his sister, Mrs Langdon, who bought his six-acre village lot, the one facing Dundas Street, bordered by the east side of Hurontario Street.

As for the homestead itself, it was at first rented out for awhile, before finally burning to the ground around the turn of the century, leaving a large empty space on the southwest corner which was to remain bare for a long time afterwards. Nothing was built on this property until many years later, when a small white frame Royal Bank building was established there.

The last descendant of Jacob Cook's family, his daughter, Mary Langdon, Cooksville's oldest citizen, died at the beginning of July in 1927, and was buried near him, in the Dixie Union Cemetery.

Chapter 3: The Chateau Clair Vineyards

WILD GRAPES WERE GROWING in Southern Ontario in the year 1639, as was told by the Jesuit Fathers who lived at the Huron Missions and related their experiences in books they sent back to France. The Missions received wine from France in little wooden kegs which seldom arrived without having lost a great deal from leakage. The wine, needed for the Masses, was so scarce that only four or five drops could be put into the chalice, and when the missionaries discovered wild grapes growing in the forest, they began to use them to make wine enough to last out the year, until the new kegs arrived.

Paul Ragueneau described himself, during 1650, as harnessing himself to a conveyance, like a horse to a wagon, and travelling through the forests around Huron, searching for wild grapes. In this way he would go, over tortuous paths and even over the snow, for a distance of up to ten or twelve leagues, in an effort to gather enough fruit to manufacture wine for the celebration of the Masses. This wine was of a poor and bitter quality, but it eked out the missionaries' supplies for the remainder of the winter months.

Two hundred years later, the new domesticated grapes cultivated by the Schillers were thriving in Cooksville. Situated on the sunny, shallow slopes of Lot 17, facing southwards towards the lake, and with good drainage and growing conditions, the grape known as the 'Clinton' variety was producing fine wine.

John Schiller's was the first commercial winery to be established in Canada. It had only a field stone vault for storage, probably constructed about 1825, and was necessarily a small undertaking, spoken of today as a 'cottage industry;' but it was nevertheless the beginnings of the Cooksville Winery which became famous under the management of the Canada Vinegrowers' Association.

In 1841, the sixty-six acres first bought by Stanous Daniell was sold again, this time to Sir William Parker, who brought his three sons, Albert, Henry, and Melville, from England, to settle them in Cooksville. By 1853, they had bought another thirty acres; and in 1856, Melville Parker was selling 'horses, cows, oxen and fat cattle' on the premises, while Albert Parker had become a land agent and commissioner who 'took affidavits in the Courts of Chancery and Courts of Common Law.'

The grapes were good on Lot 17 and, in 1864, the Parkers, along with the Honourable Francis Day, and the Robinets who had settled in

Chateau Clair, Cooksville. (Photo: Region of Peel Archives, William Perkins Bull Collection, 93.0042 #2-17)

Chateau Clair Winery, Cooksville. (Photo: Region of Peel Archives, William Perkins Bull Collection, 93.0042 #2-15)

The Brampton Times,
March 27, 1868

Dixie, formed the Canada Vinegrowers' Association. Count Justin de Courtenay arrived to become Manager and to superintend the building of a large and beautiful house on the crest of the hill, where a long lane led up to it from Dundas Street. This house they named the 'Chateau Clair.'

In the year 1866, the Vinegrowers received a special Charter by an Act of Parliament, to encourage interest in vine-growing, and the production of native wine in Canada. At that time, thirty acres of grapes were being grown by the new company, and when a quantity of wine was exhibited at a Paris Exhibition it was judged to be acceptable in quality.

Count de Courtenay advertised grape cuttings for sale at the rate of one dollar per hundred, available to anyone calling at the office of the Association in Cooksville. Persons who ordered one thousand cuttings and upward, received with them a booklet describing the culture of the vines, and explaining how every farmer could now learn how to plant and prune his own vineyard.

In 1869, the editor of *The Brampton Times* wrote an article telling that he had received a bottle of the Winery's famous grape brandy, of his surprise at its flavour and strength, and its superiority over even the

Solomon White. (Photo: Region of Peel Archives, William Perkins Bull Collection, 93.0042 #2-13)

celebrated French brandy. He stated that for medicinal purposes it had no equal, 'and we had no idea before that such a prime article could be manufactured in Canada, especially so near home as Cooksville.'

Solomon White, a native of Essex County, who had been called to the Ontario Bar in 1865, purchased the Vineyard in 1871. The Winery was in operation eight months of the year, and paying out yearly wages of $3,200. Eight men and one woman over sixteen years, and fourteen young men and three young girls under the age of sixteen were, at the time, employed in growing thirty tons of grapes which yielded red and white wines, as well as brandy.

In those days of the eighteen-seventies, huge stables stood at the rear of the Chateau, always filled with the horses and carriages of visitors, and Solomon White became known as the Squire of the village. As a Winery, though, Chateau Clair Vineyards had lost prestige with the government and when, after fourteen years, the Charter was refused, Solomon White left. Toward the end of 1876, he sold out the fruit farm and the wine establishment and moved back to Windsor, to practise law there. He was elected to the Legislature for North Essex, and served as Conservative MPP for fifteen years. He later became Mayor of Cobalt, Ontario.

Meanwhile, in Cooksville, the Winery continued in operation, with

The Streetsville Review,
January 31, 1890

B. W. Murray managing it and living in the Clair House. Mr Murray was the Registrar at Osgoode Hall, as well as a breeder of Jersey and Holstein cattle. Andrew Aikens was now living in the other house on the property; not so large and grand as the Clair House, it was named the 'Transatlantic Home,' and was situated at the front of the lot, on Dundas Street. By the year 1882, Ontario Claret was being shipped from the Cooksville Railway Station, fourteen miles west of Toronto.

At the times when the snow fell and made for good sleighing, Mrs Murray threw open her beautiful home to parties of guests of young people who belonged to St. John's Church, in West Toronto. It was reported in *The Brampton Conservator* that 'right merrily did they enjoy themselves.' Christmas parties were held for local people in this house on the hill. Mrs Mildred Belleghem wrote that her Aunt Jennie

Goldthorpe remembered once going to a Sunday School party there and thought she had never seen such a large Christmas tree in her life, and just loaded with gifts.

In March of 1891, the Murray family moved away to the northwest, and the Clair House Vineyard was sold in Toronto. It was bought by Mr Andrew Aikens of Cooksville, for the sum of $13,100, and Mr Aikens then moved into the beautiful Chateau Clair. Mr A. C. Pettit, the undertaker at Cooksville, moved into the other Vineyard house, on Dundas Street, and began operating his business with his office in the Transatlantic Home.

Mr Aikens was a member of a Toronto firm of cattle dealers and came home to Cooksville every night, in order to personally supervise the whole farm. He was a thorough and practical farmer who believed in making all the possible profits of his industry, and so cultivated and cared for the vineyards that his wine cellars were among the most spacious in Ontario.

In all, Mr Aikens had between two and three hundred acres, with over forty acres planted in grape vines; besides the new farm, he already owned another, known as the Galbraith estate and called Spring Valley Farm. The Clair House acres were worked by four men, under the control of a foreman, Mr Myers; and the trimming of the grape vines and picking of the grapes required a great deal of extra help, which gave employment to a large number of men.

Others engaged in the manufacture of wine at the time were Mr Frank Thomas and Mr T. Bersotti, each of whom bought up tremendous quantities of grapes and manufactured a first-class article, for which they had a large demand.

There was much industry connected with Mr Aikens, for in 1894 he also became owner of the Cooksville saw mill property, and had the buildings on it refitted. By 1899, he had planted two thousand tobacco plants as an experiment, but nothing more was reported on this enterprise. That year, he was manufacturing over eight thousand gallons of wine.

However, as often happens, an unexpected tragedy occurred. Andrew Aikens died as the result of an accident, and everything had to be sold. Fifty-eight acres, opposite the Clair House, went to Mr Charles Patchett for $3,600, with no buildings on the property; the Transatlantic Home and Broddy Cottage were bought by a veterinarian, Dr Murray. Mr Stevens, from Trafalgar, purchased the Spring Valley Farm.

At the Clair House executor's sale were listed: a brown stallion (Young Woodburn); a handsome mare (Harriet); 4 fillies (Maude, Little Eva, Maggie and Bertie); a good driving horse (Jim); and a light buggy and harness, brass-mounted; 1 Boar pig, and 10 Barnyard fowl. There were 2 Trucks, a Mill Belt, and 2 Kant Hooks for turning logs. Also on the property, along with sawed Maple and Oak, and Square Timbers, were 350 Apple Barrels, and a quantity of Hay, Oats, and Wheat. Mr John Thomson, of Port Credit, was the Auctioneer.

The following year, in September of 1903, the Clair House was sold to Achilles Roumegous, proprietor of the Lakeview House in Toronto, who purchased it for his son to actively manage; and in 1921, a permit to manufacture wine was still being granted by the Licence Department.

Leopold Roumegous remained as owner of the Chateau Clair Winery, and stated in 1929 that the century-old vineyards were renewing themselves that summer in a remarkable manner. From the first cultivated roots, new shoots had been growing laterally and pushing up through the soil, and in the fall of the year these new ones had blossomed, promising a fine crop of new grapes.

However, in the early nineteen-thirties, Alfred de Lautels purchased the historic and beautiful house and its grounds and the old landmark was turned into a rabbit ranch. It was the time, now, of the Depression days and Mr William Verrege and his wife were living in the former Clair House, managing the Elmwood Rabbit Ranch for the Company who owned it.

In the spring of 1932, at two-thirty one morning, Mr Verrege was awakened by the barking of his big police dog. At home alone at the time, and sleeping on the couch in the downstairs office, he found himself in a room filled with smoke. He could not get out the front door of the house, and so broke the glass out of the door and reached the outdoors, with his dog escaping behind him. Flames were pouring from the roof of the building, from the residence quarters upstairs, and although the Port Credit Fire Department poured water on the house and surrounding buildings, they were able to save only the former Winery, where the rabbits were housed. The disastrous fire demolished the Chateau Clair, one of the best-constructed old houses of early Ontario. Nothing remained of it in the morning but crumbled walls.

Over the years many legends became attached to this property, such as: that the old house was hinted to have rifle slits built into its thick walls, perhaps to be used as a 'rebel fortress,' in the days of the Sinn Fein; that secret chambers were hidden in its walls, and underground passages under the floors. People said there were wells under the old Winery, and a dozen others elsewhere on the property; and they became angry because not only cattle, but people fell down these mysterious holes.

However, the wells had probably no other history than the fact that water was needed for the wine business, and that the wine had to be stored in dark cellars; as well, not so many years before, men had been drilling for gas and oil on the property, never bothering to fill in the deep holes made by the machinery. Up until the time of its burning, the old house was still being lit by gas lamps and oil was being used for cooking.

In October of 1935, what remained of the Chateau Clair House on Dundas Street at Cooksville, was levelled to the ground. The land where once cattle were raised, where grapes and orchards grew, is today covered by large apartment buildings, and a street named Parkerhill Boulevard runs northward through the centre of the property.

* * *

The writing of this account has brought to my mind an evening a couple of years ago, when my husband and I harvested our entire crop of white Thompson grapes, from a vine we had planted ourselves in old days, when we first went to live in our farmhouse, at Chesley; that evening, our sprawling, almost totally-uncultivated, woody grapevine yielded two basketfuls. We crawled on our knees, beneath its gnarled and twisted vines, freezing our fingers in the search, and found our sweet grapes untouched by the frost – a miracle for our part of the province.

Next morning, I simmered them with water and sugar, and strained them, to make us grape juice for a whole winter, and our whole house was filled with a wonderful grape-y aroma. It is a lovely thing, to have a grapevine.

Chapter 4: Drilling for Oil and Gas

IN 1877, MELVILLE PARKER and Commander Gordon were running an oil refinery on the property adjacent to the winery; and in 1882, oil was being loaded on the train at the Cooksville Station for delivery to the Barber Brothers factory at Streetsville.

In 1892, the New Toronto Natural Gas Company had representatives in Cooksville for the location of wells, and were negotiating with several farmers on the Middle Road; they were also anxious to secure the land owned by M. W. Cook.

When oil was struck at Cooksville in 1907, *The Brampton Conservator* asked: 'Has dame Fortune something good in store for us, is the cry of the Cooksville man, or is the fickle jade but mocking us and holding out visionary hopes that may never be realized?'

The practical farmers were also asking this question when a syndicate was formed by Messrs. Thomas Bull, Dr Murray, Arthur Gordon, and Captain Eaton. The syndicate had leased over 2,000 acres and, after samples of petroleum from various parts of the area were submitted to the experts, Willis & Company, of Toronto, organized a company to raise capital, put in drills, and develop the oil.

Mr Bull, who owned land near the southwest corner of Cooksville, was the man most interested. He said that for the past two years he had been working on the project and had found oil in the area 5 miles east, 4 miles north, 3 miles south, and 10 miles west of Cooksville, and that he had been assured the samples submitted were better than those taken from the Tilbury area. He believed that the first test would produce oil in paying quantities, and that natural gas could also be found.

Four wells were drilled, and it was said that oil began to be seen on the surface; when samples were taken, a thick scum of petroleum was found. Analysis showed the samples to be rich in oil, and the leasing of much property was the immediate result. For miles along the Cooksville Creek bubbles could be seen rising up, floating and bursting, caused by the gas pressure from beneath. People reported that when the muddy bottom was disturbed with a pole, a lighted paper held close to the surface would send up a flame several feet high.

The Brampton Conservator of November 7, 1907, reported that *The Toronto World* carried a story regarding the natural gas discovery at Cooksville, and of how one man, more enterprising than most, had sunk a shaft that gave a daily supply of 50,000 cubic feet, which he was using on his own and neighbours' farms for heating, lighting, and other purposes.

Willis & Company, of Adelaide Street, Toronto, were so impressed by these reports and the demonstrations being given that they decided to install several drilling rigs immediately and bore through the clay, in order to discover what quantities of gas really could be obtained. In October, machinery was placed on the farm of Mrs Gordon, on the Centre Road, and they began with this single rig, on a farm within a mile of Cooksville. The flow of gas was so satisfactory that they intended sinking another twenty drills at other points. It was calculated that they might possibly be able to supply the city with four or five million cubic feet of gas a day, at a cost of about 25 to 30 cents per thousand feet.

In January, 1909, a derrick was erected at the rear of A. Roumegous' farm, and a drill was started to work at once by a company known as the Toronto Oil and Gas Syndicate. On February 25th, what appeared to be a great conflagration in the west end of the village, caused by the test of the natural gas, attracted the attention of many spectators.

Thomas Cox, of Brantford, had been at work and, at a depth of 500 feet, a big deposit of gas had been found. He stated that the strike was enough to supply Cooksville at once and, since it was only fourteen miles distant from Toronto, there would not be the slightest difficulty in piping it into the city and supplying gas at 35 or 40 cents. Mr Cox said that $1,000 had been subscribed in ten minutes, and he had no doubt of getting all they wanted.

Everything looked very favourable, and twenty men were being employed in the sinking of more wells. The Company intended to drill to a depth of 1,000 feet. In April, 1909, they ceased operations on Mr Roumegous' farm, and the drillers moved to the flats on the Price property, where another flow of gas was struck.

By August, the well on the Roumegous farm was producing 140,000 feet of gas per day, and Willis & Company, under the direction of Mr Cox, expected to have two wells completed and opened on October 6, for the evening of Cooksville Fair Day. A demonstration was to be made to all who chose to attend. They stated that the well on Mr Roumegous' farm was 1,075 feet in depth, and that the other, in the ravine on Mr Price's property, was 1,360 feet deep.

Mr Cox invited a number of people to witness the opening of the wells at Cooksville, and among those who came down from Brampton were: W. A. Robinson, E. T. Stork, Jos. Brownridge, and James Early. A large crowd was astonished to hear the roaring from the wells, which could be heard from a long distance; and the tremors and vibrations which shook the earth convinced everyone who watched that great quantities of gas existed beneath the surface. When burned, the flames leaped to a height of ten or fifteen feet, and Mr Smart, Government Inspector of Immigration, who was also present was delighted with the result.

The Brampton Banner and Times wrote a column about the two wells sunk by Mr Cox and Mr Bull; and on January 21, 1910, *The Streetsville Review* stated that a derrick had been erected and the necessary machinery to bore for oil was on the ground, to begin operations at the rear of the Clair House property. In September, someone took the cap off the well drilled on Price's flats and lit the escaping gas on fire, illuminating the whole vicinity.

In April, 1912, the well drillers hired by the syndicate to bore for oil on the George S. Shepard farm, southeast of the four corners, were ready to make a hole 1,500 feet deep; but the work had to be stopped when they reached solid granite. A short time later, many Cooksville residents were alarmed by what they thought was an explosion when they heard a loud roar, accompanied by the forcible shaking of houses, which caused them to run outside their homes. However, they were told that there had been an earthquake shock recorded at that time, all around the vicinity of Cooksville.

In November, a derrick and apparatus were erected for drilling a new natural gas well on Mr Roumegous' farm, and pipes for the proposed distribution of gas through the village were laid on both sides of Dundas Street. This was followed by the biggest gas strike yet. *The Toronto Star* published a story concerning this well, stating that the gas was escaping at an enormous rate, that over a million feet had escaped and the flow was on the increase. 'As the electrical steel drill was boring into the unknown depths on Roumegous' farm, a quarter of a mile from the village, the air was suddenly filled with fumes of gas that came belching forth from the five-inch casing around the drill, which was boring through shale 1,450 feet below the surface.'

Nothing was done to stop the flow or top it, as the pressure was enormous, and the gas kept spouting into the air in a purplish-blue flame. The contractors working for the syndicate had been boring wells in the Cooksville area for the past four years, but this was the largest flow struck, up to that time. The new well was the property of the Port Maitland Gas Company who refused to sell it, although they received many offers. A four-inch pipe was being constructed towards Hamilton, and they had sold the gas for the next two years at a metre rate. The head of the supply company was T. Lawlor, MP for Haldimand.

A week later, another big strike of gas was made on the Roumegous farm, and over a million feet spouted up around the casting of the drill and escaped. The men who were operating the drill had difficulty in staying on the job, owing to the fumes. This gas was spouting over 125 feet high, making a vivid picture with its purplish-blue flames. However, in March of 1913, the drilling operations were stopped, owing to the failure of the other wells to supply sufficient natural gas to run the machinery.

Oil was the original attraction to Cooksville, but this did not materialize. In August, 1913, George H. Milburn was given a franchise to run a gas pipe line along the highway from some of the wells and was urging the Council to grant him an exclusive franchise for this purpose. However, the Council did not look favourably upon his request. In the summer of 1915, through the efforts of Thomas Bull, several wells were sunk from which gas was procured, but the quantities available were still not sufficient to make the project pay, and the undertaking was abandoned.

At the beginning of October, 1916, Thomas E. Bull, who had lived in Cooksville all his life, died. He had worked long and hard in connection with the natural gas and oil wells in the area, and had become publicly known as the 'Oil King of Cooksville.' He had secured leases on numerous properties, and five different wells were drilled; some natural gas had been obtained and pipes laid through the village, and several houses were utilizing it, but there was never a sufficient supply for a profitable operation. In 1914, during a boom in Alberta, Mr Bull had left Cooksville to take part in that venture but, on his return, he had become ill and died.

* * *

Ernest Lemon, as a boy, moved from a farm at Erindale to live on Agnes Street. The brick house has long since been torn down, and stores and big apartments stand there now. But Ernie always remembered walking east from the Hotel to the creek, to a swale where the water went under the highway. He said, 'There used to be two pipes sticking up out of the ground, quite large, and we kids would strike a match at the top of the pipe and it would go 'POOF!' They had drilled for gas, and it didn't pay; but in the 1920s, it still went POOF! from the pipes coming up, which had been left there – but you could strike matches all day after that, and you wouldn't hear anything. Nobody would bother you; you could go over there and strike a match to hear the POOF! of them any time.'

Chapter 5: A Century-and-a-Half Ago

COOKSVILLE BEGAN AT THE SPOT where the Dundas road and the road to Port Credit formed an intersection. Around these four corners there grew up the little settlement of Harrisville which, quite naturally, received the name of the man who erected its first saw mill, Daniel Harris. Daniel Harris built a homestead on the Old Survey Lot 15, on the south side of Dundas, in 1809, and his saw mill was much in use for sawing the logs to build the houses of the newly-arriving immigrants.

Today, we try to save the trees, but to the people of those earliest times the trees were enemies which caused them hardship and kept them in a state of intense gloom, in the darkness of the dense forest. There was a silence in the forest but, when the winds blew and swayed the branches near the tops of the trees they made a humming sound which frightened the settlers. On the ground there was a deep padding of old, long-dead leaves and branches, where the sunlight could not penetrate; nothing could grow along the ground until the air and sun could reach the land and give it life.

Tree stumps were burned, and provided enough ashes to enable Daniel Harris to start a potashery. People used ashes from their fireplaces for making soap, but it was also a good product to sell. Small general stores which became established accepted wood ashes in return for staples, and re-sold them to the potashery, from which they were shipped out in quantities, by the barrel, from the mouth of the Credit River.

About 1830, the village was laid out under the new name of Millbrook, later changed to Cooksville in 1836. At that time, it had about 185 inhabitants, with a post daily, and three saw mills in the immediate vicinity, these belonging to C. E. Romain, Robert Rutledge, and J. Silverthorn. Later, it was James Harris who built one of the first lake vessels in the district and used it, not only for the ashes but for shipping the local farmers' grain across the lake to Niagara. There, the grain was ground and brought back again.

The road along Dundas was partly gravelled and partly macadamized as far over as Springfield-on-the-Credit by 1836, by grants of money from the Legislature under the direction of trustees appointed for that purpose. Later on, a Company received a franchise and installed toll gates to help pay for its upkeep, hiring a driver to go along weekly and collect the money from the keepers of the toll gates. With an open wagon as a stage coach, James Boyce began advertising his Dundas Street Stage.

Jacob Cook's Hotel had been erected, and his stage coach route and mail service established through Cooksville. A clerk was appointed to sort mail and it was distributed wherever convenient; there appears, in the 1895 Postal Guide published for the whole of Canada, a record of a Post Office (Peel-O) being located at Cooksville, from 1829 to 1837, in charge of Postmaster Abijah Lewis.

J. H. Savigny then became Postmaster until October 6, 1839; and on October 7, 1839, Francis B. Morley was named Cooksville Postmaster, along with his duties of issuing marriage licences. Mr Morley came to Cooksville from Lakeneath in the County of Sussex, England, in 1834 with his father, mother, four brothers and a sister. His brother, John Morley, became the tailor in Cooksville.

The Streetsville Review, January 11, 1851

Hotels were the main large buildings before Town Halls were erected; every sort of activity was carried on at the hotels, from meetings by the road builders and volunteer firemen, to auction sales and entertainments. Cattle and other farm animals were driven through the village streets to the inn yard and sold, along with the house furnishings of people who wished to leave and try their luck in some other area. Small general stores were to be found at hotels, where goods could be traded for other goods; as well, they often served as small savings banks, but paid no interest. A person could get advice on how to run the farm, or advertise there for help, such as for a barn raising in the surrounding area. Travelling peddlers came to the hotels.

35

For years, there was a recipe to be found in every hotel, with directions guaranteeing to 'destroy all kinds of bugs.' People were told to take two bushels of wood ashes from their fireplace, leach them by filtering water through them until the liquid became strong enough to hold up a potato and, when it was boiling hot, they must add 'a gallon of whale oil' to make a soft soap. A quart of this soft soap, mixed with seven quarts of water and stirred up into a good suds, was said to kill every kind of bug. The full amount needed, to buy a gallon of whale oil from any druggist was one dollar, and this would make enough suds to sprinkle over a whole two acres of potatoes. The only stipulation given was that the oil must be whale oil; no other kind would do. The advertisement did not state whether the mixture could be used in the home, but it definitely stated 'all kinds of bugs.'

Before 1850, there were three innkeepers listed at Cooksville – William Scott, in his own Hotel on the south side of Dundas Street; Moses Teeter, in charge of Cook's Hotel; and Samuel Wilson, at the Tyrone Inn.

Dr William Pool Crewe was a surgeon who bought land enough from Jacob Cook to build a fifteen-room house and set up a large practice there. He called it Stafford House, but it was more like a hospital than a house, having five rooms in it used for surgical suites. He made house calls, travelling on horse back in fine weather, or in a two-wheeled cart with sleigh runners on it, pulled by a horse, in winter. The other doctor serving the area was Dr G. C. Cotter, who was placing advertisements in the weekly newspapers.

There was, at Cooksville, an organization called the Independent Order of the Rechabites, instituted on March 3rd, 1817, and within one year of its beginning its membership numbered forty-eight. They met in a little log house quite near the four corners, on the south side of Dundas Street, with their object being 'to redeem men from the degrading and awful state of drunkenness to a state of sobriety and usefulness.' During the early eighteen-forties, the Wesleyan Methodist missionaries also held meetings in the log house.

This Order, which was very strict, permitting the drinking of no wine or spirits of any kind, flourished, and on the 28th day of May, 1848, celebrated the erection of a new Hall. Inside the corner stone of this hall was placed a document made 'in the ninth year of our rightful Sovereign Queen Victoria,' stating that 'the ground was given by Jacob Cook, Esq., one of her Majesty's Justices of the Peace, of which he has done the honour of laying the corner stone of the first Rechabite Hall in British North America this day.'

The office bearers on that day were as follows: Ezra Hemphill, James McCready, John Dunn, Edwin Ogden, Thos. Stevenson, John Morley, and Michael Readman. Members listed were: Hugh Shaw, William Stevenson, John Joy, John Bangor, Matthew Dinnin, Wm. Dwyer, W. C. Ogden, T. Williams, Dan Wilcox, J. Casey, J. McCasling, W. Chisholm, W. C. Hawkins, T. Peaker, J. Taylor, J. Johnston, P. Hogan, E. Colson, J. Jordan, W. James, E. Mortimer, J. Dixon, S. Ogden, G. Miller, G. Cook, W. Watkins, M. Robins, J. Johnstone, W. Doherty, J. Grais, D. Schiller, J. Bradshaw, J. Rider, G. Sidder and T. Robinet.

This Rechabite Hall, opened so jubilantly by all the members, and used for the meetings of the Township Council up until the opening of the first Town Hall in 1873, was perfunctorily dismissed, in 1877, as 'an eyesore in the community' and was bought by one Mrs Elgie, to be torn down for other purposes.

The Sons of Temperance had its origin in the United States in 1808, and one of the earliest in Upper Canada was formed at Toronto in 1828, being the parent association for the Province. This Society pledged its members to abstain from ardent spirits, not to give them to others unless in case of sickness.

Strangely enough, it was the hotel keepers themselves who first encouraged this movement toward temperance, because of the excessive drinking and subsequent brawls occurring in taverns, resulting in many of their furnishings being damaged and wrecked, and thus putting their proprietors out of business. The best recommendation of a bartender, in the eighteen-thirties, was his size and strength, for an important part of his work was being able to stop fights and throw out the drunkards.

The hotel men wished to be allowed to supply refreshments to the travellers and local people, but within the bounds of reason; therefore, the Society was careful to add the proviso of 'moderation' and 'for medicinal uses only' to the pledge. Whereas the Rechabites would not drink wines or liquors at all, the Sons of Temperance were never as strict, and the advertisements for hotels always gave information regarding the fine conditions of their larders, and excellence of their bars.

Around the eighteen-forties it became fashionable to serve coffee instead of liquor with desserts for dinner, and refreshing lemonade and iced water for evening parties. Silver or china jugs filled with water began to be seen everywhere, even in hotels. The hotel owners did not like it, because their main profits came from the bar rooms; they were bitter when travellers avoided the hotels which had only jugs of lemonade.

But indeed, for long years afterwards in Cooksville, at socials and after games of sports, the guests and ball players were pleased to be treated to the feasts of sandwiches, cake and lemonade, such as had been started by the Sons of Temperance.

The Methodists built their own Church on Agnes Street in 1844, a frame structure large enough to seat three hundred people; its minister was the Reverend Hughes, with the Methodist preacher being the Reverend J. Wilson. Roughcast three years later, and called the 'lath-and-plaster church,' of such fine materials was it built that over the years it was to have many different manners of use; it was to outlive any of the other buildings, and stand as a landmark on Dundas Street, for generations.

When the building was later moved around the corner and down to Dundas Street, a small written note was discovered inside its corner stone, stating that 'Wm. Curtis Stephenson, Cabinet Maker, August, 1844, worked in this Church,' and beside his note was found a hardened, black apple core.

Regarding a school, Cooksville had none, for years to come; but its children, as well as adults, attended the only school known in the district, which was a long walk from home. Cooksville children walked, or got rides as they could, down to the Lakeshore road to the school on William Cawthra's land, and some of them grew up to become teachers there. One of this school's teachers was Lucinda Miller, who came with her family from County Armagh in Ireland, in 1831, to settle in the Port Credit district when she was thirteen years old. By the time she was fifteen, she was teaching in the first school in the settlement and in 1836, at eighteen, she became the wife of David Schiller and went to live at Cooksville.

The Toronto and Home District Council was at first made up of appointed representatives from Toronto, the Counties of Peel and York, with eight of these coming from the County of Peel. On November 11th, 1842, Dr William Pool Crewe and William Thompson, representing Toronto Township in the County of Peel, tried, unsuccessfully, to have the Council approve a resolution to authorize the road surveyors to obtain the cost of improving the Centre Road and Dundas Street, with authority for levying a special rate for same. This was the first endeavour toward the building of what later became two main Provincial Highways passing through Cooksville.

After Toronto Township became incorporated, in 1850, the Council meetings were held in various halls and hotels in the new municipality; one of these was the Rechabite Hall, at Cooksville.

By 1851, Cooksville was said to be 'the liveliest village west of Toronto, being on the main travelled road between Toronto and Hamilton,' and in these early days Cooksville was well able to supply the needs of its inhabitants, for there were enough tradespeople to handle most businesses.

When a settler's suit of clothing finally wore out, he had his choice of two tailors, John Morley or John Mackenzie, to make him another. For the three shoemakers, John Ryder, William Weeks, and J. D. Galbraith, there was plenty of work because in this new and rough life, families had to walk, far and near. James Soady had a last and peg factory, equipped with a steam engine and boiler, along with a full set of machinery for making the lasts, pegs, and crimps needed by shoemakers. Mr Soady also had boot-trees, for stretching the boots and keeping them in shape. The tanner and currier who kept all of them supplied with leather was John Dunn.

Stone work was handled by the stone mason, William Oldfield; and of carpenters, there were five: John Bell, James and Samuel Harris, W. F. Magee, and James McCready. The tinsmith was William Peaker, who had a store; and Elijah Markle made pumps. Hugh Shaw was the painter; and the cabinet makers, to make the furniture, were Thomas and William Stephenson.

Village merchants of the time were listed as P. Z. Romain, F. Logan, and Thos. J. Thompson. Mr Thompson was, as well, an agent for the National Loan Fund Life and Equitable Insurance Companies. James Peacock was the butcher, and James Vyse, the baker.

In a district where horses were a necessity of life, for the work they did on the farms and in transporting produce and goods, there were three blacksmiths in the village, Eugene Guthrie, Michael Readman, and John Belcher Jr., working to keep the horses well shod. Ezra Hemphill and George Miller owned wagon shops, where they built the carts, wagons and buggies on which the farmers and their families depended. Early saddlers in Cooksville were Rogers & Morrison.

Finally, according to the Directories of 1850-51, these were the farmers and other villagers who patronized them all:

John Bighan, Jane Blevins, Richard Ezzard, Mrs Fisher, William Frickley, Jane Grimshaw, Richard Hornibrook, Stephen Morris, Charles and John McLaughlin, Samuel G. Ogden, Albert Parker, Mary Anne Royal, Robert Rutledge, William Sanders, Styles and William Stevens, John Taggart, James Thompson, Asa and Isaac Walterhouse.

Chapter 6: The Great Fire

DURING THE FIRST PART OF MAY, 1852, *The Guelph Advertiser* reported that the weather in this part of the country had been very warm, with no rain, thus keeping the growing of crops in the townships very slow. Much of the fall wheat on the higher land, around Erin, was killed by this drought. Although no mention was made of Cooksville, such had been the case there as well, for some time previously, with everything becoming exceedingly dry.

Most readers of *The Toronto Globe* were aware of Cooksville's location, but it was rare for any story from this village to ever be put on the front page of any large newspaper. However, at the beginning of June, 1852, the readers of five newspapers throughout the province, *The Hamilton Spectator*, *The Daily Colonist Extra*, *The Toronto Globe*, *The North American*, and *The Owen Sound Comet*, were able to learn of the disaster at Cooksville.

'THE VILLAGE OF COOKSVILLE DESTROYED!
A WHOLE VILLAGE IN RUINS! WHAT AN AWFUL SPECTACLE!'

These were the headlines, regarding the 'post town on the Dundas road, about 16 miles west of Toronto.' The fire happened on May 26th, after which a special reporter from *The Toronto Globe* went to visit Cooksville, and reported the information which he collected on the spot.

He wrote that about two o'clock in the afternoon, on Saturday, a fire broke out in the blacksmith shop of John Belcher. Belcher's forge stood on the north side of Dundas Street, about a block west of Hurontario Street, and between his shop and the four corners stood Romain's general store. Both Mr Belcher and Mr Romain had bought lots from Samuel Ogden, and set up their businesses around the same year, 1844.

With the wind blowing fresh and everything so dry, and only a short distance between them, both businesses were set afire, and the flames spread easterly along the entire north side of Dundas Street, crossing Hurontario and continuing onwards. They spread northward to the very edge of the village, devouring everything that stood in their path. Houses and their contents, fences, wooden pavements, and everything consumable by the flames were entirely destroyed, all the way over to the creek, where even the embankment and wooden timbers of the mill caught fire and let the water flow unchecked from the dam.

Several times, Saville's Hotel, which stood on the south side of Dundas, caught fire, and several houses on the east side of it were totally lost. The hotel keeper had, no doubt, more people to help fight the blaze and more equipment to work with, and was thus able to save the hotel; its stables and other outbuildings also remained standing. Damage was caused to furniture taken out from the hotel, but this was minor in consideration of what was happening all around.

This fire raged furiously for longer than two hours, at which time an awful storm, such as was experienced in Toronto about the same time, occurred, with torrents and floods of rain coming down on the village and quenching the fire. The rain prevented its spreading any further.

No estimate could be made for some time afterwards of the amount of property destroyed, but it was large. There were thirty-five houses and other buildings burnt, and not many of them insured for nearly the amount lost. Many families were utterly ruined and left with no homes. There could not be a reckoning of the names of all the sufferers from the fire in time for them to appear in the newspapers, but the ones the reporter was able to learn at the time were to be found on their front pages. Those listed were:
– John Belcher's Blacksmith Shop, and a building attached to it;
– P. Z. Romain's brick store and outbuildings, including his whole stock of merchandise – partially insured, but loss heavy;
– Moses Teeter's Hotel (on north east corner of Dundas and Hurontario Streets), built of brick, and owned by Jacob Cook – insured;
– Francis Morley, his Post Office and store – slightly insured, loss heavy;
– John Galbraith Shoemaker's Shop – small insurance;
– Eugene Guthrey, occupant of a dwelling house belonging to Jacob Cook – no insurance;
– Michael Readman, blacksmith, lost dwelling house, but his Shop saved;
– Widow Grimshaw, her dwelling house and barn;

– E. Guthrie, Wagon Shop;
– Mrs Blevins, Tannery and barn;
– James Vyse, Baker, dwelling house;
– Thomas Harris, barn;
– W. Perrin, house and barn;
– Samuel Wilson, Tavern and outhouses;
– John Morley, barn;
– Dr Crewe, barn and shed.

Due to the destruction by fire, numerous other families were reduced from a state of comfort to want. *The Globe* reporter wrote: 'Their pitiable condition demands the prompt action of the benevolent on their behalf.'

Thus, the village of Cooksville seemed to be left in ashes, like Phoenix, the bird of great beauty in Egyptian mythology which was said to live for five or six hundred years in the Arabian Desert and then be consumed by fire.

Chapter 7: The Hotels of Cooksville

ONLY TWO HOTELS were left standing at Cooksville, immediately following the great fire – the Saville Hotel, and the Tyrone Inn.

Situated on land owned by William Scott, who had bought eighty-five acres of Lot 15 on the south side of Dundas Street in 1833, the Saville Hotel had good stabling and drive sheds for coaches, and a large yard. After leasing it from Mr Scott in March of 1851, J. Saville had been managing the hotel, and holding auction sales of live stock there, on the twenty-first of each month. The Tyrone Inn, owned by Samuel Wilson, and located farther east, on Lot 14 on the south side of Dundas Street, also remained in operation, but by 1855, Mr Wilson had gone elsewhere, with his inn being leased and run by James Russell.

At the end of July, after the fire, Mr Saville left and J. Wallace took over its management, restoring to it its former name of Scott's Hotel. However, it did not prosper and, by 1856, William Scott had left for Whitby, with the large piece of land known as the northeast part of Lot 15 Con.1 SDS being advertised on the market, for sale. The eighty-five acres 'long sought for by many,' was offered to farmers, land speculators, and others. On the Tremaine Map of Peel, drawn in 1859, the hotel itself was designated by nothing more than a black square, with the words 'old hotel' beside it.

SAVILLE'S HOTEL,

(late Scott's)

COOKSVILLE.

THE Subscriber, in returning thanks to his old Customers and the Travelling Public, would announce that he has leased the above House, where he trusts he will be enabled to supply them with everything that may conduce to their comfort and convenience.

J. SAVILLE.

Cooksville, March 20, 1851.   15

A MONTHLY SALE of STOCK, &c., will be held at this HOUSE on the 25th of every month.

The Streetsville Review, April 3, 1852

SCOTT'S HOTEL.

COOKSVILLE,

BY J. WALLACE.

WHO takes this method of acquainting the travelling community, and his old friends, that he has succeeded Mr. Saville, in the above Hotel. He will spare no pains to merit a continuance of that support, heretofore so liberally bestowed on his predecessors.

His LARDER will be supplied with the best the Country affords, and his BAR, with the choicest Wines, and Liquors.

☞ GOOD STABLING. ☜

Cooksville, July 27th, 1852.   33-tf

The Streetsville Review, April 9, 1853

The Streetsville Review, July 7, 1855

The Brampton Standard, September 4, 1855

With the complete destruction of Jacob Cook's Hotel, on the northeast corner of Dundas and Hurontario, there was a terrible gap left to be filled, because it had been a focal point, and the post for changing horses on the stage coaches carrying the mail, as well as passengers.

Besides being a disaster for the village, the fire came as a disaster for a man named William Harris, an Irish settler who also owned extensive sheds and stables, located at the four corners of a hamlet northwest of Streetsville. Called 'Ginger' Harris, he was driving his own stage route from Harris' Corners to Toronto; at six in the morning, he left his own inn and came down the road through Streetsville, Crozier's Corners, Springfield-on-the-Credit, and on to Cooksville, the point midway between Harris' Corners and Toronto. At Cooksville, he drove in to Cook's yard for a change of horses; thus, the fire brought misfortune for him as well.

Ginger Harris was resourceful. Cook's Hotel, run by Moses Teeter, had insurance on it and was thus able to be rebuilt. Therefore, Ginger bought the whole lot himself and, by September 4th, 1854, was running an advertisement in *The Brampton Standard and County of Peel Conservative Journal*. The 'Phoenix bird,' lying in ashes at the Cooksville corners had risen up again, more brilliant than before, at great expense, by Ginger Harris. Under its new name of the Royal Exchange, the hotel was once again in business with a larder and bar second to none other in the Township. However, since Moses Teeter had died several months after the fire, Ginger had to take care of the new hotel himself.

On the northwest corner of Dundas and Hurontario Streets, Readman's Blacksmith Shop remained in business and horses could still be shod there. New sheds were put up to stable horses, and soon travellers began calling at a one-storey house near the corner, owned by Asa Walterhouse, the carpenter. John and George Schiller became stage coach drivers and kept tavern at this house, which became known as the Walter House.

THE SCHILLER HOUSE:
West of where John Belcher's forge had been, Dundas Street remained the same, and David and Lucinda Schiller were still living just outside of the village itself, in the homestead house they had built. However, this was not to continue, for David died in 1856 at the early age of forty-six years.

Following the death of her husband, Lucinda lived with her son

Schiller House, (Irwin Hardware Building, 26-24 Dundas St. E.),
c. 1989. (Photo: The City of Mississauga)

David, who built a general store at the northwest corner of Cook and
Dundas Streets. Her son Charles later became Cooksville's Postmaster;
George and John, who had become experienced at driving a stagecoach
and operating a tavern while working at the Walter House, went into the
hotel business for themselves. John Edmund Schiller bought the section
of William Scott's former property on which had stood the 'old hotel.'
This land, described as Lot 19 and part of Lot 20, on the old plan of the
village of Cooksville, consisted of three acres, and was located a short
distance east of Hurontario Street. On it, John Schiller erected a new
hotel, and named it the Schiller House.

John married Mary Jane Thompson, and together they owned and
operated this hotel near the four corners of Cooksville. It was a large
and commodious house, with a large barn, stable and shed, and had a
public hall in connection with it. There were fruit trees and a fine
garden on the property.

At the beginning of August in 1874, John and Mary Jane Schiller
sold their hotel to the Western Canada Loan and Savings Company, and
left Cooksville. John's brother George went to live in Iowa, and the
Schillers bought John Hirst's Yorkshire Hotel, in Toronto. At the
Cooksville Fall Fair of 1878, there was a Special Prize of $5.00 listed on
the programme as being given by 'John Schiller, Yorkshire Hotel,

The Brampton Conservator,
March, 1878

Adelaide Street, Toronto, for the best and greatest variety of field roots.'
This prize was won by Thos. Pallett.

The times were changing, for in those days the city hotels began
advertising that they 'kept a first-class Saloon and Restaurant, with
everything to drink,' and in the Restaurant they offered cigars, oysters,
pies, and other refreshments. A feature which drew the patrons was a
good Bagatelle, this being a game somewhat similar to billiards, played
with balls and a cue, on a board having nine holes at one end into which
the balls were struck. A sandwich and a glass of ale could be had for the
sum of 5 d. More luxurious plumbing had now been added in the
hotels, and there were by this time only two public baths listed in the
city.

Another notable change was that of the names of hotels; instead of
being called by flowery and fanciful names, or by sentimental names of
the Old Country counties, they were becoming known by the names of
their owners. The Toronto City Directory for 1880 listed: the Yorkshire
Hotel, Proprietor, John E. Schiller; however, when the Exhibition began
to be held in Toronto, among the chief hotels which promised the best
accommodations for Exhibition visitors there appeared the name, not of
the Yorkshire Hotel, but of the Schiller House.

As for the Schiller House at Cooksville, it became Josiah Green's
Pharmacy and dwelling; the ancient barn on the property was carefully
taken down by John Cunningham in 1907, removed to the CPR Station
grounds, and its timbers used in the erection of a coal shed.

After Mr Green's death, his son-in-law Hugh Bowden carried on the

Pharmacy business, and also became Cooksville's Postmaster. He altered the front of the building, making it into Bowden's Drug Store on one side, and the Post Office on the other. The public hall connected with it was variously known as Pharmacy Hall, Bowden's Hall, and later as the Orange Hall; it was used for entertainments and suppers, as well as for special meetings and social gatherings of the Dixie Anglican and Presbyterian Church groups. Years later, the old hotel building was bought by Mr Bailey, of Streetsville, for a new Butcher Shop.

At the present day, in 1996, though its outbuildings and public hall have disappeared from the scene years ago, this landmark hotel still remains standing, between Hurontario Street and Shepard Avenue, at No. 24-26 Dundas Street East.

THE COOKSVILLE HOUSE:

William G. Harris, who owned the Royal Exchange Hotel, also owned several lines of Stages running from Toronto to Brampton, Edmonton, Cheltenham, Streetsville, Norval, Georgetown, and other smaller places situated in between. He claimed to have liquors of the best quality and a larder second to no other hotels in the United Counties of York and Peel, and in all of these cases his charges were extremely moderate.

Royal Exchange Hotel,

COOKSVILLE.

(FORMERLY KEPT BY WILLIAM HARRRIS.)

THE subscriber would respectfully inform his numerous friends and the travelling public that he has opened the above house, and intends keeping it in a manner that will raise houses of accommodation in the estimation of all right-minded persons, who may favour him with a call.

F. B. MORLEY.

Cooksville, February 9, 1859. 5

The Streetsville Review, March 26, 1859

However, with the coming of the Great Western Railway through Port Credit in 1855, his stage lines were soon becoming unprofitable and he decided to sell the hotel at Cooksville.

Mr Harris then bought the Globe Hotel, at Streetsville, and sold the Royal Exchange to Francis B. Morley. On February 9th, 1859, Mr Morley inserted an advertisement in *The Streetsville Review*, respectfully informing his friends and the general travelling public that he had bought the hotel, and intended to keep it 'in a manner that will raise houses of accommodation in the estimation of all right-minded people who might favour him with a call.'

The Royal Exchange Hotel became known as the Morley House, and Francis B. Morley, who had been the Postmaster and Issuer of Marriage Licences at Cooksville, now moved his offices into a part of the hotel. Here he kept the Cooksville Post Office until his resignation on November 22nd, 1867.

Frank Morley was a genial man who enjoyed serving and entertaining people. He was a perfect host for all important meetings, dinners and parties held in his hotel. He had his own band, and this band travelled about, appearing in other hotels and halls; on occasions, he took his band to Lorne Park to play for the people who came there in the summers, from Toronto.

In 1883, a hotel licence was granted to James W. King, Cooksville Hotel; and in April of 1891, Mr King bought the Morley House for the price of six thousand dollars, taking possession on May the first. Mr King was the second son of Thomas King, the Township Treasurer, and was born on his father's farm on the Wolfe Line. Before buying the hotel, he had been a time clerk in Barber's Store, near Streetsville, and he thoroughly understood the business and requirements of the public.

A description of the hotel at that time stated that his bar, waiting rooms and dining rooms were models of excellence, and that proprietors of more pretentious hotels might profitably copy Mr King's example. It was a quiet house, and was well-furnished. It had good stabling, and auction sales were being held there regularly by the best-known auctioneer in the County, John Thomson, of Port Credit.

At the beginning of April, 1904, James W. King died, but King's Hotel remained as before, now operated by his son, James H. King. The young Mr King was one who liked to be absent from behind the hotel bar at times, to go on hunting trips in search of big bear and other wild

Cooksville House, northeast corner Dundas & Hurontario Streets, c. 1910–11. (Photo: Mississauga Central Library, Cooksville Vol. 1)

game; and it was always reported in the paper that, on his return, the patrons of his house might expect high living.

After the death of his father, James arranged for considerable repairs to be made to the shed of the Cooksville House. A new stone foundation was built, with new sheathing, and horse troughs were installed inside. Both the interior and exterior of the building were given a new coat of whitewash, making a decided improvement in the appearance of the whole area.

While all this work was being done, George Casselman, the veteran hostler at the Cooksville House, suffered an accident and had his shoulder blade broken. Another hostler also worked with Mr Casselman, his name being Charles O'Mellian.

In 1905, King's Hotel was advertised for sale and was bought by Mr J. C. Ward, who improved it still further. A couple of years later it was purchased again, this time by George Bowers who was to remain its proprietor for many years.

The first thing that occurred after Mr Bowers became the owner was the destruction by fire of the driving shed and stable which adjoined the hotel. Besides this loss, estimated at one thousand dollars, Mr Bowers had to make arrangements for the use of Mr Walterhouse's stable, in order to carry on his business. However, auction sales of milch cows and young cattle could still be held in the yard, and their success and value to the surrounding locality enabled Mr Bowers to have his own stable and sheds rebuilt.

He held shooting matches for prizes of turkeys, geese, chickens and pigeons, with some of these contest winners being John Fleming, of Lambton Mills; John Heary, of Dixie; A. Thomson, of Port Credit; J. Kennedy, of Dixie; and B. Gordon, of Cooksville.

Along with all the other work done, by February of 1911 Mr Bowers had finished renovating and improving the interior of the hotel, just in time for the holding of the Annual Meeting of the Cooksville Agricultural Society. A new hallway had been arranged as an entrance to the dining room, the front sitting room re-fitted and furnished as a ladies' waiting room, and most of the other rooms had been painted and wallpapered.

A modern steam heating outfit was next established and, besides all this work, the hotel received a thorough system of water pressure to provide all of the bathrooms, closets and wash basins with hot and cold water, in all parts of the hotel. Greatest, and most important of all, was the installation of a hose attachment to protect the hotel from the ravages of fire. Terrible fires had been wreaking havoc on Cooksville over the years, and it was a satisfaction to Mr Bowers to see his hotel thus protected.

Electric wiring for lighting was also put in at this time; and it could be stated truthfully that Cooksville now had all of the modern appliances of a first class hotel, to benefit its patrons.

George Bowers decided, at this time, to have a holiday and bought himself a new 35-horsepower McLaughlin family automobile; and the next thing reported in *The Streetsville Review* on February 1st, 1912, was that the Cooksville House had changed proprietors – that he had sold out his interest to Messrs. McCheyne & Ginn, of Toronto. Rumours were flying about that the new owners planned to make changes, for the purpose of further accommodations and appearance. However, two weeks later, the transfer of the licence was refused to them.

George Bowers himself then began to make changes in the hotel. He had the bar removed from the west to the east side of the house; a window in the east end of the front verandah was made into a door, for an entrance, and the former bar room was turned into a general sitting room and fitted up accordingly. The hotel dining room, with its entrance now directly off the new sitting room, was re-modelled with an oak beam panelled ceiling; the walls were painted with scenic decorations and finished all around in burlap. The new bar room, together with all of the upstairs rooms, was also redecorated and improved, all of this work being completely finished under the capable management of the T. Eaton Company, of Toronto.

The enterprising proprietor received so much credit for his modern, up-to-date changes, and was so pleased with the inside that he had the outside of the hotel covered with a new coat of paint. The final touch was the installation of a brand-new, three hundred dollar cash register in his bar, to keep accurate control of its receipts.

Business men took notice indeed, for the following week, in June of 1912, four automobiles were seen parked in the lot, and the members of the Peel County Council stayed for dinner at Bowers' Hotel.

Everything was going ahead, and the following year the part of the building used formerly as a garage, in the rear premises of the hotel, was turned into a Barber Shop, with a Pool Room, in charge of Alf Harris. It was a nice comfortable shop, with a metallic ceiling and walls, covered outside with metallic siding; it possessed the only plate glass window in the village, and had a revolving red-and-white barber sign outside. Inside, there was a large wall case with a handsome mirror, up-to-date barber's revolving chair, and all the other necessary furniture for the required business. A small notice inserted in the newspaper invited people in, stating 'Now, you are next.'

In 1915, a fire of mysterious origin entirely destroyed the shops and sheds, but they were rebuilt, better than before. Not only did they have a new Barber Shop, with a barber named Mark Juniper, but a further attraction which caused much surprise in the district, was the hiring of a lady barber. It was announced in the local newspaper that 'Cooksville is about the only unincorporated village that boasts a Pool Room and a lady barber – there are a lot of good things about Cooksville that need no enumeration.' Frank and Charles Harris took over the new Pool Room, with two tables in use and more planned to be added. Business was thriving.

J. O. (Ollie) Rutledge, whose barn had also been destroyed by fire, rented the new stable and shed and began running his Cooksville Livery Stables there, with both horses and autos for hire, until he was able once again to erect a new barn of his own.

In a very short time following these changes and renovations, the disturbing news came that the Temperance Societies had been successful and hotel licences would no longer be issued, despite all of Mr Bowers' efforts with regard to his accommodations. So discouraged was he that he decided to retire to his farm, known and far-famed as 'Corn Dilly,' and devote all of his time to agriculture.

The hotel, along with the Pool Room and Barber Shop within the building, was rented to Frank Harris; the sheds and stable were rented to Mr R. Coulter, to conduct a Livery and give accommodation to farmers desiring feed and stabling for their horses.

This arrangement did not last long, because Mr Bowers could not remain out of the hotel business. He now called it the Cooksville Inn, and to make up for the loss of the liquor sales, he fitted up the front sitting room as an Ice Cream and Refreshment Room for the travellers along Dundas Street. He put in a new Soda Fountain and declared that he would now serve 'first class cooling beverages to the hot and thirsty public, to the Queen's taste.'

In addition, he curtained off the large verandah facing the Centre Road, and provided chairs and tables where all of these delicacies could be enjoyed in the cool and comfortable conditions of the outdoors. He

The Brampton Conservator, September 28, 1922

The Streetsville Review,
September 30, 1915

The Port Credit News,
September 23, 1927

54

erected banners, one across Dundas Street and the other across the side lawn, calling attention to his refreshment rooms and attracting many customers.

Mr Bowers next added to the industries of the village by turning the hotel bar room into a Harness Shop. A native of Devonshire, England, he had come to Canada at an early age and lived in Toronto where he was in the harness business, and he now began to ply his former trade. Thus, he showed his ingenuity and business sense in adapting to the conditions of the day, and his hotel once again prospered. In 1923, the old verandah at the front and side was torn down, to be replaced by a handsome new cement block verandah, on three sides. For a few years, Mr and Mrs R. C. King leased and moved into the Cooksville Inn. They erected an Ice Cream and Refreshment Booth on the lot east of the Inn, under the spreading elm tree so much admired by all who saw it.

In 1927, Mr Bowers returned to the Inn once again, and spent five thousand dollars to enlarge his dining room to accommodate 125 guests; he declared, at the same time, that accommodation could be found for twice as many, at a pinch. Pretty latticed windows, and beautiful soft pastels were used for the interior decoration. Both the upper and lower verandahs were lengthened, in order to give more space for sitting-out places; and the pretty grounds surrounding the hotel were turned into a picturesque parking space. In July, his Dominion Day advertisement promised Special Chicken Dinners at the Inn; and the following September, his specialty was First Class 50-cent Meals with the best Ice Cream being served.

Mr and Mrs Pat Long took over the management in 1928 and, the following spring, Mr A. V. Devins tore down the old shed adjoining the Pool Room, which had served its usefulness. For long years it had sheltered the horses from the wintery blasts during the days of the open bar room, and recalled to many people the names of men who had once conducted its business – Ben Trimble, John F. Noble, Charles Strong, and Eddie Carr. A nice rock garden appeared upon the site, for both Mr and Mrs Devins were great lovers of flowers.

When the lease was up, after Mr and Mrs Long left for Sterling, Mr and Mrs Bowers returned to the Inn in 1931 to carry it on themselves. In summer, 1936, there were busy days for George Bowers' well-managed hotel, as many American tourists, added to the Canadian travellers, made it their regular stopping place.

On July 7th, 1937, Mr Bowers who had then been in the hotel business for thirty years, said that it was 'the best week I have had since I have been here.' *The Port Credit News* stated that he contemplated an addition to his business shortly, in the form of an Ice Cream and Soda dispensary.

Just before Christmas, in 1941, George Frederick Bowers, who had been the Proprietor of the Cooksville Inn for almost thirty-five years, died at the age of sixty-five; and the following July, in 1942, Robert Henry Edwards, one of the few remaining original stage coach drivers of Cooksville, died at the age of eighty-eight years.

Still, the Cooksville Inn remained in operation, on the northeast corner of Dundas and Hurontario Streets. Its next owner, in 1945, was Jack Braithwaite; and in 1947, Alfred P. Ward purchased the Cooksville Inn. Mr Ward had the Annex in the east side as the headquarters for his Drug Store, with Mrs E. Sweet managing the hotel business.

December of 1950 saw a Christmas party being held there, and the following spring, Mr Ward leased the Cooksville Inn to Frank Laven, the former proprietor of Mac's Lunch.

Finally, in 1954, the old Inn was torn down and the new Canadian Bank of Commerce was built on the historic site. Rodney Pinkney remembers today that, in October of 1954, on the day before Hurricane Hazel swept across the Cooksville area, the concrete was poured for the foundation of the new bank, causing a great deal of trouble for his Company in getting the work done.

THE REVERE HOUSE:

Edway Walterhouse was born in Cooksville in 1842 and, at a young age, went to Detroit where he worked at a meat market for several years. In 1866, he married Elizabeth Tewesley and returned to Cooksville to go into the hotel business.

The small Walter House, the home of the Walterhouse family, situated near the northwest corner of Dundas and Hurontario Streets, had become a stopping-off place for farmers as they brought produce into the village and picked up their supplies. Before leaving for home again, they could enjoy a bit of rest and catch up on the local news.

Edway Walterhouse took over the management of the Walter House, and changed its name. After Mr Readman's death in 1883, Louis Walterhouse erected a new blacksmith shop at the northwest corner of Agnes Street and Hurontario; and among the names listed under the heading of Licences Granted in 1884, published in the weekly newspaper, was that of Edway Walterhouse, Cooksville Revere House.

In 1889, the hotel was leased to Mr Riesey, formerly of Halton, and two years later Mr Walterhouse decided to move the building closer to the sidewalk at the northwest corner of Dundas and Hurontario Streets. There were extensive stables, which had been built after the great fire for stage coach operations and, with the added blacksmith business, the hotel was doing well. By the beginning of September, 1891, the Revere House had not only been moved, but had been 'raised' (by the addition of another storey); the entire building had been covered with a veneer of red brick, with a balcony built across the front.

Accommodation in the hotel was now said to be superb. It was a good and quiet house, and after ten years of being leased to Mr Riesey and his new partner named Mr Carpenter, the Revere House had become very well known in the district.

In 1895, the Editor of *The Streetsville Review* wrote: 'It would not seem right to mention Cooksville and not say anything in reference to

Ward's Drug Store, (in old Revere House), northwest corner Dundas & Hurontario Streets, c. 1920-1930. (Photo: Region of Peel Archives, 81-3390M, N164-93)

the Revere House and its obliging proprietor, Mr Ed. Walterhouse. The large hotel is handsomely furnished throughout and has the best of accommodation for both man and beast. The bar is always supplied with the best brands of liquors and cigars. The table is one of the grand features of his hostelry, and one meal at the Revere House would do you good; try it and see for yourself.'

Although Edway Walterhouse owned the Revere House, it had long been leased by other people, thus allowing him the freedom to go about pursuing other careers, one of which was breeding horses. During the season of 1895, he owned a celebrated trotting stallion named 'Aberdeen Star,' which he described as a golden chestnut, foaled in 1886, and bred by R. Watson, of Brampton.

The horse had a fine pedigree, well-advertised, and each season Mr Walterhouse had a regular route, taking his horse from his own stable at Cooksville and keeping appointments with other horse owners. The route was to Erindale, Streetsville, Centerville, Ashgrove, and Georgetown, where he would stay over; then it was on to Norval and Edmonton, travelling north to Brampton, as well as to other small villages east of Hurontario Street. Wherever arrangements could be made, for the breeding of fine new horses, Edway Walterhouse travelled with his stallion.

Another of his ventures, in conjunction with the managing of the Revere House, was operating the saw mill. His father had been a carpenter by trade, and Edway Walterhouse carried on the business of the saw mill. In 1902, he purchased a new 60-inch chain saw, which enabled him to cut any size large logs. The mill was thoroughly overhauled and was able to handle timber up to sixty feet long.

Mrs Walterhouse was pleased to have as her visitor for several months, in 1903, a remarkable lady to introduce to her friends, in the person of Mrs Tewesley, of Detroit. Mrs Tewesley was her mother, a bright conversationalist who had interesting reminiscences to pass on about days of her girlhood when she visited Cooksville. People were all the more amazed to learn that Mrs Tewesley was now 104 years of age, having been born before the turn of the century.

In 1905, Cooksville's only then-active industry was the saw mill, and there were changes coming to the Revere House now, after so many years. First, the hotel was painted red. It was fenced in, its yards and sheds were closed to the travelling public; and at the beginning of February, 1907, Cooksville people noticed that the inside of the premises was being neatly painted and decorated by Mr J. K. Morley.

At this time, the Revere House underwent a real transformation when its former bar room was fitted up as an office for the Sterling Bank. The new Cooksville bank was a branch of the Port Credit Sterling Bank situated at the corner of the Stavebank and Lakeshore Roads, open for business two or three days a week. Its first manager was Herbert Thompson, who stayed until 1910 when Mr Connor came.

The Sterling Bank occupied the front of the Revere House building until 1911, when it was closed owing to insufficient business. However, arrangements were made for the Union Bank at Islington to move into the premises, and the Revere House then began to be called the Union Bank Building.

Rooms in the building were still being rented, to overflow guests from the Cooksville Inn, as well as to workers in the neighbourhood. Riches and Riches, a legal firm, moved in with their entrance on the Hurontario side; and they were followed by Mr Gordon Jackson, a lawyer who began his practice with an office in the rear of the building. Mr Jackson's hours were on Monday, Thursday, and Saturday afternoons.

In 1911, there was held a meeting in the Township Hall to consider the establishment of a municipal telephone system in Toronto Township. Up until then, Cooksville's Central office of the Bell Telephone Company had always been located in the Post Office but, in March of 1912, their main office was installed in Mr Walterhouse's old hotel, on the west side of the building, adjoining the bank. The door into the telephone office opened off Dundas Street.

Finally, the Revere House was gone; but Edway Walterhouse lived to see all of these changes. When he died, at the beginning of March, 1923, his funeral was held in the same house in which he had lived for nearly sixty years, and he was reported to have been the oldest hotelkeeper in Peel County, both in years and numbers of years conducting the business. As for the Revere House, it remained standing until the 1960s, when the Dundas Highway was widened into four lanes.

Chapter 8: The Corner Store

ALTHOUGH ACCOUNTS APPEARED in the larger newspapers of the day, nothing else seems to have been written for us about what was done to assist the Cooksville people who lost their stores and homes in the great fire.

Peter Z. Romain, a merchant who had owned the general store half a block west of the four corners, beside John Belcher's blacksmith shop where the fire started, was not only a storekeeper but a Commissioner of the Court of Queen's Bench. Pierre Romain's family, of Italian descent, had settled before 1820 at Point Levis, Quebec, later moving to Cooksville. The name of Elizabeth Romain, age 51, wife of Pierre R., is to be found listed as having been buried in 1832 in the Dixie Union Cemetery. Their sons Charles, William, and Peter Romain received an education at Upper Canada College, in Toronto, and were prominent in business at Cooksville. Charles was a lumber merchant who owned a saw mill close to the village, and the Romains owned land on Dundas Street, Lot 15 SDS.

At the time when William Harris was building his Royal Exchange Hotel on the northeast corner, Peter Z. Romain was actively working on getting a new general store into operation on the south side. By 1854 he was again advertising his wares in the local papers, announcing that Cooksville was still going ahead. He thanked his friends and customers for the liberal support he had met with in years past, and informed them that he had just received from Quebec, Montreal, Boston and New York, one of the choicest selections of goods ever offered in the Province, and for cheapness they could not be equalled in either Town or Country.

He had bought for cash, enabling him to sell at lower prices than for goods bought on credit. He declared it was no trouble to show the goods, and no grumbling if they didn't buy; that he had marked the

The Streetsville Review,
November 25, 1854

goods in plain figures, and there would be no deviation in prices. 'So Heave Ahead, my hearties. I fear no competition, for I can't be beat or undersold,' he declared; and signed himself, 'Respectfully, P. Z. Romain, Cooksville, Nov. 8th, 1854.'

However, Charles Romain went to Toronto to go into politics, and was later to be appointed Collector and Inspector of Inland Revenue. Peter left the Cooksville store, and soon began advertising a new assortment of fresh Teas, Porto Rica and Cuba Sugars (granulated, crystal, crushed, ground, broken loaf, and loaf), as well as family groceries and Fresh Fruits. His new Goods had been received and were ready for sale by July 1st, 1858, at the Ontario Warehouse, Upper Town, Streetsville.

* * *

In 1859, John Galbraith owned a general store near the northwest corner of Dundas Street; and by 1877, the two principal storekeepers in the village were Mr Galbraith, and T. G. Goulding. At this time, the McClelland family was living on what was then called the 'back line.' George McClelland had come with his family from Bambridge, County Down, Ireland, at the age of twenty-seven years, and in February, 1873, less than a year later, had settled on the farm north of Cooksville. The McClellands carried on the business of farming for ten years, after which George formed a partnership with his brother John, and undertook the operation of the general store on the southeast corner of Dundas and Hurontario Streets, situated on land then owned by Miles Washington Cook.

George McClelland married Anna Langdon, who was Mr Cook's niece, and at first they lived upstairs in the apartment over the store. It was a fine store, built of solid brick, and the McClellands prospered. For Christmas, in 1890, George was advertising 'Cottonades, Shirtings, Prints, Ginghams, Cretonnes, Etc.; Boots & Shoes, Wall Papers and Borderings; Groceries, Glass and Earthenware.' Mr McClelland stated that his prices were moderate, and he would sell for Cash or Produce.

The following year, he wrote descriptive paragraphs in *The Streetsville Review*. His advertisements made interesting reading, such as: 'Boodle! Boodle's another word for money. Money is a very useful article in the hands of a prudent man. Many prudent men find that goods purchased at the store of G. McClelland, Cooksville, save their purses and also prove satisfactory as to quality. Go thou, and do likewise.'

The Streetsville Review, December 12, 1890

George McClelland's Store, southeast corner Dundas & Hurontario
Streets, 1900. (Photo: Region of Peel Archives, N 166-7)

In 1891, George was agent for the Norwich Union Insurance Society and the Peel Farmers' Mutual Insurance Company, of Brampton. In 1895, he owned the best-stocked and largest store in Cooksville, doing a very large and profitable trade in every sort of general wares. He asked: 'Do you eat? If you do, why not buy your groceries at our store? Farm produce taken in exchange, at highest market prices.'

Mr McClelland served the public well; for thirty-two years he was the Treasurer of the Township, and it was said that in all that time he missed but two meetings. For over thirty years, he was Treasurer of the Cooksville Agricultural Society; when the Hydro electric service became available, he was made its Secretary-treasurer; in connection with the Township's inner affairs, he became both Assessor and Collector.

The property behind the store faced Hurontario Street, and here, in 1910, George McClelland erected a handsome brick residence. For many years, all along the frontage of this part of the lot grew stately locust trees, which were now converted into cordwood in order to provide an extensive front lawn. The new house was built in bungalow style, bricked up one storey, with a spacious verandah on two sides, and bay windows all around. It was fitted up with an electric furnace and bath, with the convenience of both hard and soft water inside. This house had an extra room, built expressly as an office for Mr McClelland, where he could attend to his other positions besides that of being a storekeeper.

He did not sell the store at this time; but in December, the business was taken over by Mr Alfred Scott, of Burnhamthorpe. The store then began to be known as Scott's Grocery.

People were still using wagons and sleighs pulled by horses to travel about, and there was a bit of excitement caused around the corners on one Thursday, in February, shortly after Mr Scott's arrival on the scene. Mr John Wismer came to purchase supplies, and hitched his horse up in front of the store. When he left, and began untying the horse, it ran away, galloping down the Centre Road (Hurontario) and all around Mr McClelland's new house; it then raced back up to Dundas Street, continuing west until it collided with a post. The horse became stuck between the post and a fence, near Mr Pardy's harness shop, and in its efforts to free itself, it wrenched the shutter door from Mr Stephens' house. Finally, in its fright, it broke away from the sleigh and galloped for home. The sleigh was damaged, and had to be extricated, but no one was hurt; the horse was found to be safe at Mr Wismer's stable.

63

Four Corners of Cooksville, looking east, 1920s, showing Copeland's Store on southeast corner, and new white frame Royal Bank on southwest corner, Dundas and Hurontario Streets. (Photo: courtesy of the Copeland family)

The next fall, in 1911, Mr Scott had a new gasoline tank put in at the corner of Dundas and Hurontario Streets, with a pump attachment for the use of automobiles. This was an absolutely new venture, at a time when automobiles were just beginning to be seen on the Dundas Highway. However, after this improvement to the store, in December of 1912, Mr Scott moved back to Burnhamthorpe, leaving the business to the management of Mr William Copeland.

* * *

Born in 1880, William Charles Henry Copeland lived with his family in a stone house on the south side of Burnhamthorpe Road and east of Tomken Road, where he farmed until 1912. After Mr Scott left, the Copeland family moved down to Cooksville with their four children, named Violet, Charles, Marie, and Hazel, and the store became Copeland's General Store. Two other children, born at Cooksville, were Florence, and a baby named Lorna Beatrice who died in 1919 at the age of eleven months.

Mr Copeland became the first County Constable in the Cooksville area, and write-ups of his work in this line began to appear in the newspapers, such as of the time when he arrested two youths, each about eighteen years of age, in the shed at Britannia Church. These young men, from out-of-town, were in possession of a loaded revolver and several rounds of bullets, as well as jack knives, search lights, and other hardware stock. They had stolen a car, robbed a hardware store in Barrie, and sought refuge in the shed. Constable Copeland was called as a witness and had to go to Barrie to give his evidence, which was considered a long journey in those early days of the year 1921. Another example was a case where he was called upon to arrest an aged man for stealing forged cheques.

In 1922, the most important sale by the Harris and Long Real Estate firm was that of the 165-foot frontage property on which the grocery store building formerly owned by George McClelland was situated. Since there now arose a need for a new postmaster, and he now owned a proper facility for a post office, Mr Copeland applied successfully for the position and the Cooksville Post Office was installed in his store. At this time, the building which housed both the general store and the post office became known as the Copeland Building.

Within two years, the store had become one of the liveliest retail establishments in Peel County. Mr Copeland had to add a new Dodge

British American Service Station, southeast corner Dundas & Hurontario Streets. (Photo: Mississauga Central Library, Cooksville Vol.1, F176)

The Port Credit News, May 4, 1928

car to his delivery system and, besides the groceries, in the springtime he set out an unusually large display of plants, in both flowers and tomatoes, which sold rapidly.

There had long been a one-gallon gasoline pump, which had to be operated by hand, but now he added a Bowser electrically-operated gas tank with clear vision, and a rapid-service filling hose attachment for the motorists. Mr Copeland also began handling Pennsylvania Oils and Gas, which were rated high among the gasolines then on the market. While keeping on with the business of operating Cooksville's grocery store on the corner and serving gasoline and oil to the public, William Copeland was appointed High County Constable of Peel but, after two years' time, he resigned this position.

At the end of March, 1927, *The Brampton Conservator* reported that 'Cooksville's Old Landmark, The Corner Store,' was to be moved, that an oil company had bought the land on which the store stood, in order to erect a new Gas Station.

Much interest was taken in the removal of the old building at the southeast corner of the Centre Road and Dundas Street. How could this be done? Built of solid brick, and dating back from the time following the great fire, the store was estimated to weigh over two hundred tons. 'Impossible,' said many wise people. 'A brick building cannot be moved. It will crack and perhaps fall to pieces.'

Nevertheless, it was jacked up, steel T-rails of regulation length were installed beneath it, and three double lines of rails were laid down, on which the building was to be carried eighty feet to the east. The work was done so carefully that, during the operations involved in the preparation for the move, not even a hair crack was to be found inside or outside the building.

Business was continued as usual in the store and the post office, delayed only for the time during which the actual movement to its new location took place. Mr E. A. McKay, the contractor from Port Credit, by means of a jack and cable, completed this work without any mishap; and so it was moved, stock and all, without any damage, and was one of the first so handled in the County.

A new British American Service Station was opened the following September, on the land formerly occupied by the General Store and Post Office conducted by the Copeland family. It was leased to Grant A. Edwards, of Toronto, a well-known Ford dealer. A unique feature of this new place of business was its water service; the water was pumped from an eighty-foot well, and there was running water for cars, as well as for drinking purposes. All British American products were sold, and there was a Battery Service, Vulcanizing Department, and also a wrecking truck. The building in connection with these services was modern in every respect, with steam heating, and no stones were left unturned to make the station the best possible.

The following year, Mr Copeland continued advertising such Week End Specials as Breakfast Bacon, Strawberries, Lettuce, New Cabbage, and Fresh Fruit – all to be delivered by calling Phone 3, Cooksville.

There was much excitement around the corners on a Friday morning in mid-August of 1931, when a young man from Hamilton stopped at the Service Station to fill his motorcycle tank with gas. For reasons of gas overflowing his tank and going on the hot cylinder of the engine, a serious fire was started, destroying not only the motorcycle but the gas pumps as well. The blaze was so hot that the paint on all the surrounding buildings was blistered off.

The British American tank wagon, which was standing near the pumps filling the large tanks at the time when the fire started, was driven to a safe location and no damage was done to the truck or its contents. Luckily, neither the attendant nor the motorcyclist were injured. The Oil Company's employees demonstrated that they believed in doing business in a hurry, for within a few hours of the fire, gas was being sold out of cans which had been brought out from the city, and by evening, two new gas pumps were in place and operating. The four corners of Cooksville had become much changed.

Free deliveries were made when the Copeland family had the corner store. Charlie Copeland delivered the groceries up the Tenth Line northwards, and Violet took them down the south line. The orders came in by phone; the persons would phone in summer, and in winter too. The girls had to get the groceries ready and, when it was winter, Charlie placed them in the sleigh before he went. He hitched the horse to the sleigh, and ran along beside it. He delivered the orders right up to Britannia, where the 401 highway is now, at least four or five miles, and all the while being so considerate of the horse that he wouldn't even ride on it.

The sleigh had lots of room to put the grocery boxes in it, and over the years deliveries were made on a regular schedule; they had a day for the north, a day for the south, a day for the east, and a day for the west. All four girls, Violet, Marie, Hazel and Florence, helped, and never forgot, especially delivering by sleigh in the wintertime. The bills were sent out to their customers on the 15th and 30th of the month, always hoping that people would pay. Some people paid with produce; some people gave eggs, or vegetables, or something like that, towards the cost of their groceries.

Since Mr Copeland was the Postmaster, all four girls helped to sort the mail as it came in; and after Mr Copeland died, on New Year's Day of 1948, while in the general store he had operated for thirty-five years, his son Charles took over the business. His daughter Violet took her father's place and became Postmaster. Listed in the Postal Records at Ottawa, regarding Postmasters on the Staff at Cooksville Post Office 2618, below her father's name, can be found the name of Miss Violet Marion Copeland, January 5, 1948 to May 31, 1960. Charles Copeland built a new grocery store on the east side of the original store and carried on, selling not only groceries but grains and feed for animals and chickens, as well.

The original corner store that became Cooksville's Post Office, as many people remember it to the present day, has been used over the years for many other types of businesses, from a drug store to a hairdressing salon, yet still retains its original appearance and can be seen standing, in 1996, at 14 Dundas Street East, near the four corners of Dundas and Hurontario Streets.

Chapter 9: The Village Tradesmen

IN THE EARLY DAYS, each small village had its own tradesmen who laboured manually to supply such necessities and services as were likely to be needed and bought and paid for in the village itself, as well as in the surrounding farming community. There was also to be found in Cooksville, at the turn of the century, a lodge known as No. 233, Ancient Order of United Workmen (AOUW), which provided a meeting place where the tradesmen gathered to compare ideas. In the event that any of its members met with a disaster, the group banded together and gave whatever assistance it could.

It would be hard to judge which of the tradesmen were of most importance to the life of the village. One might say the blacksmiths, because for over half a century horses were used for every type of undertaking, from working on the farms in this agricultural area to carrying the families to town for their supplies; all of these horses had to be shod. It was the blacksmith, hammering and shaping the iron shoes on his anvil, and fitting them onto the horses' hooves at his own forge, who kept things moving and running smoothly.

Cooksville had Michael Readman, who was born in 1810, at Durham, England. He came to Canada in 1832, and for nearly forty years carried on his trade as a blacksmith. There was a brief time when he left the village to join a Captain Austin's Company and shoulder a musket during the Mackenzie Rebellion of 1837; it was said that he lay in the old windmill near Gooderham's distillery for a couple of nights, and marched from there to Montgomery's Tavern to find it burning. He was an enthusiastic hunter and, when game for food became scarce, he spent a few weeks in the fall 'up north,' hunting for deer. Aside from these expeditions, Mr Readman lived quietly, pursuing his trade, for nearly forty years. He died at the beginning of June, in 1883.

* * *

Louis Walterhouse, born in Cooksville in 1848, took his trade from his father, Isaac Walterhouse, who had been a notable blacksmith before

Walterhouse Blacksmith Shop, northwest corner of Agnes and Hurontario Streets. (Photo: Mississauga Central Library, Cooksville Vol.1, #327)

the village was built. Louis was still carrying on the family business in 1891, at his own shop located on the northwest corner of Agnes and Hurontario Streets. In 1923, this fine brick building, which had long served its purpose as a blacksmith shop and was one of the best-known in the Township, was converted into a two-storey residence by its owner, Louis Walterhouse. Frank Walterhouse had worked there with his father, but when their business closed, a new blacksmith shop was erected by Joseph Allen behind his home, located on Cook Street, back of Schiller's Store property.

* * *

From 1898, Jerry Doherty's shop was in operation, and was bought in 1904 by Robert S. Whaley. The slippery conditions of the roadways in the December months made harvests for the blacksmiths, who had to work overtime to accommodate their numerous patrons wanting their horses' shoes provided with a means of keeping them from slipping on the snow and ice. The simplest way was to have the blacksmith replace some of the regular nails with ice-nails; when the ground was well covered with snow, these ice-nails stayed sharp. But when the ground was unusually slippery, sharp calks had to be screwed or welded to the shoes. Farmers and villagers tried to be at the smithy at seasonable hours, on those cold mornings; but they all expected to be served first.

In 1911, Mr Whaley erected a new blacksmith and wood working shop on his lot on Dundas Street, adjoining Mr Bowers' hotel. This

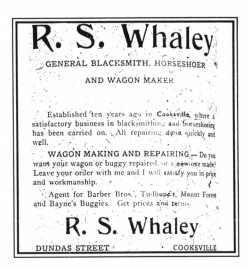

The Brampton Conservator
August 19, 1915

71

shop was built of concrete, two storeys high, with a paint shop above it. The contractors, Messrs. Richie and Wilson, fitted the building up with all modern requirements for the rapidly expanding business; there was even a telephone installed for the use of the customers, and it was wired for electric lights. After it was completed and Mr Whaley moved in, the shop had such a fine appearance, fitted up as it was in such style, that it began to be known as Cooksville's new Carriage and Blacksmith Shop.

Robert Whaley remained in this business until the beginning of March, 1917, when he purchased ten acres of land fronting on Dundas Street, from Mr John Ezard and began to devote his energy to market gardening and stock raising. The blacksmith shop was turned over to Frank Walterhouse, a descendant of one of Cooksville's original blacksmiths, Isaac Walterhouse.

* * *

In 1891, along with the blacksmiths, there was a wagon builder's shop owned by Charles R. Colwell, who also enjoyed the good will of the community. Born in 1842 in Gloucestershire, England, Mr Colwell was brought to this country by his parents when he was only three years of age. He learned the trade of carriage building and carried on this business on Dundas Street, at the western side of the village, for over forty years. He was widely known as a first-class workman, and was treasurer of the Ancient Order of United Workmen for many years.

The AOUW held Annual Concerts in the Town Hall, as well as Oyster Suppers in the Pharmacy Hall. On one occasion, visiting members from Mimico, Derry West, Port Credit, Springfield and Streetsville met at the Cooksville Lodge room and marched in a body to the Methodist Church, where a service was preached by the Reverend J. W. Morgan, of Malton, and special music was sung by the church choir. After their parade, the members returned to the lodge room and thanked Mr Morgan for his sermon; a short speech was given by a representative from each of the visiting brethren, and the Cooksville Lodge treated everyone to lemonade to bring the evening to a pleasant close.

The value of the AOUW in the village was clearly demonstrated in June of 1900, after a disastrous fire consumed the workshop owned by Charles Colwell. His stable and outbuildings, with part of their contents, and a quantity of valuable lumber were lost. The fire began at noon on a Sunday. A small stable owned by Mrs Wilcox, from which the fire spread, was also burned. The neighbours nearby turned out in force and, with the assistance of some bicyclists who happened to be passing along the road at the time, prevented the fire from spreading to the Agricultural buildings at the fair grounds, and Mr Ellingham's barn.

Mr Colwell had no insurance and was devastated by his loss, but at the beginning of August the members of the AOUW held a benefit entertainment on the fair grounds with the object of assisting him to rebuild the buildings destroyed in the fire. Attendance was very large. Previous to the programme a football game was played between the Cooksville and Streetsville teams, resulting in a win for Streetsville by 3 goals to 0.

The Meadowvale Band rendered plenty of lively music, and there were other musical attractions as well. The grounds were well-lighted by illuminators put up by Mr D. MacDonald, while Mr Charles Gill, in charge of the affair, did a large business from several booths set up on the field. After the concert the two football teams were treated to sandwiches and lemonade, described by *The Streetsville Review* as being 'very relishable;' and with proceeds amounting to over fifty dollars, the Lodge had a good-sized purse to hand to Mr Colwell.

However, in 1905, Charles Colwell was forced to retire from his trade owing to poor health, and the wagon shop was then taken over by Mr Stephens, of Streetsville. As for the Ancient Order of Workmen, they continued to prosper in Cooksville, holding many grand garden parties and entertainments. With bonfires lighted, refreshment booths well supplied with ice cream, fruit, candies and cigars, sandwiches and soft drinks, and with various Bands in attendance, they delighted all those who were admitted to the grounds at an admission price of 25 cents for adults, and 5 cents for children.

They provided help for the tradesmen wherever possible. *The Brampton Conservator* reported in 1915 that meetings were still being held in the Cooksville Town Hall, by the AOUW, but these gradually tapered off.

* * *

In 1846, there were four boot and shoe makers at Cooksville, one of these being James Soady. Mr Soady had settled on property at the eastern end of the village, near where the CPR Station was built, and he later owned land located east of the property belonging to Miles Washington Cook, on the south side of Dundas Street.

In the beginning, James Soady made boots and shoes by hand, attaching the soles to the tops by pegging, but by 1850 he was owner of a last and peg factory. This factory was equipped with a steam engine of 5 or 6 Horsepower, complete with a boiler, fly wheel, pump and governor. It had a full set of machinery for the making of pegs, lasts, crimps, and boot-trees. A last was the wooden form on which the boot was fitted; the boot-crimp drew and shaped the body of the boot, after which it was pegged to the sole by means of wooden nails, or pins; the boot-tree was the instrument used for stretching the boots and keeping them in shape.

In 1850, J. D. Galbraith and John Ryder were making boots and shoes; but by 1866 John Galbraith was advertising his wares in a General Merchandise Store, as a dealer in groceries, hardware, and dry goods.

At the time when Cooksville had a population of 400 people, in 1873, J. R. Morley, James and Walter Soady, Asa Walterhouse, John and William Weeks were the shoemakers of the day. William Weeks' son, born in Cooksville and also named William, succeeded his father in business in the old-fashioned way, and continued to live in the same

Cobbler's Shop and Residence, erected 1850, Cooksville, Ontario. (Photo: National Archives of Canada, C. P. Meredith Collection, August, 1925, Neg. PA26978)

Cooksville Carriage Works

Manufacturer of Buggies, Wagons, Cutters and Sleighs.

Repairing and Painting a Specialty.

Agent for
Tudhope Carriages and Cutters.

J, H. Stevens, - Prop.

For Sale ! A Bargain !!

A STEAM ENGINE, of 5 or 6 Horse Power, with Boiler, Fly-wheel, Pump, and Governor, nearly new.

Price, £100 ; £25 down and the remainder in three annual instalments with interest.

—ALSO,—

Will be sold with or without the Engine, a full set of Machinery for making Pegs, Lasts, Crimps and Boot-'Trees. Enquire of

J. SOADY.
Steam Last Factory.
Cooksville.

February 21st, 1855. 7tf.

house. When the younger William Weeks died at the age of seventy-six, in February of 1928, the old shoemaker's house was considered 'a fixture of the village.'

* * *

William Peaker bought half an acre of land from Jacob Cook, on the north side of Dundas at the corner of Cook Street, in 1847, and set up in business as a tinsmith. He produced such items as lanterns, candle moulds, candle sticks, tin cups and scoops, and stove pipes; all of these items were made and shaped by hand.

By 1866, Mr Peaker was also selling stoves in his store on Dundas Street. He later went into business with Mr E.O. Runians, of Brampton, while his son John continued operations at Cooksville, and this was the business which, for many years to come, was known as Peaker and Runians Hardware.

In 1871, John Peaker, now thirty-three years of age, set up an office in his father's store on Dundas Street and, on March 31st, was appointed the village Postmaster. He handled the mail there until he died, in 1873, and afterwards Hannah Peaker fulfilled these duties until the end of November in 1877.

The white dwelling and store, located on the northeast corner of Dundas and Cook Streets, shown in a picture familiarly recognized today as 'the old Cooksville Post Office,' was first inhabited by the tinsmith, William Peaker.

Chapter 10: The Schiller Stores

IN 1878, THE SAME YEAR that his brother John sold the Schiller House and George left for Iowa, David Schiller put up an unpretentious building at the northwest corner of Dundas and Cook Streets and entered into the flour and feed store business. Charles Schiller bought the tinsmithing premises owned by William Peaker, situated on the opposite, northeast corner. By constant industry and honest dealing these two Schiller brothers developed profitable businesses, and Lucinda Schiller, who had been a widow since 1855, continued to live with her eldest son, David.

Charles Alvin Schiller was appointed Postmaster at the beginning of April, 1885, and the following year a telephone office was opened in his premises at the corner of Cook Street. The telephone had been invented twelve years before, and this first Cooksville telephone was used for long distance calls only. However, Charles did not live long; he died in 1887, at the age of forty, and by 1891, his widow Margaret was conducting a grocery store, and had become well-known as the village Postmistress. In March of that year she had the whole store and post office re-painted, with the work being done by James Morley.

By this time, also, it had become necessary for David Schiller to make additions to the building which housed his business. He was still running the flour and feed store, which his customers found very convenient.

In 1895, Margaret Schiller, in her large and profitable general store, was described as being 'a woman of good judgement and business tact, buying her goods in the best market.' It was said that she kept constantly on hand the best groceries, ladies' dress goods, hats and caps, boots and shoes, and in fact everything kept in a first-class general store. She took butter and eggs in exchange at highest market prices.

Her son, Donald D. Schiller was appointed agent for the Jones Locked Wire Fence Company and began inviting people to write or call on him and get prices, at the Post Office Store, Cooksville. He was a

The Streetsville Review, July 4, 1895

convincing salesman. He explained in his advertisements that with the old, plain type of fencing, the livestock could go through as they pleased, due to the easily-spread wire. He said that his horse, Duke, walked right through the woven fence, and his hogs simply raised up the wire and went under it wherever they liked; as for the barbed wire, it would ruin the animals. Now, with the new type of fence, of much heavier weight which allowed no sagging, his stock could no longer roam about the farm at will, nor feed on the fields of grain.

Thus the two Schiller families were now forming a good business section, for farmers and villagers alike, located in that little block around the Dundas and Cook Street corners. However, at the end of September, 1896, Margaret Schiller decided it was time to leave, and her valuable store and premises were put up for sale by auctioneer John Thomson, of Port Credit, and the whole property was bought by Mr H. H. Shaver.

Margaret Schiller, besides raising her family and running the store, had been not only a worker in the Methodist Sabbath School, but also a member and worker in the Sabbath School of Dixie. At the end of October, 1896, the congregation at Dixie met in the Church and presented her with an address of their thanks, beginning with the words 'Our dear Mrs Schiller, our late villager;' and along with this address, read aloud to everyone at the meeting, she received a purse of money. Following the presentation, she moved away from Cooksville and went to live in Toronto, where her son Donald had gone to become a plumber.

The Streetsville Review, July 9, 1903

78

Meanwhile, David Schiller, who had always been engaged in the flour and feed business, then began to undertake selling the general store goods himself, along with his own supplies for farm animals. In 1903, he was selling whole season's supplies of salt, bringing it in by the car load.

On October 18th, 1905, Mrs Lucinda Schiller, who had then been a widow for over fifty years, died at her son David's home. She had lived to the great age of eighty-eight years, and was now laid to rest beside her husband in Dixie Union Cemetery. At this time, her grandsons, Thomas and James, were both involved in running the general store with their father and, in 1912, T. D. (Thomas) Schiller was appointed Tax Collector for District #2 in Toronto Township, at a salary of $125.00.

The following year, the Schillers found it necessary to again enlarge their premises and in June, 1913, Mr H. H. Shaver purchased their original building and had it taken up to a lot on the Centre Road, opposite the Cooksville School.

By the end of July much progress had been made on a new store at

Schiller Tombstone, Dixie Union Cemetery, Mississauga.
(Photo: Verna Mae Weeks)

1877   1915

COOKSVILLE

Schiller's
General Store

**SERVICE AND QUALITY OF ALL GOODS
UNEXCELLED**

Thirty-eight years' dealing with residents of Toronto Township is surely the best guarantee of satisfaction obtainable. Your patronage solicited.

Clean, Fresh Groceries, Ames-Holden McCready Shoes,
W. B. Hamilton's "Model Shoes," Dry Goods.
Hardware, Paints and Oils.
Neponset Ready Roofing.
Agency for Hobberlin's Tailored-to-Measure Clothes
Tailors to Canadian Gentlemen.

Leave your 5 gal. can or barrel and have it filled with best Canadian Oil at 14c gallon.

Thos. D. Schiller

PHONE 46

The Brampton Conservator, August 19, 1915

the corner of Cook Street, on the same spot where the old one had stood. The cement walls of the basement were completed, and the frame work of the first storey erected. The store was sixty feet deep, with ceiling over ten feet high, commodious enough for the accommodation of the growing business and increasing prosperity of the village. The family's new dwelling rooms were situated above the store, and by October the whole building had been completed. Messrs. Geo. McClintock & Son had painted it throughout, and it was declared to be one of the finest stores between Toronto and Hamilton.

However, all the upheaval, excitement and work entailed in setting up this grand new structure proved to be too much for David Oscar Schiller. He died very suddenly in the following June, 1914, at the age of sixty-four years, leaving the business in the hands of his two sons, Thomas and James.

Thomas Schiller (called Tommy by the Cooksville people) was the one who carried on as proprietor of the general store, while his brother James became a barrister, being called to the Ontario Bar in 1915. An advertisement inserted in the local papers gave information that besides clean, fresh Groceries, the store kept on hand two types of Shoes, Dry Goods and Hardware, Paints and Oils, and Ready Roofing; it was the Agency for Hobberlin's Tailored-to-Measure Clothes; and people could come into the store and leave their five-gallon containers to be filled with the best Canadian Oil, at 14 cents a gallon.

Thomas became the owner of a Motor Car, a Regal, and thereafter was the agent for these new model automobiles in Cooksville. Always ready, as his father before him, Thomas looked for ways to add new stock to the shelves in the store, and in 1922 he made Men's Pants a specialty.

Following World War I, James Schiller had gone to practise law in St. Catharines and, after their mother's death in 1923, the old Schiller property once owned by David and Lucinda on Lot 17, was bought by Mr F. C. Colorco for the purpose of erecting two new brick bungalows.

Thomas Schiller gave up the store property and sold it to Mr E. Spiers, of Bracebridge. Ten thousand dollars worth of stock had to be cleared out within fifteen days, in order to give possession to the new owner. Placing a double-sheet advertisement in the newspaper, Thomas described this 'stupendous undertaking,' stating that he had ripped, cut and slashed prices to such an extent that the public could buy as never before in the County. He advised people to 'Come early. The prices will shout louder than any words that can be put in type. Let nothing keep you away from the greatest of merchandise buying opportunities.'

The public took advantage of his giant sale, thus allowing Thomas and his wife, who had been Miss Pearl Wylie of Cooksville, to make their great change and move away to St. Catherines, where James was now practising law.

Thomas Schiller died in 1930, at St. Catharines; and in 1938, Margaret Schiller, widow of Charles Alvin Schiller, the Postmaster, died in Rome, Indiana, on her eighty-sixth birthday.

Schiller's former general store became one of a chain of Superior Stores, still remembered by some as Sam McCord's Store. This building erected by David Oscar Schiller in 1913, on the same site as his original flour and feed store, remains standing today at 51 Dundas Street West, on the corner of Cook Street.

Chapter 11: The Butcher Shops

THERE IS NO BUTCHER listed for the village of Cooksville in the Canadian Gazetteer for Canada West, in 1846. In those days, there were 'beef rings' with lists of farmers who owned cattle, each of whom would take his turn at having an animal slaughtered by the members of the group, with the families sharing the meat. Although called a beef ring, pigs and other animals were slaughtered as well. This manner of supplying meat for each other was somewhat after the fashion of the old-time quilting bees, or barn raising bees held in the district, with neighbours joining together in the work and benefits.

In the 1850-51 Toronto and County of York Directory, James Peacock's name appears as the butcher; and in October, 1854, *The Streetsville Review* printed a small notice stating that 'James Eliott, butcher, serves Streetsville, Springfield, Cooksville and Port Credit,' this being the first knowledge of a travelling butcher in the Cooksville area.

Thomas Codling was Cooksville's butcher in 1866 and, in 1876, Mr Coombes was actively engaged in the butchering business there; later on, another wholesale butcher was Mr Alcock, who moved into the Gummerson house on the Centre Road.

A story was told in 1894, of Mr Rutledge who had a wagon which he filled with loads of meat and drove to the Toronto Market. Near the end of November, Mr Rutledge set out with his wagon as usual, but when he arrived in the city that day, his horses suddenly became frightened by a noise and ran away. The butcher was thrown violently from his wagon to the pavement, and one of the wagon wheels passed over him. He was so severely injured, having some of his ribs fractured and one of his lungs damaged, that it was several days before he could be pronounced out of danger of losing his life.

There were many runaways listed when teams of horses pulled the wagons; horses were very apt to become startled and this fact, coupled with the loading and handling of live animals on the wagons, often caused such incidents.

In 1912, Thomas Stewart, of Cooksville, was loading pigs onto his wagon at Mr Birkett's farm in Dixie, when either their squealing or the sudden attack of a dog frightened his horses. They made a bolt out of the lane, collided with the gate post and crossed the road, where one horse fell backwards into a deep ditch and held the other horse fast to the side of the wagon. A considerable amount of effort and work was required to extricate the team, from the wagon and each other, causing great damage to the harness and wagon. However, Mr Stewart was grateful that his horses were not much injured. Nothing was said of what happened with regard to the pigs. Thus, even at such a late date in our history, we read of hardship in managing to supply the people with meat.

In the summer of 1913, Mr Joyce opened a new butcher shop, filling a want which had long been felt in the village, and in no time at all began doing a good business.

His success was quickly noted by Mr G. E. Ellingham, who erected his own new butcher shop the following year, on the corner of his property on Dundas Street at the corner of the Township Hall roadway. This building was a one-storey, brick-faced structure, with a concrete floor and foundation. A handsome circular-top, plate-glass window adorned the front, and the inside of the store was fitted up with a refrigerator, and all necessary furnishings needed for selling meat to the public. Hydro electric light was installed.

In August of 1915, Gabriel Ellingham was not only the butcher, but also a poulterer and provision merchant. He dealt in fresh and salt meats of all kinds – ham, bacon, lard, tongue, and cooked meats; poultry could be bought, as well as vegetables in season. Orders could be placed at the store through the telephone by calling 6, Cooksville.

G. ELLINGHAM

BUTCHER, POULTERER AND
PROVISION MERCHANT

Dealer in Fresh and Salt Meats of all kinds,

Ham, Bacon, Lard, Tongue. Cooked

Meats, Etc. All kinds of Vege-

tables in Season.

PHONE 6 - - - - - - - COOKSVILLE

The Brampton Conservator, August 19, 1915

This store was much admired and well patronized, with nothing untoward to speak of happening except for an accident which occurred on a Friday evening in 1920, at the four corners. Mr Ellingham and his son were driving along Dundas Street, returning with their loaded truck from Toronto, when their truck and another coming up the Centre Road, on its way to Brampton, crashed into each other. There was not much injury done to either truck, but Mr Ellingham was thrown out onto the roadway, along with several carcasses of meat he was taking to sell in his butcher shop.

Besides the store, he owned five acres of land at the rear of the fair grounds, on which there stood a large barn he used as a slaughterhouse, but in 1922 he sold this land to the veterinarian, Dr Hopkins. He did not need his barn or the land any longer because he was getting all of his meat from Toronto.

In February, 1931, G. E. Ellingham was still busily working in his Community Meat Market, and claiming at that time to be the oldest butcher in Peel County. When interviewed by a writer from *The Port Credit News*, he told that he had been born near Erindale Station at a time when it was known as Springfield-on-the-Credit, and that he had started up in the business in 1876, with his late uncle Mr Coombes. In those days, he had peddled meat through the country with a team of horses, on his route to Clarkson, Sheridan, Erindale, Dixie, and other points. Part of the week, he would travel east of Cooksville, and the other days, west.

He used to go to Port Credit and do a rushing business at the hotels, which were numerous in early days. There were three hotels in Cooksville, two in Dixie, three in Port Credit, and one in Erindale. Cooksville Fair was a great day in Cooksville, and the hotels were busy places from morning till night on Fair Day.

Edway Walterhouse, who ran one of the hotels in Cooksville, would buy from $75.00 to $80.00 worth of meat for Cooksville Fair Day, and he would sell meals for 25 cents. Other hotel keepers, over the years, were James King, Frank Morley, and John Schiller; and the bars in those days did a rushing business, when eight or ten expert bartenders were brought out from Toronto to quench the thirst of the Fair enthusiasts.

Mr Ellingham told that lambs could be bought for $3.00 each, and the same price would apply to pigs. It was common to buy a whole flock of lambs in the spring and take them when they were required; the lambs would be paid for as he got them, two or three at a time. He could well remember driving 144 sheep from the Toronto market to Cooksville, when it took three hours to make the trip.

'One good sheep dog was of more use in those days than three men,' he said, 'as the dog could drive the sheep along the road to perfection.' He said that the meat was good, and that the farmers fed these animals well; they grew lots of peas which they fed to their cattle.

While the newspaper editor was at the meat market, a man came in and purchased a pig's head, and when asked what he would have charged for one of the pigs' heads in early days, Mr Ellingham replied, 'Anything you could get for it, and that wasn't much. The best pork could be bought by the quarter at 4 cents per pound, and the best pig I ever bought was from John Davis, whose daughters now reside on the Centre Road.'

He remarked that live cattle at the present time (1931) were about the lowest price they had been in fifty years. 'A half-century ago,' he said, 'one could buy 3 pounds of steak for 25 cents, a pound of butter for 15 cents, 3 dozen eggs for a quarter, and a shank for soup – why, I've given hundreds of them away.' He remembered that a good beast could be bought, in 1880, for $75.00, and that the best beast he had ever purchased weighed 600 pounds; he got it from John Currie. He stated that the price of beef on the hoof at the time, in 1931, was between 4 and 5 cents a pound.

When Gabriel Ellingham finally gave up his business, he continued to live at the back of his lot on Dundas Street, and his Community Meat Market became Mary's Meat Market.

* * *

On a Saturday in November, 1921, James Bailey, of Streetsville, opened a meat market in the former Post Office in Mr Bowden's building, and Mr Halsey moved into the village to take charge of it. Mr Halsey was a practical butcher who had been operating a rural meat route, and making many friends around the Churchville district.

A handsome mammoth meat refrigerator was installed in the shop;

The Port Credit Weekly, October 5, 1950

THAT . . .

TURKEY
GOOSE
OR
CHICKEN
DINNER

Chickens ⸺⸺⸺⸺⸺⸺32c to 38c lb.
Geese from ⸺⸺⸺⸺⸺⸺⸺25c lb.
Turkeys ⸺⸺⸺⸺⸺⸺38c to 40c lb.
Beef, Lamb, Pork and Veal.

JAMES BAILEY
FAMILY BUTCHER
COOKSVILLE

WE DELIVER   PHONE 93

The Port Credit News, November 7, 1930

and new wall fixtures and paraphernalia were set in place to make it more attractive. In a couple of weeks' time, Mr Halsey had a new assistant on the staff, Mr Gill, who moved down from Streetsville and went to live in a house on Hook Avenue.

In December, 1921, *The Brampton Conservator* reported that the finest display of Christmas meats ever seen in the village of Cooksville was to be found in Bailey's Butcher Shop, consisting of 'tons of the choicest beef, pork, mutton and fowl – among them being Mr William Pinkney's baby beef, which had been a prize winner at the Toronto Exhibition.'

Shortly afterwards, the upstairs quarters over the Butcher Shop was rented to a new barber, Mr Hadlow, who had just arrived with his family in Cooksville.

In May, 1923, James Bailey purchased, from Martin Crofton, the 50-foot frontage east of the building, which included the corner of Shepard Avenue along which the property extended 150 feet. He added another motor truck to his business, in order to cover the territory both east and west of the village; the interior of the new truck was finished in white enamel, insuring increased service, sanitation, and satisfaction to the customers.

Mr Bailey prospered so well that, at the beginning of June, 1926, he was able to purchase from the Hugh Bowden estate, the building in which his butcher shop business was conducted. He became known as Cooksville's 'family butcher,' and for Christmas, 1930, he was offering for their Christmas dinners every sort of fowl and meat – turkey, goose, or chicken, as well as beef, lamb, pork, and veal.

Chapter 12: The Bakeries

DURING THE 1840s and up until the great fire, James Vyse was the baker at Cooksville, but his dwelling was lost in the fire and, afterwards, nothing more seems to have been reported about him there. Later on, in 1866-67, William Cox had taken over the business of being the village baker.

William A. Burrows was born in Colchester, England, and as a young man had operated a coal business there. He arrived in Canada in 1911 and took up a new life and trade as a baker, delivering his baked goods to his customers by horse and wagon. For a quarter of a century, he was a

Mr Burrows, of Cooksville, delivering bread, c. 1915.
(Photo: Region of Peel Archives, N164-99)

familiar figure in the district, liked by all the children along his route because they knew that he always carried a pocketful of candy. Mr Burrows lived on the Centre Road and, after his retirement, was particularly fond of doing all his own gardening, right up until his death in 1937, at the age of 88 years.

* * *

At the beginning of April, 1917, Miss E. Walterhouse had a new frame building erected on her property on Dundas Street, about half a block west of Hurontario Street. This building was to be occupied as a bakery and, within a few weeks, the new bakery was opened up for business by Harry Fullwood.

Right from the beginning it was a success; Mr Fullwood's goods were declared to be nice, clean and tasty, and several batches of his pies, bread and cakes were readily disposed of. However, the following November, the bakery was discovered on fire and before anything could be done to save the contents, by those who went to help, they were totally destroyed. The small building, of light frame construction, was greatly consumed.

It was the spring of 1921 before Mr Fullwood again began

advertising his Cooksville Model Bakery wares, announcing that they could now be had, strictly fresh, as far away as Gill's Grocery Store in Streetsville. He was taking orders for wedding and birthday cakes, as well as his 'celebrated Fruit Cake, at $1.50 a 5-lb. slab, 35 cents a lb.' He stated that all cakes were made with butter and new laid eggs, and were 'the Pride of Peel County.'

In October of that year, *The Brampton Conservator* reported that 'To Cooksville's Bakery goes the honour of establishing a low record in the price of bread since the War started it upwards.' Mr Fullwood was then making up over 32 sacks of flour into bread each week, and selling it at 16 cents a loaf. A few weeks later, he said that with flour selling around $6.60 a barrel, there was no reason that the public should pay more than his new price, 15 cents for a double loaf.

Harry had his own methods for cleaning his bread baking pans. He said that the usual way of cleaning them with soap and water spoiled the pans, and a better way was to scrub them with ashes, afterwards rubbing them with a kind of crumpled-up paper. As for the baker himself, he always looked spotless in his shop, wearing a white T-shirt, a large white apron, and a white baker's hat on his head.

Mr Fullwood left for England at the beginning of January, 1922, but returned to re-open the bake shop on April 1st. Within a week, the Model Bakery was in full swing again, and Harry had plans to build a Lunch and Ice Cream Parlour beside it. There were now many motor cars passing along Dundas Street in front of the Bakery and, by the middle of May, his Refreshment Parlour was opened and began doing a good business.

Meetings were held in his Refreshment Parlour, such as those for the planning of a new outdoor skating rink on the Fair Grounds near the Town Hall, in order to provide skating for both the children and adults.

In December, Mr Fullwood had on display in the Bakery an unusually large line of fancy boxes of Chocolates and Bonbons, and 'presentation' boxes of Cigars and Cigarettes for Christmas gifts. He had made several hundred pounds of Christmas Cake for the local trade, and was adding new showcases, as well as an extension of a Tea Room. By the end of the year he was talking of extending his premises even further, due to his constantly increasing business, and had many improvements in mind for the year 1923.

Once again he returned from England, and this time installed a new electric oven, which would enable him to sell bread at 14 cents a double loaf. He had an English-built mixer on its way from England, to be ready for the opening of the Bakery in the new spring season.

In June, 1923, local people learned that Harry Fullwood had been granted a gold medal in competition in London, England; he had also produced a new dainty in food products, on which he had placed three patents. For some time, he had been experimenting on a Souffle, with the successful result that its taste was as good as its looks; it was said to 'tickle the palate.'

United States baking concerns became interested in the new product, and various representatives of large bakeries began arriving in Cooksville, the most enthusiastic of these being a man from a Boston bakery. Harry received many congratulations on his efforts, saying that the Souffle would surely prove a great seller in the bakeries of the cities.

In March of 1924, the Model Bakery was selling bread at 14 cents a double loaf, made by baking two small loaves in one pan, where they rose and joined in the middle, and yet could still be easily broken into two separate loaves. However, this low price did not stay in effect long; by the end of July the price in the city had risen to 20 cents, and Mr Fullwood's loaves were 18 cents. This necessary change was because of the sudden increase in the price of flour, due to a shortage of wheat.

The following year saw Mr Fullwood once again returning to Cooksville, after a two months' stay in England. He placed his usual advertisement in *The Streetsville Review*, this time giving the information that his Tea Room and Ice Cream Parlour would re-open in March, with not only Cigars, Tobacco and Candies, but a fresh stock of Groceries as well. The specialty of the Bakery, in 1925, was Pastry made with table butter, and Pure, Unadulterated Bread.

The Model Bakery was so well-known by 1928 that Fullwood Fruit Cake was selling by the ton, and being shipped to all points. People came from a long distance away to buy his celebrated fruit cakes; and not only the fruit cakes, but his extra-large, round meat pies, called Melton Mowbrays. Mr Fullwood and Mr J. Jones, who worked with him, were both British, and they knew how to bake these pies in the exact way they were baked in England. Both fruit cakes and meat pies were placed in lovely cardboard boxes, and were actually mailed in bags. There were bags filled with them, piled up at the Post Office, and they went by mail from Cooksville.

Besides Mr Jones, the Bakery gave employment to a number of other Cooksville people, one of whom was Mary Bonhomme who worked

Fullwood's Cooksville Bakery; at left, Roffey's Barber Shop, 1920s.
(Photo: Miss Mildred Bonhomme)

The Streetsville Review, March 12, 1925

there one summer. Today, Mary's sister Mildred remembers that sometimes there was trouble with the well behind the Bakery, and Harry would call on her father, Albert Bonhomme, to go over and take care of the problem. After these visits, Mr Fullwood would take the Bonhomme family half a dozen butter tarts, which Mildred recalls as being different from anyone else's; Harry's butter tarts had a little piece of cake on the top of each one.

At this time, Mr Fullwood had a little competition along the line of baking, for there appeared in *The Port Credit News* an invitation for people to come and attend a sale of Homemade Bread, Buns, Cakes, Tarts, Etc., at the home of Miss L. Ellingham. Commencing on June 1st, 1928, Miss Ellingham began having her sales to the public, on each Saturday morning.

On December 7th, 1928, Mr Fullwood advertised in *The Port Credit News* to the effect that the last ton of Fullwood Fruit Cake had been sold, but 'In response to many requests, I have decided to make one more ton. The price is still 5 pounds for $1.50, and 7 pounds, almond iced and decorated, for $2.50.' He was ready to start for the Old Land on December 8th; the cake was all ready, but the customers must order early to ensure delivery in time for Christmas.

In April, 1930, after spending the winter in England and other places, Mr Fullwood came back to Cooksville, once again opening the Bakery with a choice supply of Bread and Pastry. He remained in business, for thirty-five years, with his 'Fruit Cake Bakery' becoming ever more famous. It would have been hard to find a person, near or far, who had not heard of Fullwood's Fruit Cakes and Melton Mowbrays, shipped the world over.

Harry Fullwood maintained the Bakery up until April, 1956, when failing health caused him to cease operation. He died a few weeks later, and the building remained unoccupied until July, 1956, when this historic link with the past, on Dundas Street, was demolished. Nothing remained on the little lot (at 19 Dundas Street West), next door to the cement block building to the west of it, except a white sign, a pile of boards, and the old bakery oven.

Chapter 13: The Pharmacies

AT THE END OF OCTOBER, 1879, Josiah Green bought the Schiller

House, on the south side of Dundas Street, east of Hurontario Street. It was in good repair, with a frame public hall beside it. Although these two buildings were not connected, they were close together, with a stairway between them; at the top of the stairs was a landing which led into the hotel on the left, and into the hall on the right. At the rear, the lot consisted of three acres of land on which stood a large barn, an orchard of various fruit trees, and a fine garden.

Josiah Green was a druggist who operated a shop on Queen Street, in Toronto, and another at Lambton Mills. After he bought the hotel in Cooksville, he converted one side of it into a drug store and the other side into his dwelling.

When the Drug Store was in full operation, Mr Green was described as a 'genial young man who will always be found ready for business.' He always kept a large stock of drugs, patent medicines, and other wares such as seeds on hand, for which he had a large demand. He was one who mixed his own brand of cough mixture, and sold it for 25 cents a bottle.

In 1898, the Drug Store was being managed by Mr Green's son-in-law, Hugh K. Bowden, who hired young John Morley to decorate and paint the premises. By the beginning of September, 1900, many repairs and improvements had been completed which made a great difference for the better in its appearance. The balcony running across the front of the building was said to be 'all right for the purpose, and would no doubt be used from time to time.'

Mr J. F. H. Green purchased a house from Mrs S. South in 1903, and moved into it, leaving the Drug Store building and Hall for Mr Bowden's complete use. Instead of Pharmacy Hall, the frame building then began to be known as Bowden's Hall, where many suppers and entertainments were held by village organizations. The Hall was located even with the Drug Store building, and had an entrance right off Dundas Street; downstairs, it was used as a warehouse for the drug store, and the upstairs was one huge room, with seats along both sides and a beautiful floor for dancing.

After managing the business for some years, Mr Bowden purchased the premises, and hoped for the continuous and generous support which had been forthcoming in the past. He added greatly to the variety of stock in the store, selling prescriptions and family recipes, Horse and Cattle medicines, all of which he was legally qualified to compound.

He also kept on hand such first-class articles as Syrup of White Pine and Tar Compound, for all coughs and colds; Canadian Cattle Spice, the best and cheapest stock food known; Carbolated Sheep Dip, for all animal vermin; Soluble Creosote, a valuable disinfectant and antiseptic; Water Glass Egg Preserver; Diamond Lye, and Grape Saline.

In 1907, the great barn at the back of the property was taken down and removed to the CPR Station grounds, where it was once again erected for use as a coal shed.

H. K. Bowden continued advertising in the newspapers, as Mr Green had done before him, and the business prospered. The store now carried a line of goods supplied by the National Drug Company, identified by the name Na-Dru-Co Specialties; a new patent medicine was a Linseed, Licorice and Chlorodyne Cough Cure. Mr Bowden now had cosmetics, such as Royal Rose Talcum Powder, Ruby Red Cold Cream, and Shaving Sticks on his sales lists, and offered free samples to anyone who wished to try them.

The Streetsville Review, October 3, 1912

There were sometimes accidents involving horses around the Drug Store near the four corners, such as the time when William Brunskill was driving a team of horses hitched to a double wagon, travelling west along Dundas Street. As he was passing his father's place, where Grenville Drive is now, the kingbolt attaching the wagon to the axle came out and allowed it to strike the horses, causing them to break away suddenly and run the wagon into the ditch. Mr Brunskill was unable to hold them, and they got away. At the bridge over the creek, they collided with Albert Kee's buggy and startled his horse so that it, too, dashed into the ditch, throwing Mr Kee out and smashing itself loose from the buggy. Mr Kee's horse galloped into Bowers' shed, where it was caught.

Meanwhile, Mr Brunskill's team had continued racing along Dundas Street until it reached Bowden's Pharmacy and ran in between the verandah and the hitching rail, where yet another horse was tied. All ended in a great mix-up, with the horses' legs being cut and the harnesses and rigs being much damaged.

One day, Hugh Bowden was injured, being thrown from his wagon while getting supplies for a party. A few years later, when motor cars were becoming more frequent along Dundas Street, Josiah Green was returning home from Toronto in his market wagon; as he approached the Third Line (Dixie Road), a car struck the wagon, breaking it from the shafts. Mr Green was pitched out bodily, just missing a telephone pole, but luckily not much hurt.

In 1915, the Pharmacy was continuing to carry a large stock, and Mr Bowden's advertisements were giving the information that he had been a legally qualified druggist since 1871, and should be fully competent to attend to all requirements of the trade. As a Registered Pharmacist, he solicited their patronage, giving his telephone number 62, Cooksville.

At the end of August, 1917, Hugh Bowden was being congratulated on his appointment as Cooksville's new Postmaster and, by October 10th, the new Post Office had been opened in the Pharmacy. Considerable improvements were made at this time to the former hotel building. The old front of the premises was taken out, and two plate glass windows, 5 feet by 6 feet, were put in on either side of a centre doorway; an extra window was added for the Post Office Department. This Post Office, which had combination and call boxes, occupied all the west side of the Pharmacy; the rest of the store continued to be used for selling drugs and patent medicines, with stationery and confectionery, tobacco and cigars all contained inside counter showcases.

The whole store was newly papered, painted and decorated, and was brilliantly lighted up by hydro electric light furnished by a single Commercial Lamp of 200 Watts. Several hanging lamps were installed in the Post Office Department, which was arranged for the prompt and efficient receipt and despatch of the regular and local mails.

Mr Bowden, born in Ireland, had qualified as a druggist at a young age and worked for a time in Toronto. He had taken charge of Mr Green's Drug Store in 1895 and, after twenty-five years, was still successfully conducting the business until his death, at the age of 72 years, in October, 1920.

The following month, Mrs Bowden moved from the brick building and went to live with her daughter, Mrs R. Whaley, across the street. Mr Rutledge took over the Post Office, while the Pharmacy was continued under the management of Mrs Bowden. Later, the upstairs rooms were rented out, and Mr Morley lived there.

* * *

At the end of October, 1922, Mr P. J. Christie, PHM. B., then living in Streetsville, purchased a large red brick house on the north side of

The Streetsville Review,
November 30, 1922

Dundas Street, opposite the Methodist Church. This had been the Rutledge home, but alterations were now made and fixtures installed for the opening of a new drug store. In November, Mr Christie informed the public that he was now carrying a large stock of drugs and toilet goods, remedies and patent medicines, with extras such as Stationery and School Supplies, Oils and Turpentine. Residents could also leave their Kodak films to be developed there, and no doubt many of the old snapshots still in existence in this area were ordered to be developed in Christie's Drug Store.

* * *

By 1928, Cooksville had two drug stores in operation. Jesse Jones opened his store in the white-painted frame building, located at the southwest side of the four corners, which had been used by the Royal Bank before their new stone Bank was erected. Mr Jones was druggist there until the beginning of September, 1935, when Alfred P. Ward arrived from Owen Sound and took over the business.

In September, 1947, Mr Ward's Drug Store was re-located in the front part of the old Revere House hotel, having its front entrance opening out onto Hurontario Street. Various restaurants and other businesses in Mississauga today have pictures hanging on their walls for their patrons to look at and admire, which show Ward's Drug Store at this location.

However, at the beginning of November, 1947, Alf Ward purchased the Cooksville Inn from Jack Braithwaite and hired Mrs Sweet to manage it for him, while he set up his Drug Store in the Annex at the east side of the hotel.

Chapter 14: A Farming Community

IN 1891, COOKSVILLE had great natural advantages besides being one of the neatest and cleanest villages to be found anywhere. Its streets were wide, and just sandy enough to absorb the water which fell during rainstorms; once the frost had left the ground, its roads were not as muddy as in the heavier clay soil places. It was located on gently sloping land which drained easily, and was far enough away from the lake and river to have no swampy areas.

It was an ideal spot, with beautiful scenery along Dundas and

Hurontario Streets. Hurontario Street came down from the north, bounded on both sides by fertile farms; looking either to the north or south from Dundas Street, during the warmer months of the year you could see fields of fruit and vegetables spread out in large or small acreages and plots of land. Also, from the top of the hill on Dundas Street, you could look down on a beautiful view of Lake Ontario.

Many acres of grapes were grown, by people who had started them from cuttings bought at the old Chateau Vineyards. Orchards covered large acreages, where the CPR railroad tracks crossed Hurontario, with apple, plum and pear trees. Peaches were grown, but these could not always be depended upon; farmers did not bestow much attention on them. Still, there were occasional years when the peach trees blossomed well and produced an abundance of the luscious fruit.

In 1922, during the time the farm of J. F. Smith, consisting of 73 acres located just south of the overpass, was rented to Mr Duff, there were between five and six hundred cherry trees in full bearing growing there, with the rest of the property being mainly covered in apple trees. Apple packers travelled about this area around the turn of the century, buying up nearly all of the fruit from the orchards, at a price of from $1.00 to $1.25 per barrel.

People kept cattle, tying them up for grazing near their homes, to supply their families with milk; herds were raised on pasture lands and slaughtered for the wholesale markets in Toronto. James Hook held sales of choice cattle, auctioned off by John Thomson of Port Credit; and Dr Hopkins, the veterinarian, sold many fine animals at handsome prices. One heavy farm team sold for nearly five hundred dollars.

A well-known Cooksville auctioneer was J. R. Long, who not only sold animals but wrote 'The World's Greatest Auction Treatise,' offering his services for a number of breeders' and farmers' sales. His clients owned notable Holstein, Shorthorn, Angus, Hereford, Clydesdale, and Percheron breeds, from such faraway places as Ottawa, Port Perry, Waterloo, Simcoe, Moose Jaw, Arcola and Keeler, as well as from the Saskatchewan Breeders' Association. Mr Long's advertisements stated that 'Live Stock Salesmanship is one of the Arts.' He guaranteed that the farmers' sales, in his hands, would bring them more money, and offered to send them his literature. It was true that some of these sales brought in from $6,000 to as much as $11,894.00.

John Cunningham owned a gigantic feed store by the Cooksville Station, where everything in the feed line for cattle, horses or hogs grown in the whole district could be got from him. In 1910, he was selling Shorts (bran mixed with coarse meal or flour) at $21.00 per ton, and plain Bran at $20.00 per ton. Cottonseed meal was sold at $39.00 a ton, stated in 1917 to be 'a good feed at a reasonable price.'

Very close to the Station was the farm of William Pinkney, who bred Yorkshire hogs and won big prizes at the Royal Winter Fair. Mr Pinkney's son James was the veterinarian who built a second home and office beside his father's original homestead, and reached by crossing the railroad tracks, driving along a lane and up a slight hill. This red brick house was well-known to many Cooksville people who took their sick pets in for treatment. Nothing stands there today but large apartment buildings, and a few old apple trees which so far have refused to die.

In 1913, *The Toronto Globe* told the story of an early Cooksville apple orchard existing on a 40-acre farm, near where Confederation Drive now runs north from Dundas Street. George Hamilton had bought the place in 1908, with its wild and woody, uncared-for trees. He was advised to forget it, as a waste of time, but he ploughed up the land in spite of all good advice to the contrary. It took three weeks to get the plough through the ground because it was packed down so hard and had so many weeds and shoots growing out of it. He pruned the trees a little later, and by fall collected 100 barrels of scrawny apples off the entire farm.

In the spring, Mr Hamilton applied eleven carloads of manure and cultivated the soil again. This time he had the trees pruned by an expert, and sprayed them four times through the growing season. The second picking yielded him 600 barrels of better quality apples. The third summer, 1,500 barrels of apples rated at 90-per cent quality were obtained from this formerly neglected orchard. In 1913, Mr Hamilton's apple harvest was recognized as excellent; 500 barrels of the much-favoured Duchess Apples, along with many wagonloads of others, were taken by teams of horses to the market in West Toronto.

This West Toronto Market was most convenient for market gardeners like Josiah Harris, who could handily travel there along Dundas Street by wagon, to sell the produce he grew in Cooksville. Besides the fruit from his apple, pear and plum trees, Mr Harris grew grapes, currants and rhubarb; and on the lower part of his farm he cultivated celery and lettuce, corn, cucumbers and pumpkins.

The great concern, in 1913, was the fact that the hours of opening the hotels at Lambton Mills and Humber Bay were eight o'clock in the morning. The market gardeners who travelled along the Dundas highway from Cooksville, Dixie and Summerville all set out in the early hours before morning light in order to reach the hotels by five o'clock, put up their horses, meet their buyers, and be on their way toward home again long before eight. Since the eight o'clock opening caused them great inconvenience, they banded together with other market gardeners coming from Streetsville, Lorne Park, Oakville, and Port Credit to present a petition to the Honourable Mr Hanna, asking him that the hours be changed.

A gardener who grew carrots, in 1921, was Rupert M. Pickett, who placed straightforward advertisements in *The Streetsville Review* offering 15 tons of carrots, in good condition, at $8.00 per ton. It was a good year for carrots, with thousands of bags being harvested in the district in one week. Celery and cabbage were not as plentiful; potatoes and apples were not nearly as much in evidence as they had been the year before. The green crops were not keeping well, and as a result the prices rose considerably higher between harvest time and Christmas.

However, agriculture was a business which changed with the weather and various other conditions, from year to year. In February, 1922, Fred

The Port Credit News,
September 23, 1927

Brunskill, agent for the W. A. Freeman Fertilizer Company, of Hamilton, announced a reduction in the price of the company's products, which he guaranteed to be free from useless ingredients, and whether this had the right effect to bring about a change in the potato harvest was a question. By July of that year, hundreds of bushels of Early Potatoes were being marketed at a money-making price; Harrison and Archer, wholesale and retail potato dealers who specialized in new potatoes, were taking two crops off the land in one season.

Cockshutt Implements and Parts, from an old reliable firm, were being sold in 1922 by Walter C. Irwin. He supplied every type of farm implement needed to produce the best results for all the farmers in the Cooksville area. The farms were not all spread out at a distance from the village. James Harris and W. J. Lowe were raising feeder cattle on a farm on the Dundas highway, adjoining the Cooksville Brick Yard.

* * *

In 1912, Price's dairy farm, located at the eastern limits of Erindale, was shipping milk to Toronto by motor truck, but during the winter months the trucks went only as far as Cooksville where the milk was transferred to sleighs. Sometimes a loaded truck got stuck in high drifts and could not get through; the milk then had to be shipped in from Erindale Station. They had difficulty even in spring and summer, for when the truck got out of condition and had to be left in Cooksville for repairs, the wagons had to draw the load.

A disastrous accident happened in July, 1912, at the Dundas Street crossing by Cooksville Station, as the dairy wagons were on the way to the city. About 9 p.m., just as the last wagon was clearing the track, the Detroit Express train struck it, completely demolishing it and scattering milk bottles, cases, and cans in all directions. The horses broke loose and ran for some distance before being caught. A quantity of milk was saved, but the train was delayed while damage to the engine was repaired.

An early milk carrier for Cooksville was Mr Shean, who lived first on the Centre Road, afterwards moving into E. Walterhouse's house at the rear of the Revere House in April, 1916. A dairy service was later established by Jack Crawford, who had been serving the Dixie district for the previous eight years. In 1922, he extended his services to all parts of Cooksville, making deliveries in bottles and selling 21 tickets for a dollar. In January of the following year, when Mr Crawford gave up his

Cooksville Dairy

Pure Jersey Milk from Government Tested Cows. Milk and Cream, Butter and Buttermilk.

MILK 9c QUART

EFFICIENT DELIVERY SERVICE

CYRIL CLARK, Owner, Phone Cooksville 18 r 5

The Port Credit News, April 8, 1932

Rural Mail Route owing to his growing milk business, his dairy was welcomed by everyone in the village.

The Brampton Conservator of May 15, 1924, announced that the Hillside Dairy had started delivering pasteurized milk in and around Cooksville. This company was a small plant with a daily capacity of 150 quarts, and had but one delivery truck. Located on the Dundas highway at the eastern end of Cooksville, and operated by Sayers and Son, it was purchased in November, 1933, by James Newman, who came from Hamilton where he had been in the dairy business with his father.

After five years, when more space was needed, Mr Newman constructed a new brick building on Hurontario Street, north of the Cooksville Inn. 'Chief bottle washer' and 'pasteurization foreman' at the new location of the Cooksville Jersey Dairy, in 1938, was Francis McCarthy; Jimmy Newman and Fred Reeves delivered milk each morning through Cooksville, Dixie, Port Credit and Streetsville; and Bert Harper collected the milk for the day's supplies from district milk producers.

A popular product manufactured in the Cooksville Jersey Dairy was ice cream, which they sold in their own Dairy Bar constructed at the front of the plant in 1949. By 1953, the company was employing 50 people and distributing their dairy products throughout South Peel; and

PLANTS FOR SALE.

———

A quantity of Strawberry Plants, all the leading varieties, for sale.

HENRY DAVIS,
Cooksville.

The Streetsville Review, April 30, 1903

BERRY PICKERS WANTED.

———

15 Berry Pickers wanted for picking raspberries. 2c a box for first two and last two pickings, and $1\frac{1}{2}$c a box for all other pickings.

S. E. HARIS,
Cooksville.

The Streetsville Review, April 30, 1903

by 1955, this privately-owned Cooksville dairy had 30 trucks on the road, serving 25 routes. The topping from a quart of their Jersey milk could be beaten up in a bowl, thick enough to completely cover the top of a lemon pie with a full inch of delicious whipped cream.

* * *

Since milk and honey seem to go together, we should take note that, in 1902, a great beekeeper of Cooksville was Harry Sibbald. He actually kept his bee colonies at Claude and Belfountain, north of Cooksville, and his harvest that year was eleven tons of honey.

However, the man best known in Cooksville for his beekeeping was Adam Brunskill, who lived near Dundas Street West and Grenville Drive. He owned a market garden, and along with it a large apiary behind his house. In 1893, he was said to have produced up to 30 tons of honey each year, which he sold for 7 to 10 cents per pound.

On April 30, 1908, *The Brampton Conservator* printed an advertisement for Mr Brunskill, offering 60 Colonies of Italian Bees for sale, and stating that the Queen bees were the offspring of imported mothers. He was a serious beekeeper, striving to improve the bee colonies, and in the summer of 1917 he held a beekeepers' demonstration on his apiary grounds. Several other prominent beekeepers attended the demonstration and delivered addresses; a refreshment booth set up in his garden that day yielded $13.40 for the Patriotic League.

In May of 1927, at the age of 76 years, Mr Brunskill was still active on his small farm, gardening and tending to his bees.

* * *

Situated as it was, in a location with such fertile sandy soil, Cooksville was well able to supply the markets with strawberries and raspberries, which grew there to perfection. In 1891, special attention was given to the raising of currants and berries; the yearly output of strawberries from the Cooksville area was enormous, and the picking of these and other small fruits gave employment to a host of women and children.

In the springtime of 1903, Henry Davis, of Cooksville, drew attention in *The Streetsville Review* to his sale of strawberry plants, of all leading varieties; and in the same newspaper that April, Samuel Emerson Harris was advertising for berry pickers to pick his raspberries.

Mr Harris offered as wages two cents a box for the first two and last two pickings, and one-and-a-half cents for all other pickings.

July was the month for the strawberry harvest, and in 1910 *The Brampton Conservator* reported under the Cooksville heading that the berries were plentiful, with boxes and labourers not sufficient to pick the magnificent crop. Some records were made during the few weeks, with 3,000 boxes being picked on a Monday from Deputy Reeve Lush's patch. Mr C. A. Gill, that year, sold 147,000 berry boxes, and had orders for 70,000 more, which the factories were unable to fill.

Mr C. B. Crawford, of Cooksville, introduced a new strawberry called 'Rango,' in 1918. It was large, firm, and had good flavour; it ripened to the tip, and was a beautiful light red colour. Charlie Crawford did not own an extensive farm, but he began to be famous due to originating the new strawberry. His intensive study of the berries and his experimental plot in Cooksville attracted many prominent Canadian fruit growers, and all who saw it complimented him on his achievement. It was pronounced to be the most remarkable ever produced in the strawberry world, due to the fact of its being not only large and of rich colour, but a heavy producer; the stems bore eleven and twelve berries to each one.

In 1922, Mr Crawford had 43 varieties in his experimental plot, but all attention centred on two varieties; the newer one, though not as large, was a heavy producer, with the mother plant sending out five stems of from 9 to 12 mature berries; the baby plants each carried two or three stems, with berries being ripe, green, and in blossom.

This local fruit grower suggested at the time that the Education Department should close the schools a couple of weeks earlier in June than was customary, opening that much sooner in the fall in order to enable children to help pick the fruit, which would otherwise go unpicked. Since some people already kept their children out of school to pick berries, it seemed unfair that these should be handicapped in their examinations because of enforced absence from school.

In 1923, Mr Crawford became an agent for selling berry boxes, baskets and crates. People had to order early due to the large crops and shortage of baskets. The market stands along the highway that year were selling strawberries at 10 cents a box.

Again, during that season, after five years of labour perfecting another new berry, Charlie Crawford was being noticed by famous experts. This strawberry was named 'Crawford's Excelsior,' and

The Brampton Conservator,
May 17, 1923

produced stems containing 11 and 14 berries, some of them measuring two inches across. Harris & Long mailed samples away to American interests and they began negotiating for the plant's marketing rights. The Canadian growers were very reluctant to see its control given up to those in the United States, who were said to be offering a price in the five figures; but they hoped to be given preference at a lower price. Nevertheless, they agreed that the new berry was a wonder, and accorded Mr Crawford a great deal of credit for his achievement on its perfection.

In the same year, 1923, Mr Crawford was advertising, as well as various other strawberry plants, Cuthbert Raspberry Canes, and Two-year-old Walnut Trees. He was an avid horticulturist, raising his crops quietly, in his garden plot in Cooksville.

* * *

In 1929, George Laver was growing two varieties of raspberries new to the district, called Viking and Latham. He owned five acres of land, closely planted in fruit. Since he was employed at the Hydro Sub-station, located not far from his home at Hurontario Street and Upper Middle Road, Mrs Laver, also an ardent gardening enthusiast, took charge of much of the work on the farm.

The large bushy plants of the Lathams produced heavy crops of berries. Originating in Minnesota, these canes were particularly sturdy and carried thick clusters of fruit in an upright position. The Vikings were a cross-variety between the Cuthbert and Marlboro, and earlier in production. These new berries were developed at the Vineland Experimental Station in Ontario, and grew on heavy canes almost an inch in diameter. The best advantage of Mr Laver's raspberries was that the bushes did not die over winter, and were also able to withstand the wettest weather in spring.

* * *

Mr John E. Bell was a tenant on the Cook farm at the four corners for about nine years and, in 1903, bought part of a farm south of this on the Centre Road, known by everyone as 'Corn Dilly Vally.' By 1908, he had erected a greenhouse on this property and planted a four-acre patch of strawberries.

At the beginning of July, 1910, owing to the dry, hot weather, there was a bumper crop of strawberries and Mr Bell had upwards of thirty pickers at work. On a Saturday and a Sunday morning, 135 cases of berries were taken off the plants; and the following Monday it was reported in *The Brampton Conservator* that, on the fruit farm of Mr J. E. Bell, Cooksville, Mrs Bert Rogers had broken the record for picking berries. Beginning at eight o'clock in the morning, she had stopped half an hour for a lunch in the forenoon, an hour at noon, and half an hour again for another lunch in the afternoon. Mrs Rogers had stopped picking berries at 5.45 p.m. and, when counted, it was discovered that her berry boxes numbered 412 quarts.

Mr Bell's plants were prolific; in 1912, over 100 cases of berries were picked on a Monday and Tuesday, from one picking. One of the girls employed picked 382 boxes on one day, for which she was paid well over five dollars. Mr Bell was busy, taking two loads to Toronto, and two to Brampton; and at the price prevailing that season, he took in over five hundred dollars.

The following year the strawberries again came in early and had as fine specimens as any in the county, and John E. Bell was again able to make many such trips, with the products from his farm. He had then 23 acres under cultivation in fruit, with a total value that year of ten thousand dollars.

In 1915, he bought a new Reo motor truck to market the products of his Evergreen Fruit Farm. He began securing peaches from a commission company in Toronto and bringing loads of these out to Cooksville, as well as to Brampton. At the beginning of October, he brought back 230 baskets on a Tuesday, 180 on Friday, and 271 baskets on Saturday, all of which were quickly sold. Mr Bell had built a box on his truck which held three tiers of baskets, and in that way he could bring peaches and other fruits from the city in perfect condition, without any danger of their being bruised.

The following year, after taking off the crop, Mr Bell sold 16 acres of his fruit farm on the Centre Road to Mr Murdock, of Toronto, for about nine thousand dollars. He kept the remaining acres, which were then in orchard, and afterwards concentrated on this part of the business.

* * *

Besides the outdoor farming, there was farming carried on in greenhouses, on smaller acreages. In 1908, John E. Bell erected a fine greenhouse on his property on the Centre Road, south of Dundas, and in 1912 his son built a large concrete root house, ready for storing his big crop of roots. Later on, John Bell Jr. built a larger greenhouse in which he installed a new heating apparatus; it was described as one of the largest hothouses in the Township. In 1922, he built a second

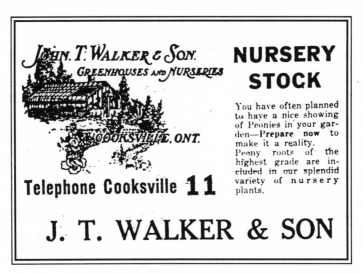

The Port Credit News, September 18, 1935

greenhouse, north of the first one, and the next year these were both bought by John T. Walker and Son for the purpose of growing flowers. By 1927, John T. Walker & Son's Greenhouses and Nurseries were in full production, with the nurseries planted on the entire twenty acres belonging to the farm.

In 1923, J. J. Milligan, a florist from Toronto, set out 20,000 gladiolus bulbs and 2,000 asters on five lots of the old Gordon estate on Dundas Street West, east of the Brick Yard. He planned on building a greenhouse in connection with his flower sales.

With the success of the hothouse-growing industry at Cooksville, Anson Forster erected one on his small farm on the west side of Hurontario Street, up near the railway overpass. Yet another appeared and became established as the floral and nursery business of Miss F. E. Miller, located at the west end of Cooksville.

* * *

In the early times, grocery stores usually bought their eggs from market gardeners, and in many cases took eggs and butter in part payment for their goods. But in 1921, both eggs and butter were scarce, owing to the fact that farmers were now taking them to sell at the city market. The plea in the Cooksville section of *The Streetsville Review* was: 'Won't some of the nearby farmers take pity on us poor souls in town and market some of these commodities here? Let the local merchants have some.' There were plenty of fowl being shown at the Cooksville Poultry Show that year, but a scarcity of eggs for sale.

In September, 1922, Mr English, a former blacksmith, leased an acreage on the Moody farm at the corner of the Centre and Middle Roads and began operating a poultry farm. The following month, a new regulation regarding the sale of eggs was passed by the government, stating that after January 1, 1923, eggs were required to be graded and sold as 'selects,' 'firsts,' and 'seconds.' Penalties were imposed on anyone selling eggs other than as graded through the packing houses. The packing houses had to grade according to the age of the eggs, which then had to be passed and stamped, the same as the government-inspected meats.

Roy Pallett was a breeder of Wyandotte chickens on free range on his poultry farm on Dundas Street, and bred many prize winners at the leading poultry shows. Called 'the Wyandotte man' by local people, they agreed that his birds were second to none in Canada, with his winnings being in the strongest competitions, at the largest exhibitions. *The Brampton Conservator* of May 24, 1923, reported that 'Mr Pallett helps put Cooksville on the map.'

J. Sandusky, G. H. Crump, and W. Roland Hill, of Cooksville, started a large poultry-raising business, but the years of 1924-25 were bad ones for them on account of continued spells of dampness, especially during February, when the weather varied between frost and high temperatures. However, they persevered and, by 1926, they were supplying thousands of dozens of eggs to the Toronto market, and producing broilers at the rate of 1,500 per season, with roasting fowl at 2,000 per season.

They stated that the larger flock paid the profit, and at that time the gross profit on a hen worked out at eight dollars, with the net profit of five dollars, providing the flock was large. Electric lights were used in the hen houses, to get the hens up early and keep them up late at night, thus increasing the number of eggs laid. These poultrymen sold eggs for hatching, as well. Incubators used in the larger plants had a capacity of from 500 to 6,000 eggs. A plant with 2,000 hens could be operated by two men, taking care of twenty colony houses, three laying houses, and other buildings.

William A. Callanan, with Holstein heifers, on Rosemount Farm, now Huron Park. (Photo: Mary Anne Kelly)

Callanan Farm Equipment (Mower, Cultivator, Reaper) – on side of hill, Dundas Street, above Huron Park. (Photo: Mary Anne Kelly)

Holstein cattle at Rosemount Farm Gate. (Photo: Mary Anne Kelly)

However, *The Streetsville Review* gave the news on July 11, 1929, that the breeding house and contents of the Cooksville Poultry Farm, on the Centre Road north of Dundas Street, had been totally destroyed by fire. The breeding house was 40 feet by 25 feet in size, and contained incubators with 3,000 eggs valued at $2,000, with no insurance. The following January, there was a shortage of fresh eggs in the community, with the wholesale price then being 60 cents per dozen.

* * *

Large farms surrounded the village of Cooksville. They were situated in those hazily-defined places: between Cooksville and Erindale, bounded on the west by Erindale Station Road, where once the Dundas road toll gate stood; between Cooksville and Dixie, bounded on the east by where the railway tracks crossed Dundas Street at the First Line (Cawthra Road); south on the Centre Road (Hurontario Street) toward Port Credit, as far as the Upper Middle Road (The Queensway) where once the red brick Hydro Sub-station stood; and north above the railway overpass to the 'back line' (Burnhamthorpe Road).

The farming people received their mail along the rural postal routes branching out from the village, identified by a Rural Route Number, Cooksville. These were the people who came into the village to shop and trade, and exchange the news of the day, and they considered themselves to be quite as much a part of Cooksville as any who lived in that tightly-knit little village around the four corners.

Chapter 15: The Town Hall

THE TORONTO TOWNSHIP RECORDS state that the first Council meetings were held in the Streetsville Hall, the Rechabite Hall at Cooksville, and various hotels in the Municipality; and in 1873, a permanent Town Hall was constructed on the fair grounds at Cooksville. This red brick building took two years for completion, and cost the tax payers two thousand dollars. The first Council meeting was held in the new Hall on October 4th, 1873, with R. Cotton as Reeve, Melville Parker and George Savage as Deputy Reeves, and John Eakins as Clerk. The first By-Law passed at that time was #273, for the purpose of granting a loan to the Cooksville School Section. Thus, with a population of 500, Cooksville became the seat of the Toronto Township Council.

Cooksville Town Hall, 1900.
(Photo: Region of Peel Archives, 81.3307M, N166-14)

In June, 1881, a grand concert was held in the Town Hall, with instrumental selections by Cooksville's own Brass Band, readings by J. W. Fletcher, and choruses sung from the operetta 'The Pirates of Penzance.' Tickets for admission to this performance cost 25 cents.

An interesting resolution on the agenda for a Council meeting in April, 1896, was that of asking the Township Clerk, William Cook, to have the pathmaster, poundkeepers, and fenceviewers notified of their appointments by postcard. The Reeve of Toronto Township at this time was Sir Melville Parker.

Besides meetings and entertainments, benefit concerts were held, such as the one on January 18, 1899. The evening was pleasant, which resulted in a crowded Hall. People from villages throughout the Township came to add their talents and make this concert a success. Al Hare and Miss N. Duck, of Port Credit, played instrumental music duets before the programme began.

Since the Chairman, Mr Blain, was late, Captain Mercer opened the show by asking everyone to join him in singing 'The Maple Leaf,' after which Miss Pallett, from Dixie, gave a recitation entitled 'How Jamie Minded the Baby.' Aggie and Millie Hare sang a duet, 'The Rag Doll,'

The Brampton Conservator,
June 10, 1881

and for an encore, Aggie and Charles Hare sang 'The Happy Birds.' A quartette made up of Messrs. Statten, Beamish, Taylor, and Hardy then rendered 'Dreaming the Happy Hours Away' in such good style they were loudly applauded.

At this point, Mr Blain arrived and gave an address on the object of the benefit concert. Other musical selections and humorous recitations followed; Miss Pallett recited several times, each one seeming more humorous than the one before. Mrs Parks contributed a fine old song, 'The Man Behind the Plough,' while Captain Mercer and Miss Pettit entertained everyone, in the proper military spirit required, with 'The Soldiers of the Queen' and 'A Sailor Aboard the Maine.'

Comedy was injected by Mr Beamish and Mr Hardy, with 'The Size of Your Wife,' and Mr B. Sprowl described the ways of the world, and his misfit suit of clothes – all being received with great applause and appreciation by the audience.

A moving picture show given in the Hall in 1909, was so new at the time and received such meagre advertising that it was poorly attended. *The Streetsville Review* of February 2, 1911, reported that the building was to be repaired and decorated; and in March, the old seats from the Town Hall were sold at auction by John Thomson, for twenty-four dollars.

The Town Hall was used for special meetings, such as the Fruit Meeting of February 23, 1915, when the fruit growers of the entire district were invited to come and present their problems to the experts. Paul Fisher, BSA, an orchardist of Burlington, dealt with serious questions regarding their fruit farms; J. W. Stark, BSA, of the Department of Agriculture, Brampton, conducted a discussion on

Commercial Fertilizers. Everyone was welcome to join in the discussions, led by R. M. McCullough, of Snelgrove, President of the Farmers' Institute, and George Downey, of Bolton, Secretary of the Farmers' Institute.

The Brampton Conservator reported the regular meetings of the Township Council, as well as those of the Judges' and Magistrates' Courts, which were also held regularly. Cooksville had the Pharmacy Hall, where Council meetings could be held at such times when the Town Hall was not available, due to its having to be decorated.

In the year 1885, Cooksville had been the possessor of a far-famed Brass Band, but this band had, at last, to be dissolved, because of deaths of bandsmen or of their moving away from the village. By 1920, only three of the members remained, these being J. K. Morley, William Weeks, and Joseph Goldthorpe and, at that time a movement was begun to organize a new band; and when Mr Varley, a musician of wide experience and ability, moved into the village, he wished to become its leader. Much enthusiasm was shown in the project, and a number of pupils came to learn from Mr Varley, along with a few others who had already had some experience playing in a band.

In August of that year, a Garden Party was held on the fair grounds near the Town Hall, to assist the members of the newly-formed organization. A good crowd turned out, led by the popular Mr Burns, of Port Credit. Booths were set up, and the Port Credit Brass Band did their part in livening up the evening's affair. Will J. White and Jules Brazill provided a comedy show, and the booths did a good business. With all these efforts put forward to help Mr Varley's cause, a tidy sum of money was collected, and everybody wished him 'Good Luck!' with his new Cooksville Band.

The Town Hall was put to a special use during 1920-21, when the new Cooksville School was being built; it was turned into a fine temporary school, with plenty of space around it for a schoolground. A couple of months later, a new porch was erected at the entrance, which immensely improved the appearance of the whole place. Not only a porch, but a complete re-decoration was done, and a new heating apparatus installed.

An enjoyable concert, presented in Cooksville Town Hall on March 11, 1921, was said to be the best concert held in the old Hall for many years. It was a comic sketch about 'That Rascal Pat,' cleverly done by three of the Tuxis boys, assisted by young ladies from Cooksville. Archie

Armstrong was congratulated on his exceptionally clever make-up, as Pat; Harry Duff and Harley Long, as Pat's two masters, were also admired.

A patriotic sketch, given by Miss Hazel Duff (Canada), Miss Bessie Tolman (Scotland), Miss Irene Hodge (Britannia), Miss Neita Tolman (Ireland), and Mrs H. Pawson (Wales) was unique, and gave great pleasure to everyone. Ansel Hopkins played 'Ben Hur's Chariot Race,' and Miss Gladys Stewart and Miss Neita Tolman gave readings. The Hall that evening was packed to its fullest capacity. *The Streetsville Review*, in a write-up the following week, gave first place in entertainment to The Trail Rangers and their Jazz Band, and complimented the Tuxis Boys on their latest songs. The following year, the Alta Vistas Tuxis Square returned to give another performance, this time a play, 'Dot, the Miner's Daughter.'

Mr Varley Sr. was now in charge of the Township Hall building, and other projects were being presented. At the end of May, 1923, the Department of Agriculture presented a demonstration of running water systems which could be supplied for the rural homes of the Township, and gave information about the installation, operation, and cost of operation.

BY POPULAR REQUEST

The Alta Vistas Tuxis Square

OF THE

Cooksville Methodist Church

WILL REPEAT THE PLAY

"Dot, the Miner's Daughter"

IN THE TOWN HALL

COOKSVILLE

Saturday, April 8th

The Streetsville Review, April 6, 1922

A narrow roadway led south from Dundas Street straight down to the Town Hall and, in 1923, when developments and improvements were taking place in the village, this Township Hall Road was badly in need of repairs. For three weeks in April it was not only a disagreeable sight, but an almost impassable approach to the Town Hall. Cars and trucks became mired in it; the mud was so deep that pedestrians lost rubber boots off their feet in it; neither villagers nor school children could reach the Town Hall with dry feet. Even *The Brampton Conservator* carried a message about the low spot inside the gates of the Cooksville grounds, urging one of the Council members to take the hint and have the section levelled up, stating that only a few dollars would make it as it should be.

In January, 1925, the Township Council decided to vacate the Hall and hold their meetings henceforth in R. S. Whaley's residence on Dundas Street; and in one month's time, the Township Clerk and Treasurer was housed in the new quarters. The name of the Clerk-Treasurer was Miss Eva Harris, appointed at the rate of fifteen dollars per week. The Hydro Department still occupied the Town Hall, and installed new furniture there. It was not until April, 1927, that work

July 1st, 1927, Diamond Jubilee Parade to the Fair Grounds, Cooksville school children passing southwest corner Hurontario & Dundas Streets; background, new Royal Bank building; on right, the first Royal Bank building. (Photo: Miss Mildred Bonhomme)

118

began on building an extension and making other improvements which would allow the Council members to move back to the Hall.

The work was finally completed, just in time for the additional accommodation required for the special celebration of Canada's Diamond Jubilee. The Trustees of each School Section in the Township were especially requested to have all school children attend this great event; and on Saturday, July 2, 1927, a public service for everyone in the Municipality of Toronto Township was held on the Cooksville Fair Grounds, at the Town Hall.

The following month, in August, the Cooksville Fife and Drum Band also celebrated this Diamond Jubilee by holding a dance in the Town Hall, serving refreshments, and providing music by Brown's Orchestra.

Chapter 16: The Cooksville Fall Fair

LONG BEFORE THE TOWN HALL was erected, the Fall Fair was being held at Cooksville. One of the earliest fairs in the province, it was listed among the first 30 established, beginning in 1836 with the Governor of Upper Canada contributing 50 Pounds towards the prize list.

The old minute books had disappeared but, in 1928, when Colonel T. L. Kennedy searched through old newspaper files in the Parliament Buildings at Toronto, he came across one paper containing a report of a Cooksville Fair Board meeting held on February 11, 1851. The document stated that the Fair had been held during the month of October, 1850, and the Treasurer's statement reported receipts of seventeen pounds, six shillings, with expenditures amounting to twenty pounds, six shillings.

Under the banner of the Toronto Township Agricultural Society, the Fair was held on these grounds continuously until 1858, when a change was made which moved it to Streetsville in alternate years.

On October 10, 1892, *The Streetsville Review* reported that, at the Toronto Township Fair in the cosy little village of Cooksville, glorious weather and crowds of people made the Directors glad, and caused the Treasurer's purse to overflow. Streams of vehicles filled with people poured onto the fair grounds from the four main thoroughfares; hundreds came by train, and scores more came on foot.

The special train from Toronto was crowded, while three trains from the west swelled the crowd to vast proportions – 'and yet, this was only a township fair, without any circus performance to attract the giddy multitudes.' People crowded the grounds to enjoy the side shows, candy, popcorn and peanuts; as well, there were men selling cheap jewellery, a phonograph man; a woman in tights, and a man with long black hair whose voice was like a fog horn; and eloquent soap box orators.

Breeds of cattle and horses, sheep, swine, turkeys and chickens were shown. There were Red and Yellow Mangolds, Turnip Beets, Red Carrots and White Carrots, Root Celery, Winter Radishes, Citrons, and Yellow Pumpkins. Apples, mostly of sorts never seen today, were the Snows, Cayuga Red Streaks, Fall Pippins and Ribston Pippins, Blenheim Oranges, Manitoba Apples, Box Russetts, Swazies, Pomme Grises – all these, besides the Northern Spy, Baldwin and Greening types. The fruit was declared to be superior to that seen at the Great Industrial Exhibition in Toronto.

At the Fair were displayed Crocks and Firkins of Butter, made in the homes by the housewives; Bottles of Domestic Wine; Honey in the Comb; Hop Yeast Breads, and Canned Fruits. Every sort of Craftwork and Sewing, from Raised Berlin wool work to silk patchwork Quilts; to Rag Mats and hand-hemmed Handkerchiefs, were all put proudly on display. Implements, as well as Lumber Wagons on Thimble Skeins, Fanning Mills, and Iron Harrows were all there to be examined and admired, as well as bought.

A most interesting event of the day, in 1892, was a bicycle race, watched by thousands of delighted spectators; and King's Brass Band furnished great music. The Press was well represented by a reporter from *The Toronto News*, Mr Charters of *The Brampton Conservator*, Mr Forster of *The Oakville Star*, and the editor of *The Streetsville Review*. Of such interest was the 1892 Township Fair, at Cooksville.

In 1894, a Band competition was held, First Prize for which was $20, and $10 for Second. People were told that 'Speeding in the Ring' was the great feature, greater than ever before in its history; and the advertisements stated: 'Everybody is going. Do not stay at home to keep house, but go; the house will not walk away.' This Agricultural Fair was truly the most important event looked forward to by the whole Township.

However, when there were more members of the Fair Board from Streetsville than from Cooksville, the people of Streetsville voted to keep the Township Fair in that community. Since it was too far a trip

120

for them to go to the Toronto Exhibition by horse and buggy, and being left without a Fair, the people of Cooksville formed their own new Agricultural Society in 1897. Under the guidance of Dr Moses Aikens of Burnhamthorpe, a well-known physician who bred trotting horses, the first all-Cooksville Fair was organized and held in 1900.

The change of name to Cooksville Fair, held by the Cooksville Agricultural Society, made no difference in its popularity. In 1902, there were 4,000 people on the Fair Grounds to see the show of Cattle, Sheep and Pigs. In Pigs, R. F. Duck and Son won red ribbons with their Lakeview herd; R. N. Switzer, of Streetsville, had the best Shropshire Sheep; in Poultry, the top exhibitor was J. H. McCauley, of Britannia.

The ladies put on a large display of handiwork in artistic designs in cotton, silk and wool; fruits and butter by the basketful; and dressed fowl (turkeys, ducks and chickens). During the afternoon, the Victoria Industrial School Band enlivened the proceedings. They had a midway with a striking-machine, but only an odd person could strike the machine and ring the bell at 200 lbs.

While these events were going on, a good exhibition of speeding events was taking place, these races being won by Hilda B., Lulu, Little Kate, Sleepy Joe, and Frank C. There were classes for Lady Drivers, Saddle Horses, and Hurdle Horse Races, as well.

The following April, 1903, a gang of men was employed to re-fence the Fair Grounds, and enlarge the horse ring and race track from one-quarter to one-third of a mile around. The driving track, in the shape of an oval, and properly fenced-in to protect the public from danger, was completed in time for the opening of the October 8th Fall Fair.

In 1907, a substantial new grandstand was erected, capable of seating upwards of 400 spectators; underneath, it was filled in for the suitable display of agricultural exhibits. The old building formerly used for this purpose was then used for the showing of Poultry; and new public conveniences were added to the grounds. A bandstand was built near the horse ring, and improvements were made to the entrance gate. All of these improvements brought a great increase in the number of special prizes awarded.

The Brampton Conservator declared the Fair of 1907 the best in half a century, with delightful weather bringing 1,000 persons by train from Toronto, in addition to all those from the neighbouring districts. So many visitors pressed through the narrow gates that the ticket takers had a difficult time; afterwards, it was variously estimated that the

Cooksville Fair. (Photo: Mississauga Central Library, Cooksville Vol. 1, #41) crowd numbered between 4,000 to 6,000 people, all enjoying themselves on the Fair Grounds.

The Cooksville district farmers excelled in growing roots, fruits and vegetables, and that year the size of the potatoes, squash, cauliflowers, cabbages and other roots astonished everyone who inspected them; it was a splendid showing of what the southern portion of the county could do. Persons from the city remarked on the accommodation furnished by Ward's Hotel; they said that the 25-cent meal at Ward's would put to shame many of the half-dollar feasts served in the city hotels. Mr Ward also refused to sell any person a flask or bottle of liquor during the whole day of the Fair, and there was no sign of drunkenness in the village; everyone returned home at an early hour.

Nothing seemed to slow the progress of the Cooksville Agricultural Society. In 1909, 250 horses were shown, of which 150 were in the carriage and roadster class, 65 in heavy draught, and 30 in the special events. Of cattle, there were 76 entries of Ayrshires, Jerseys and Holsteins. That year, the special train from Toronto was met at the Centre Road crossing by the officials in charge of the Fair, and all marched toward the grounds, led by the Port Credit Band.

The visitors ate hot tamales, and ice cream cones; at the booths, they 'took a shot at Old Aunt Sal,' 'dropped the Ring over the Cane,' and played 'Hoop-La.' Bankers, policemen, blacksmiths, lawyers, working folks, clergymen, Members of Parliament – one and all, old and young, mingled together and made as merry as a lot of school children on a holiday. George McClelland took in the cash, as in other years, but he had more shining quarters jingling in the pouch on the way to Mr Thompson's bank than he ever had before.

Six thousand persons celebrated Thanksgiving on the grounds of the Annual Fair in 1910; every available stable, shed and yard was filled with vehicles used by the farmers and others arriving. There was held, on that day, a sham battle at Erindale, in which 4,000 soldiers engaged, and when it was completed at about 2.30 p.m., a number from there came over to join the crowd in Cooksville. Among these was Major T. L. Kennedy, of Dixie, who was President of the Society. J. K. Morley was the most active man of the day, making out entry tickets and keeping the machinery of the show in motion, ably seconded by his assistant, Sergeant Schiller, of Cooksville.

A new ticket office and entrance to the Fair Grounds gave better accommodation to the attending crowds in 1912; and in January it was

Major T. L. Kennedy's Regiment on the Cooksville Fair Grounds, 1914.
(Photo: Mississauga Central Library, Cooksville Vol. 1, #123)

decided that, under the able presidency of William Baldock, the Society's financial standing was good. The Treasurer's report showed a balance of $1,426.53.

At the Annual Banquet of the Cooksville Fair Association, held in Bowers' Hotel at the end of February, upwards of forty officers and directors met, together with their friends; and in the fall, they were happily congratulating the new President, J. J. Hopkins, on his efforts, towards the continued success of the Fair.

The following year, in 1914, under the establishment of district representatives of the Department of Agriculture in Peel, School Fairs began to be held in Cooksville. These Fairs were to the school children what the larger Township and County Fairs were to the grownups, with the children electing their own directors and taking care of the work, as far as their own schools were concerned. They had the full management of the School Fairs and prize lists in their own hands, just the same as their elders had for the Fall Fairs.

Department of Agriculture representatives stated that it was the first step in the development of young leaders, and it was leadership that was much needed in agriculture. W. H. J. Tisdale, District Representative, said, 'What we want are men and women who are not afraid to voice an opinion, and the management of the Fair is something that inspires confidence and develops self control.' Thus, it was arranged, and the first Toronto Township School Fair, held under the auspices of the Peel County Branch of the Department of Agriculture, took place at the end of September, 1914.

The following week, the Squadron of Governor General's Horse Guards, under Major T. L. Kennedy, camped on the Township Fair Grounds, and music for the Fair, that year, was provided by the Band of the 36th Peel Regiment. Much interest was created by the exhibition Hurdle Race, which was contested by the officers of this cavalry troop. Colonel Sanford Smith, with his horse 'Silver Buckle,' came out the victor in a close finish. In the Saddle Horse Class, this military unit scored a distinct success, Colonel Smith placing first, and Lieutenant O'Brien, second.

In 1917, a new Poultry building provided room for increasing entries; special cars from the city were provided by the Toronto Suburban Railway, and the famous 110th Battalion Irish Pipe Band entertained at Cooksville Fair.

A list of Special Prizes donated in 1918 offers a little insight into the qualifications and conditions to be met, for a few of the entries in this great Fair:

Lady Drivers Class, open to all comers. 1st prize a Silver Medal
    valued at $10, given by Ryrie Bros. Jewellers, Yonge St., Toronto.

Roadster Farmer's Turnout, to be bona fide property of the
    exhibitor, and must farm at least 50 acres of land.
    1st prize $5, given by Whittaker & Sons, Oakville.

Single Wagon Horse, must be shown in a single wagon suitable for
    delivery purposes. 1st prize $5, given by Brown's Copper &
    Brass Rolling Mills, Ltd., New Toronto.

Best Team Suitable for Light Delivery, manners and speed to be
    reckoned in making the award. Special prize $10, given by
    The Canada Bread Company, Ltd.

Best Dappled Grey in Harness, suitable for delivery purposes.
    1st prize $5, given by Robert Simpson & Co.

The 1920 Fall Fair was notable for the fact that Ernest Drury, Premier of Ontario, and Manning Doherty, Minister of Agriculture, attended. At 3 p.m., Mr Doherty delivered an address; and a $100.00 prize was offered for a racing event under the regulation of the Canadian National Trotting and Pacing Horse Association. Other Prizes were given for the best-decorated automobiles.

The Streetsville Review, March 10, 1921

The following year, for the first time, the Cooksville Fair became a two-day event. The poultry house at the exhibition grounds was now equipped with 102 folding wire coops, and 70 stationary coops, affording enough accommodation for 600 fowl. Turkey raising had become a popular pursuit, with one woman marketing over 1,800 pounds of turkey at nearly one thousand dollars that year; another sold 125 birds at over seven hundred and fifty dollars.

By 1922, the Poultry Show had been worked up from a dozen or so exhibits in the beginning to over 800 entries, all said to be a wonderful tribute to the President, Roy E. Pallett. The Auto Polo Contest was an exciting attraction; and the gentleman who judged the Butter said that the quality in the Township was superior to entries at either London or Ottawa.

However, a very unfortunate affair ended what was to be a happy event for 1,500 children of West Toronto. These children had been transported to the Fair Grounds by 135 cars and trucks, for a picnic under the auspices of the West Toronto Business Men's Association. Just as they were about to be served with the refreshments they had brought with them, they learned that the fair grounds land had been leased and they were not allowed to stay. They had to start off again for home without enjoying their picnic.

These West Toronto Business Men had always been strong supporters of the Fair, and the taxpayers of Cooksville were much upset when they heard of the affair. They denounced the lease and declared that, if thirty-five dollars were so essential to the Treasury, they would subscribe to it themselves, in order that the young people of the village and from other points could enjoy the fair grounds as a playground property. They extended their sincere regrets to the city children and their friends who had brought them for the picnic, and hoped that the breach would be healed.

At the next Agricultural Society Board meeting, there was a record attendance with every part of the Township being represented, and it was decided that the grounds should not be leased for pasturage purposes, but remain open as a playground and picnic park during the days and evenings. It was agreed that any animals found on the premises should be impounded and their owners prosecuted, in conformity with the Township By-law for animals running at large.

In 1923, nine covered stalls were erected for race horses at the Fair, and a new stand for the race horse judges added. Visitors at the Fair

Cooksville Shale Brick Company Horses, shown at the Cooksville
Fair and Toronto Exhibition. Driver is Harry Auld; with Bob Cox,
machinist in the mill room, 1925. (Photo: Mississauga Central
Library, Cooksville School Collection F 235)

who knew good horses, that year admired the Clydesdale team exhibited
by the Cooksville Brick Company, an unbeaten pair as to size, weight,
conformation, and overall attraction.

After the extension to the Town Hall was completed in 1927, and
more space could be allocated to exhibits, the Agricultural Society's
directors decided to spend considerable money on the race track. Two
hundred loads of new material were put down to turn it into first class
condition, since a better track would assure that more race horses would
be brought to the Fair. To give the spectators a better view, the posts
enclosing the track were given a good coat of white paint.

Each year, new attractions were added. Horse Shoe Pitching Contests
began to be held, and Ladies' Softball Tournaments, as well as Perfect
Baby Contests. Later, a new sound equipment system was installed so
that music could resound over the Fair Grounds, and important events
like the results of the judging could be announced through the
amplifiers. Midget Auto Racing, and Greyhound Races were held, and
always the admission remained the same – 25 cents.

In 1930, the Horse Show was great, the weather splendid, and one of

the features of that Fair was the Special Prize given for the Best
Collection of Vegetables, which went to James Guthrey & Sons, of
Dixie. This same exhibitor won the special prize for the largest
Pumpkin, which topped the scales at 75 pounds. A newsman asked the
Judge as to the weight of the pumpkin and, when he raised it from the
ground, the Judge replied, 'It weighs every bit as much as a bag of
potatoes.'

Four Ladies' Softball Teams competed, with contestants being
entered from Cooksville, Georgetown, Clarkson, and Port Credit; and
the beautiful Silver Trophy, the gift of the Fair Association, was
presented to the team from Georgetown. Edward G. Smith, of Malton,
carried off the J. Lockie Wilson Cup for the Horse Shoe Pitching
Contest, after a very exciting finish. All ages took part in the Programme
of Sports, from children under the age of seven to the race for single
men.

In the Fruit Class, James Guthrey & Sons captured the J. H. Pinchin
Special Prize of $10.00 for the majority of prizes; Mr H. B. Stewart was

FIRST DAY

"Batter. Up !
Let's Go!"

Girl's Softball Tournament

Beginning at one o'clock sharp, standard time,
Tuesday, October 4

COOKSVILLE VS. STREETSVILLE
BRAMPTON VS. LAKEVIEW

Prizes given to each member of the winning teams
in first two games.
Prizes donated by Cooksville Hardware.
Winning teams play off for Cup donated by the
Society.

ADMISSION 25c

The Port Credit News,
September 23, 1927

Men Who Made the 1929 Cooksville Fair a Huge Success

ENERGETIC PRESIDENT AND DIRECTORS OF BIG ATTRACTION

The layout shows: (1) Howard J. Walker, Cooksville, convener of the flower show; (2) George Duck, Lakeview, president of the fair; (3) Fred B. Pense, Port Credit, secretary; (4) Harvey Stewart, Dixie, first vice-president, in charge of the vegetable classes; (5) Fred Watson, Dixie, in charge of the fruit; (6) Martin Crofton, Cooksville, convener of the horse section; (7) 'Sea Crest,' four year old jumper, owned by Martin Crofton; (8) J. W. Dale, convener of the sports committee; (9) Gordon Harris, treasurer. (*The Brampton Conservator*, October 3, 1929) second. The Home Baking Department had the best exhibition of its kind ever seen in Cooksville; there was such a demand for home-baked articles that the exhibitors sold them 'like hot cakes' at the close of the Fair.

Keen competition was shown in every class – Cattle, Sheep, Swine, and Poultry. Rabbits, in the Poultry Shed, were much admired; the next year a special inducement was offered to breeders of different types of rabbits. The Flower Show entries were very large, one lady remarking to the Press that she had never seen dahlias like them.

The Port Credit News reported that, with no exaggeration, the Horse Show was the best in the history of the Fair, and the sole purpose of those in charge was to give the visitors a real horse show – 'and they sure got it.' Martin Crofton, Chairman of the Horse Committee, was congratulated upon the splendid horse show, and one horseman said, 'It was the keenest contested class I was ever in, and I have been competing for many years.'

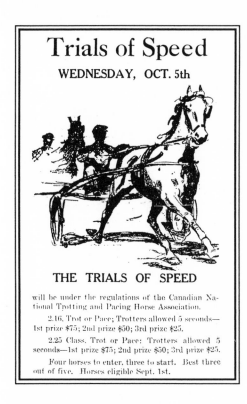

Trials of Speed
WEDNESDAY, OCT. 5th

THE TRIALS OF SPEED

will be under the regulations of the Canadian National Trotting and Pacing Horse Association.

2.16. Trot or Pace; Trotters allowed 5 seconds— 1st prize $75; 2nd prize $50; 3rd prize $25.

2.25 Class. Trot or Pace: Trotters allowed 5 seconds—1st prize $75; 2nd prize $50; 3rd prize $25.

Four horses to enter, three to start. Best three out of five. Horses eligible Sept. 1st.

The Port Credit News,
September 23, 1937

The Port Credit News, September 8, 1935

The First Prize Baby at the Fair, judged by Dr Frank O'Leary, of Toronto, and Dr George Watson, of Lakeview, was the little son of Mr and Mrs Robert McLeay, of Credit Grove.

At the end of the 1930 Cooksville Fall Fair, Gordon M. Harris, the Treasurer, stated that 'The Merry-Go-Round did a rushing business, especially by the young folk, and after all, who isn't young at the Cooksville Fair?'

* * *

The last Cooksville Fall Fair was held on September 14 and 15, 1951, one of the contributing factors to its end being the declining interest on the part of district residents; Colonel Kennedy, of Dixie, attributed its real cause to the advent of urban life into the area. He said, 'The best fairs are in communities far away from the cities, where there is interest in agriculture and everyone knows their neighbours.'

Chapter 17: School Section No. 2, Cooksville

THE CENSUS OF 1861 listed one School House in Cooksville, and the Register of 1866 stated that the Common School there averaged 40 scholars, being taught by James McKinnon.

In 1873, a new building built of red brick stood on Hurontario Street a short distance north of the Dundas highway; on its cornerstone were the words 'Cooksville Public School, School Section No. 2, Cooksville, A.D. 1873.' This original one-room school had a bell tower, was heated by a pot-bellied stove, and its first class was taught by Miss Cavell.

Children carrying cloth school bags came from as far as two miles distant, walking along the sandy Middle Road (Queen Elizabeth Way) and up the gravelled Centre Road to Cooksville Public School; in winter, their fathers brought them by horse and bob-sleigh. They took lunches from home, carried in honey pails and left sitting in rows until it was time to eat. At noon, boys went outdoors to play 'Fox and Hounds,' running as far over as Cooksville Creek, and northward to the railroad tracks.

By 1877, there were two rooms, heated by two stoves, with a woodshed at the back. Years afterwards, some of the school children recalled that when Jack King's father owned the Hotel on Dundas Street, their teachers, Miss Walterhouse and Miss Thurston, bustled about in long full skirts, tending the stoves.

Old Cooksville School, s.s. #2, Hurontario Street, north of Dundas Street. (Photo: Mississauga Central Library, Cooksville Vol. 1, #14)

As early as March 10, 1877, *The Brampton Conservator* carried a full report on an entertainment given, by the Literary Society, in a room of the Cooksville School, so crowded with people that standing room was hardly to be found. The programme opened with a chorus by the school pupils, followed by two songs by the Misses Bull, whose voices were said to be in perfect harmony. Instrumental music was provided by Professor Latham, the popular teacher of the Cooksville Band, on the violin, and Joseph King on the cornet, accompanied by the organ.

A. H. Wilmot and A. Brunskill played solos at the concert. Miss Soady and Miss Barnard gave readings and recitations, and Mr Tracy read a very active story, as well; but an article entitled 'Farming Life,' by Francis Morley, was judged the reading of the evening. John Price and Jenny Cook, and Mr Tracy's two small sons, all pupils of the Public School gave excellent dialogues. This part of the programme was followed by a splendid play entitled 'The Widder Bedotte.' Miss Brodie played the part of the designing and disappointed widow, ably supported by E. O. Winters as 'Mr Crane,' and Miss Annie King as 'Millissey.'

Thus came to a conclusion one of the first Literary Society entertainments performed in the school, under the chairmanship of T. D. (Thomas) King, which proved to be a great success. The admission to all concerts was set at 1 cent per ticket.

The Annual Teachers' Convention was held in the schoolhouse on Friday, November 9, 1894, with 29 teachers present, chaired by Mr O. G. Copeland, of Elmbank. Inspector Allan Embury opened the proceedings with a lecture on Reading, and on analyzing poems. History was the next to be dealt with, outlining a plan of teaching this subject to beginners by using pictures and biographies for the lessons. Mr Embury laid great stress on the early teaching of Physical Geography, contending that a landscape or a map should be to the child a living book which might be read. The daytime session closed with the topic of Primary Arithmetic.

In the evening, Mr Embury spoke in the Methodist Church, giving his views on the relationship of the public school to national life, and so engrossed was the audience that not a move was made, nor an eye turned from the speaker, for an hour and a half.

At the end of November, Mr O. G. Copeland was engaged as senior teacher of School Section No. 2. At this time, Cooksville was said to possess one of the best public schools in the county, and in April, 1896, the pupils gave Mr Copeland a flattering address and a diamond pin and tie; he received, as well, gold cuff links from the boys, and a china cup and saucer from the girls.

The Streetsville Review of March 5, 1903, listed 'Cooksville's Senior School Room – in order of Standing:'

Sr. IV – James Schiller, John Walterhouse, and Harold McClelland.

Jr. IV – Norman McClelland, Oscar Brunskill, and Thomas Fenwick.

Sr. III – Stanley Pellet, Susan Kee, and Jessie Rose.

Jr. III – Wilfred Parks, Allan Harris, and Johnston Pinkney.

Also, in 1903, the following from this school passed the Entrance Examinations: Lena Murray, Hannah Goldthorpe, Ella Pettit, James Schiller, and Harold McClelland. They wrote these examinations at Toronto Junction.

In August, that year, a new maple floor was laid in the School and pronounced to be quite an improvement.

When Mr Taggart was Principal of the School, in July, 1905, six out of seven pupils passed the Entrance, written at Brampton High School.

A grand concert consisting of songs, recitations and comic dialogues, and music by a mouth organ quartette, was held in the Town Hall on an evening in February, 1908. Admission to this event was set at 20 cents for adults, and for children not scholars of the village school, 10 cents, with all proceeds being used towards the purchase of books for the School Library.

For a short while, the trustees of S.S. No. 2 had a difficult time of it, trying to keep a principal at Cooksville School. Mr H. M. Brown gave up his duties at the end of 1909 and moved with his family to the city. The following year, 1910, the new appointee, Mr Buchanan, was offered a more remunerative position in the city and also left the village. At that time, Miss Guthrie was asked to take charge as principal until another could be found. In spite of an increase in the minimum fixed salary, there appeared to be a scarcity in the teaching profession.

The great innovation in the public school system in 1914 was the beginning of the rural school fairs. The children were given a list of materials, such as Oats, Barley, Mangels, Corn, and Potatoes, from which to choose and take home to plant. Settings of Eggs were also given out – four or five settings to each school. These eggs were obtained from the Guelph College, from a bred-to-lay strain of Barred Rocks or White Wyandottes.

The plants grown, and the chickens raised, were to become the personal property of the pupil and to be exhibited at the School Fair at the central point in the Township (Cooksville), in September. Prizes were also to be given for Baking, Sewing, Writing, Weed and Seed Collections, Insect Collections, Weed Naming, and Apple Contests. The boys were to bring Colts and Calves to show, and this feature was calculated to create as much interest as anything else in the Fair.

A special Silver Shield was to be given to the school putting up the best general display, and a Silver Cup to the child winning the greatest number of prizes. The parents were asked to come out with their children, bring their lunch baskets and make a regular day of it; they were asked to give it a trial, and if it did not prove beneficial to the children, not to enter another year.

At the end of April, 1914, the village was so prosperous, as evidenced by the crowded condition of the Public School, an order was issued from the trustees that the teachers should send home all pupils under seven years of age, which was according to the regulations of the Public School Act. In charge of the Junior Room was Miss Kate McPherson.

The following year, the parents were enthusiastic about the School Fair, everyone agreeing that it was the right way to get the little folks interested. One mother reported that the week after the Fair, the year before, her daughter said it was the best thing that ever came into the country schools.

Another parent stated that his son Jack had hatched nine Barred Rock chickens from the eggs the Department of Agriculture distributed; he had fed them all himself, and looked after the chickens almost day and night, all summer. Then he had shown them at the Fair and got one first prize, and two second prizes. His sister grew a plot of Golden Bantam Sweet Corn; she could be found in her garden nearly any hour of the day, and her ten ears of corn got fourth prize. That night she had said to her mother, 'I didn't get much of a prize, but I'll do better next year if I have to live in my garden.' The boy wanted to apply for eggs again, and his little sister wanted flowers.

The 1915 Second Annual Toronto Township School Fair was a success, in spite of the rain which fell on the grounds. The School Fair Association set up a 'War Booth,' and sold sandwiches and refreshments to aid Red Cross work, the total receipts from this being fifty-five dollars.

A moving picture camera was sent out from Toronto, and pictures were taken of the loaded vans of children on their way to the School

Fair, of the judging, the livestock, and sports. The film was to be used by the Department of Agriculture at evening meetings held in connection with a Better Farming Special, in Brampton. *The Conservator* reported that: 'Townspeople and others who never had an opportunity of attending a School Fair may see it almost as real, on the screen at the meeting.' Dr Creelman, President of the Ontario Agricultural College was a guest at the Fair, and was greatly pleased with the whole programme.

Some of the prize winners for the crops they grew, and for the care they gave their plots were, as follows:

Oats – Louie McKay, and Belle Ritchie
Potatoes – Margaret Pickett, and Arnold Guthrey
War Plot – Edmund Phillips, and Harry Pickett
Ensilage Corn – Henry Pickett, and Douglas Dunton
Sweet Corn – Archie Shaver, and Fred Scott
Mangels – Laura Fieldhouse, and Wilbert Davidson

In other classes, the results were listed in the local newspapers and a few of the entries and their winners are given here:

Leaves of the Common Trees – Lillie Walker
Bouquets of Cut Flowers – Agnes Hodgetts
Basket of Flowers from a Border – Helena McArthur
Vegetables from the Home Garden – Willie Harris
Plate of 5 Winter Apples – Percy Clarkson
Plate of 5 Fall Apples – Josie Featherston

For the Collection of Weeds, pressed, mounted and correctly named, a prize was won by Mary Armstrong; for Weed Seeds in bottles and correctly named, by Jean Dawson.

Judged best in the Poultry Classes, were as follows:

Pullets, from Eggs distributed in 1915:
– Anna McCarthy, and James Bloor
Hatched from eggs laid by pullets reared in 1914:
– Karl Kane

For his Pair of Pigeons, the winner was Milton Skinner; and for a Pair of Rabbits, Wilfred Chadwick.

In the contest naming the most types of Apples, Eva Wolfe received a prize; for naming the most Weed Seeds, Melvin Pickett.

In Domestic Science, the girls exhibited Hand-Made Aprons, and this class was won by Edna Graham.

In the class for 'One Piece of Cloth Showing Best Work in mending a three-cornered tear, patching, and making three buttonholes,' the winner was Mary Armstrong.

The boys did Manual Training projects, and Alex O'Brien made the Best Tool Box; in another class, for 'Other Forms of Handy Farm or Home Device,' the winner was Milton Skinner.

Any pupil who wished, boy or girl, could enter the Baking Contest, and the best-tasting goodies were found to be:

2 Loaves of Bread – Lillie Walker
1 Layer Cake – Laura Garbutt
1 Apple Pie – Rosa Bonner
6 Cookies – Sarah Pallett
1 Lb. of Fudge – Dorothy Pallett

In the Drawing Class, for pupils in the Second Book and under, the most beautiful crayon drawing of the Union Jack was done by Lorne Treanor; for those above the Second Book, the best map of Peel County was made by Mary Block.

Winners of the Livestock Judging, on the Fair Grounds, were:

Heavy Colt, led by pupil – George Dunton
Colt, best trained by pupil – George Chadwick
Dairy Calf, led by pupil – Percy Clarkson
Beef Calf, led by pupil – Willie Ellis.

* * *

In September, 1915, the two teachers were Miss Weyman (Senior), and Miss Northwood (Junior), and the need for an enlarged school was so apparent that the trustees considered opening an additional room and engaging a third teacher. A meeting of the School Section supporters was called to discuss the problem. The building had been in use for over forty years, and attendance now numbered 114 on the Roll, with only the two teachers. It was decided to take down the old building, saving the bricks to be used for a new building; the Town Hall could be divided into three compartments and used as a temporary school.

When the School re-opened in September, 1917, Miss Annie Fligg was the Principal, and Miss Jermyn was in charge of the Junior Room.

The new three-room Public School, constructed by Mr H. Elgie, of Toronto, opened in 1921. In addition to the Principal, Mr Dyer, the local staff now consisted of three teachers: Miss Thurston, Mrs Gillespie, and Miss Wallace. There were 14 Cooksville boys and girls attending Streetsville High School; and the following June every pupil

New Cooksville School, east side Hurontario, north of Dundas
Street. (Photo: Mississauga Central Library, Cooksville School
Collection F201)

who wrote for the entrance in 1921 was successful. For the new term,
Brampton and Weston were to be receiving their quota of High School
students from Cooksville.

However, in less than one year's time the new school was again
overcrowded. The annual meeting held in the schoolhouse in January
brought out the largest crowd that ever attended a school meeting in
Toronto Township, with 100 or more ratepayers present. When Trustee
Hodge read the financial report, it showed expenditures of $37,500, and
a surplus of over $5,000 in the bank.

In June, 1922, a new teacher, Miss Watt, took over her duties in the
Cooksville School, and was replaced in September by Miss Flummerfelt
as the Kindergarten teacher. The following year, work was put into full
swing on a two-room addition at the south end of the school building,
by contractor Mr Warren, of Mount Dennis. Joseph Allen succeeded J.
J. Lavidiere as caretaker of the school.

Throughout the proceedings of building and change, the Public
School entertainments had still been carried on, as well as the School
Fairs and everything else, as usual; and in April of 1923, notices went out
regarding a meeting to discuss the Continuation School. But only a few of

the taxpayers attended, and those who did were not in favour of incorporating an Assembly Hall in the building. The question of a heating system was brought up, but this problem was left to the trustees.

A sidewalk was built on the east side of the Centre Road, from Dundas Street north towards the schoolhouse, this project paid for by the Cooksville Women's Institute. By August, 1923, the two-room addition to the school had reached the ceiling line, and part of it was ready for opening day in September.

Two years later, in 1925, the children of the village were enjoying an outdoor skating rink in the school grounds, around which Trustee Frank Walterhouse suspended a row of electric lights over the ice. New flush toilets had been installed in the building; and the next innovation was to install a gramophone to provide music for the children to march in and out of school. In January, George Beamish became the new caretaker of the school.

The Cooksville Continuation School was now a reality, with an enrollment of 23 students, and at the end of December, 1926, the Literary Society held an interesting meeting. President Laura Pallett opened the meeting with words of welcome, and the reading of Longfellow's poem 'The Three Kings,' followed by 'O Canada,' and the song 'How d'ye do?' by all. The minutes were read by Secretary Clara Denison, and Juanita Beamish read, from the Bible, the Story of the First Christmas.

Miss Flewelling offered prizes to those standing in the first three places in each class, each of whom were asked to give speeches on the closing day. The class enacted a sketch entitled 'Today is Monday,' showing in an exaggerated way the invasion of our school system by a number of outside interests, some helpful, some not; it contained a hidden lesson in its nonsense. Faith Cowan then played a piano solo, and Tony Pavanel read a paper of jokes, all much enjoyed. The Reverend M. Harden spoke a few words, and the meeting closed with 'God Save the King.'

The Brampton Conservator reported, on Friday, May 26, 1927, that maple trees were planted at Cooksville Public School. The first tree was planted by Mrs Amy Guthrie, a former teacher in the school; she was assisted by John A. Ezard, who once had been her pupil and was now Chairman of the Public School Board. The second tree was planted by Reeve J. J. Jamieson, assisted by the Principal of the school, W. R. Beatty. It was the year of the Diamond Jubilee, and the school was decorated with flags and bunting. The British Coat-of-Arms, a piece of work done by the students, hung facing the audience. The teachers, Miss Flewelling, Miss Greta Cunningham, Miss Margaret Myers, Miss Smith, and Mr Beatty led the classes in singing, after which a grand programme was enjoyed by everyone.

The pupils of the new Middle Road School, which had been built just east of the intersection of Hurontario and the Middle Road (Queen Elizabeth Way), were now coming to play softball at the Cooksville school grounds. On May 23, 1928, the Middle Road team had only seven players, and Cooksville had to play two men short. Since there was only one fielder on each team it made for the large score of 33 to 19, in favour of Cooksville. The Cooksville team players were: James Keane, Harry Price, Frank Frances, Arnold Varley, John Jamieson, Frank Thomas, and Russell Rowett. The Continuation School, under the direction of their teacher Miss Greta Cunningham, put on its first Field Day in June, 1928. She was assisted by Dr F. E. Hopkins, and Messrs. John Cunningham and G. H. Tolman. Two Silver Medals were presented to the boys and girls receiving the highest points in athletics, won by Elda Harris and Decarr Turpel, each of whom received 28 points; Agnes Hopkins and Harry Christie were in second place, with 22 and 27 points respectively.

Mr Beamish had the rink in fine condition in January, 1929, for the Winter Carnival. Mr Forster drove over with his sound truck to supply the music, and merriment broke out each time the needle stuck in a crack on the record and played the same line over and over. The students greatly appreciated the rink, and sent their thanks by way of a note in *The Port Credit News*.

In July, 1929, it was learned that all sixteen students from Cooksville who wrote the entrance examinations at Port Credit passed. Clara Ezard won the Warden's Medal.

On Carnival Day, the next year, nearly 200 boys and girls from the five rooms took to the ice, most wearing pretty, or striking, costumes. The Women's Institute served 43 pounds of hot dogs in the school basement, and it took a dozen ladies to serve the eager line-ups for this delectable free lunch. Following the Carnival, the hockey team from the Public School played the Continuation School, beating them by a score of 3-0.

Cooksville had good hockey players and, at a match with Dixie in February, 1929, they were winners by a 12-0 score. However, later in the

Carnival Day, at school. (Photo: Mississauga Central Library, Cooksville Vol. 1) same month, Riverside (Port Credit) came up to play on the Cooksville rink. On their way up for this game, the truck carrying the Riverside team had a blow-out, which ended in their having to walk the rest of the way; the Cooksville team was already assembled when they arrived. Both teams were anxious to begin, and the puck was dropped at half-past four. This game ended with a score of 8-4, after which Jack Dearness reported, in the *School News*, that 'Riverside gave their yell and departed triumphantly for home.'

At the end of February, 1930, Cooksville School was again overcrowded. One of the rooms was being used for the Continuation School, which was felt to be doing good work because the students did not have to leave their home town to complete their first two years of High School work. Mr J. J. Jamieson, seconded by William Copeland, moved that the trustees get together with the school inspector and give consideration to the matter.

At the Annual Meeting, the question of teaching music in the school caused a lively discussion. The Board was given authority to have the teaching of music as part of the students' education, but the trustees objected, saying that there were only four teachers on the staff, and five would be necessary before the teaching of music could begin. A vote was taken, with a majority of one vote in favour of Music not being introduced into the Cooksville School. It would have to be deferred until a later date. However, the Continuation School was kept on, to the satisfaction of the parents.

For the Annual Ice Carnival in February, 1931, forty prizes for the competition were donated by the Women's Institute, the Business Men, and the staff. The list of prize winners at this carnival shows that, on the Public School rink at Cooksville in those days, it was not unusual for girls to take part in speed skating and puck handling.
– Senior Girls, fancy dress – Mary Bonhomme, Hilda Varley.
– Junior Girls, fancy dress – Genevieve Gridelet, Jane Dulmage, and
　　Eileen McDonald.
– Junior Boys, fancy dress – Jimmy Walterhouse, Bill Belford.
– Senior Girls, comic – Doris Kitney, Vera Walterhouse.
– Junior Girls, comic – Olive Miles, Eileen Baker, Mary McDonald.
– Senior Boys, comic – Clarence Hepton.
– Junior Boys, comic – Edward Heron, Jack Bull.
– Senior Girls, speed – Margaret Law, Vera Walterhouse.
– Junior Girls, speed – Eleanor Marshall, Kathleen Creighton.

Rhea Green's Class, Cooksville Public School. June, 1932.
(Photo: courtesy of Joe Bandiera)

BACK ROW: (L to R) Monica Bonhomme, Margaret Christie, Bernice Kee, Gladys Harris, Christine Crowley, Rose Brogna, Vera Varley, Evelyn Garbutt, Irene Sproule, Mary MacDonald.

2ND ROW: Ross Tommy, Gordon Rowatt, Howard Key, Tony Franze, Bill Whaley, Joe Kane, Walter Corum, Ted Herd, Jackson Cunningham, Joe Bandiera.

3RD ROW: Katina Brait, Jean MacKay, Fanny Milburn, Betty Goldthorpe, Julia Creighton, Miss Rhea Green, Rita McTiernan, Olive Miles, Annie Harper, Gladys Cook.

4TH ROW: Geo. Woodall, Julius Smith, Rodney Pinkney, Victor Arthur, Arthur Rowatt, Geo. Welk, Cleveland Harris, Austin Hepton, Edward Heron, Joe Perrin.

– Senior Boys, speed – Charlie Whaley, Bill Whaley.
– Junior Boys, speed – Gordon Rowatt, Frank Keane.
– Youngest Boy Skater – Billy Bull.
– Youngest Girl Skater – Ellen McDonald.
– Senior Girls, puck shooting – Doris Kitney, Olive Walterhouse.
– Junior Girls, puck shooting – Jean Malpass, Eleanor Marshall.
– Senior Boys, puck shooting – Billie Brooks, B. Pavanel.
– Junior Boys, puck shooting – Edward Heron, Joe Keane.

Fancy Skating:
– Senior Girls – Margaret Law, Doris Bull.
– Junior Girls – Fanny Milburn, Eileen Baker.
– Senior Boys – Billie Brooks, Arnold Varley.
– Junior Boys – Harold Brunskill, Jack Gates.

At the end of the Carnival, the Second and Third Forms (grades 10 and 11) defeated the First Form (grade 9) and the Public School by a score of 9-2 in a hard-fought hockey game.

THE SCHOOL FAIR:

The School Fair continued to be a very important event each year looked forward to, and remembered for all their lives by the children who took part in it. *The Brampton Conservator* of March 4, 1919, reported that ten years after it was organized, with three schools taking part, 357 rural school fairs were held in Ontario; the pupils had 69,848 home plots, and made 111,823 entries. It was estimated that about 250 people saw the first school fair, with 58 pupils taking part, while in 1919, 92,600 children and 107,590 adults attended the school fairs of Ontario – truly a wonderful growth.

In 1919, the Ontario Department of Agriculture distributed Seeds and Eggs to 78,946 pupils in 3,278 rural schools of the province. *The Agricultural Gazette* stated that there were also distributed:
– 1,890 bushels of Potatoes
– 432 bushels of Grain
– 12,575 packages of Root Seeds
– 30,700 packages of Vegetable Seeds
– 21,900 packages of Flower Seeds, and
– 11,045 dozens of Eggs, of a bred-to-lay strain of Barred
    Plymouth Rocks.

These figures give us, today, some idea of the magnitude of the school fairs. Thus, for a Cooksville School child to say that he or she won a prize at the Cooksville School Fair was something of which they could be rightfully proud. Even today, many children of old Toronto Township, now grown old, still recall with pleasure the Cooksville School Fair.

In 1919, a Pastoral Landscape Sketch won the Drawing Contest for Percy Grice; James Pinkney (who was later in life to become Cooksville's veterinarian), had the best Spring Calf, as well as the best Mutton Lamb, both animals being halter-broken.

A Drawing of a Carcass of Beef, naming the various cuts, and giving the approximate costs of each, was best done by Frank Shaver, who also made a drawing of his home farm, showing the location of the buildings, size of the fields, crops thereon, and also the brush, streams and roadways. In those early years, boys on the farms were well-versed in the business of farming.

The best box containing a School Lunch for One, was packed by Annie O'Brien; Richard Sandusky made the best Chicken Feed Hopper for a Hen House; Dickie MacMullen made the best Bread Board; and the best Rope Splice on a 3-4 inch Rope, (or larger), was done by Frank Whiting.

In Public Speaking, a 3-Minute Address on Any Subject, Vera Cunningham was the winner. Mollie Gordon won the Girls' Hitching and Driving Contest; and the best Boy Horseback Rider was Joseph Pinkney.

The Best-dressed Doll, by a girl ten years and under, was shown by Gertrude Greig; and in the 2nd Class and below, Hattie Whaley was decided to have written, in the neatest and best handwriting, 'The Alphabet in Small Letters, the Roman Numbers and Figures from 1-10.'

The best Short Poem, on any original subject, 4th or 5th Class, was composed by Kenneth Denison; and the best Essay, 3rd Class, was written on 'If a Dog Could Talk,' by Marjorie Bunting.

The best Freehand Writing of the Poem 'A Man's A Man For A' That,' by pupils in the 3rd Class – Mary Osman, and Morris Amos; and, of the Poem 'In Flanders Fields,' in the 4th and 5th Classes, – Florence Marshall, and Margaret Gladman.

The Peel Board of Agriculture Championship Medals, for 1919, donated to the boys obtaining the highest number of points, were won by Frank Shaver, 40 points; and James McCarthy, 31 points. The Peel Women's Institute Championship Medals for the girls with the highest

Mutton Lambs being placed at School Fair.
(*The Brampton Conservator*, November 11, 1920)

The Port Credit News,
September 19, 1930

points went to Dorothy Pallett. 68 points; and Vera Cunningham, 31 points.

The first School Fair for the County of Peel was held at Cooksville on September 13, 1920, and James Pinkney, S.S. No. 2, Cooksville, was awarded the Championship Medal, with 89 points.

The Championship Shield, presented by Major T. L. Kennedy, MLA, was awarded to S.S. No. 8, Burnhamthorpe. Major Kennedy himself was one of the happy spectators at the County Fair.

Despite heavy rains and disagreeable weather, the School Fair of 1925 was still a success. Rain did not dampen the ardour or spirits of the children, and all day long they splashed through the puddles and ran about enjoying themselves. The Foot Races were called off, and the School Contests held in the schoolhouse. The Agricultural Hall on the Fair Grounds was decked with as fine an array of handiwork by the children as that visible on the Fall Fair Day, the week following.

When we learn that there were 56 entries in one class of Apples, and 32 entries in a certain class of Cake, with other exhibits just as high, it was indeed an honour for any child to obtain a prize, and no cause to feel disappointment by the parents if their child was without a winning ribbon.

The School Booth received a great patronage; and a feature of the Singing contest was that, following their rendition of 'O Canada,' Cooksville gave forth their booming School Yell:
Boom Chicka Boom, Boom Chicka Boom, Boom Chicka Ricka Boom,
Boom, Boom, Boom. Wah Hoo Wah! Wah Hoo Wah!
Cooksville, Cooksville,
Rah! Rah! Rah!
The grown-ups, who were present in great numbers, enjoyed the day with 'Young Canada.'

The 1930 School Fair was the most successful in the County yet, with entries totalling 1,296, an increase of 582 over the year before.

In Public Speaking, Irene Cook was Second, and Doris Bull was Third. Frances Jones had the best White Leghorn Cockerel.

Doris Bull had the best show of Coreopsis Flowers; Ernest Laver, the best African Marigolds; and Everett Hepton, the best Phlox. Louise Gummerson's Zinnias were the best, and her Living Room Bouquet also took First Prize. In the Fruit Section, winners were Fern Goodison's Tomatoes, and Keith Laver's Bartlett Pears. For her Model of a Dog, Grace Cook took the Prize.

Chapter 18: Village Sports

THE ATHLETIC FIELDS for sports at Cooksville were on the four-and-a-half acre piece of land they called the fair grounds, and the hometown people were proud of their teams who played on them. A big day, in Cooksville, was the 24th of May (Victoria Day), when sports and games were always held on the fair grounds.

FOOTBALL:

Football (soccer) was most popular in 1900, and when an opposing home team representing one of the other small Toronto Township villages came to Cooksville and the referee called out 'Let's play ball!' the players went at it with alacrity. If the visiting team was late in arriving, the players waited on the field, set to play; if the visitors failed to show up, the Cooksville players made up a scratch team and had the game anyway.

Cooksville's football team, in 1900, was most apt to win against Port Credit and, after this happened twice in the month of June, the Streetsville newspaper reported, 'It is said that the Cooksville team had a couple of new players on and this is the reason they got the game.'

In 1901, under the Clarkson heading, a report told of a game their team, the 'Crescents,' had with Cooksville. This game began at 7 p.m. and, for the first thirty minutes, Cooksville's team had things pretty much their own way, with the score at 1-0. In the second half, the Crescents braced up and, for twenty minutes, bombarded the Cooksville goal but were unable to get past Goldthorpe and Hopkins, the staunch Cooksville defense.

Darkness fell, and a misunderstanding arose between the two teams, for which two reasons the referee called off the game. The two captains, Clements and Harris, decided to play off on neutral grounds, and to begin earlier, at 6 p.m., so that darkness would not intervene. Whether this game ever took place on the neutral fields of Streetsville, we will not know because, in those early days, sports reporting was neither as accurate nor as pervasive as today; no matter, the Clarkson people had a good show and lots of excitement at that game.

The main feature of the day at Cooksville on the Queen's Birthday, 1902, was the Football Tournament, in which three teams entered the contest – Cooksville, Streetsville, and Clarkson. It was decided that the Streetsville and Cooksville teams should play first, and the first half of the game was decidedly close; both teams worked hard, with no goals scored. In the second half, the Cooksville players' superior weight told the tale, and when time was called the score was two goals to none, in their favour.

The tournament continued. After a short rest, the second game commenced. The Clarkson team had the advantage, as their team was fresh and Cooksville's team tired by the previous hour's struggle. Nevertheless, Cooksville was able to overcome their second opponents of the day, and won by a goal, 2-1. Following the tournament, it was said that Referee Billy Golden, who had come up from Port Credit to handle both games, had trouble in preventing scrapping and foul playing; but all agreed that his decisions were fair.

On the fair grounds, that day, track events were also held, such as the 100-Yard Race, High Jump, and Putting the Shot. There was also a prize for Throwing the Baseball. About four hundred people watched these events, and the receipts taken in were enough to cover expenses.

In the final game for the year 1902, Cooksville defeated Port Credit on their own home grounds, thus winning the Championship of the district.

Cooksville Football Team, 1903.
(Photo: Region of Peel Archives, 81.3324 N 166-18)

The following spring, in April, 1903, the Football Club had a group photograph taken in Toronto, and people said 'If the boys play as well this year as they look in the photo, they are winners.'

A meeting was held at King's Hotel to organize for the coming season; and it was arranged that the local team would play the Toronto Junction CPR Shop team a friendly game on the fair grounds, on Good Friday. This meeting, on April 2, 1903, was well-attended by very enthusiastic supporters, and the following officers were recommended:

Honorary President – Dr Sutton, MD
President – H. H. Shaver
Vice President – G. Ellingham
Secretary Treasurer – J. W. Heary, of Dixie
Captain – P. Goldthorpe
Manager – S. K. Kennedy
Committee – Jas. S. King, J. A. McTaggart, and A. Thomas.

With nearly all of last year's players, and several new men to choose from, the prospects for a successful season were bright. One week later, the Toronto Junction team, Champions of West York the year before, drove out in two large vans to the fair grounds and met defeat at the hands of the Cooksville team, by a score of 2-0. Although three of the regular players, Sam Kennedy, Goldthorpe, and Sutton, were not in the game, two additions, McTaggart and Mitchell, played well. About three hundred spectators watched the game, fifty of these being 'lady enthusiasts,' who all cheered for Cooksville, and the write-up in that week's newspaper read: 'No wonder our boys won. Keep on with the good work, girls.'

At the beginning of August, 1903, the Gutta Perchas, of Toronto, came out to play a friendly match, which Cooksville won easily, 3-0. The visitors arrived, about thirty strong, in a large van, and after the game, they were entertained at the Cooksville House by the local players.

That summer, the Cooksville team played against the city teams of the Toronto Carpet Company, and the Gore Vales. Near the end of August, they went to play their return match with the Gutta Perchas on the Exhibition Yards, in Toronto. This Gutta Percha team was very strong, having six members who had belonged to the Ontario Champion Scot's team. The game was played on a fine Saturday afternoon, and was fast and interesting from start to finish. About five hundred people watched the play and, at the end when time was called, the score stood at a one-all tie. After the match, a supper was provided at the Parkdale House.

Cooksville's line-up in this game was: Goal – King;
Backs – Goldthorpe and T. L. Kennedy; Halves – J. Kennedy, Cullham, and Thomas; Forwards – Hopkins, Sutton, McTaggart, Heary, and Garbutt.

In late September, John Heary, the star player of Cooksville's 'crack' football team, had two of his fingers broken while playing in a game with the Scot's Champions of Ontario, at Dixie. He was immediately taken to the doctor to have them set, and on his arrival back was delighted to learn that the Intermediate Champions had been defeated by his team, 3-1. In November, they defeated the Canada Foundry Company's team, 3-0.

The Cooksville football team was in the Intermediate League of Toronto and, at the end of the 1903 season had won four and tied one of the five total games played. They were given hearty commendation by *The Streetsville Review* reporter, who stated that they were easily the leaders of the Western District of Toronto, and would have the honour of playing off with the winners of the Eastern District for the City Championship; he wrote that Cooksville should be proud of their team, as their success was remarkable. Whether or not this 'final' game for the Championship was ever played, or what the outcome was, we do not know, but what we can tell is that Cooksville people were, indeed, proud of their 1903 home town football team. On July 15, 1905, the Cooksville Tigers met the Erindale Electrics in a friendly football game on Hector's field, at Erindale. The play was very rough at times, on both sides, but the Tigers won, 2-0. The two goals were scored early in the first half, the first by Sutton, the second by Heary. A large crowd witnessed this game, and it was said that considerable money changed hands. Afterwards, the Tigers were given refreshments at O'Brien's Parlours.

A second game by the Tigers and Electrics took place the same week, in Dixie, and was also won by the Tigers, 1-0. A strong wind made scoring difficult, and in the second half, with the wind against them and the play all in Erindale territory, Cooksville made repeated shots on their goal. But Erindale's goal tender was alert, and stopped every shot but one hot one by Jack Harris. Pat Lamphier, the referee, had his hands full keeping the play going smoothly, until the game was called short of time, owing to darkness falling on the field. Before leaving for home, the Erindale visitors were provided with a supper at Henderson's Hotel.

On the 24th of May, 1907, a team from Lambton came to the fair grounds and gave the Cooksville fans an exciting time before they were finally overcome by two goals to none. On the holiday, three years later, following a baseball tournament under the auspices of the Cooksville baseball team, a large number of visitors stayed on to watch the football match between a team from Dixie and one from Islington. In this game, the Dixie boys won easily, 5-0.

At a meeting of the employees of the Cooksville Shale Brick Company, in the spring of 1923, a Football Club was organized.

That year, on the Annual Field Sports Day, the gates of the fair grounds opened at 12.30, and the programme started off with a football game between the new Shale Brick team and a pick-up team. Gunns Limited, from West Toronto, had assured them that they would come out and play, but when the great day arrived their players did not show up. It was later learned that the Gunns team had accepted a game with another city team, without having the courtesy to notify the committee of the Shale Brick Company. However, a team of volunteer players took the field and a good game was played, resulting in a score of 2-1, in favour of the Brick Company's team.

BASEBALL:

On the Agricultural Grounds at Cooksville, on May 24th, 1907, the baseball game played between Streetsville and Cooksville was extremely exciting when Cooksville scored run after run; 'especially,' as the Cooksville district reporter for *The Streetsville Review* explained it, 'after they got an umpire who understood his position and kept it.' The ball diamond was located close enough to Thomas Bull's high board fence, near the race track, to enable young Cooksville boys to sit along the top of it and watch the games free, still being close enough to cheer on the home team.

However, it was a different story when their Cooksville players travelled north to Streetsville for a game. The sports headlines in *The Streetsville Review* of June 6, 1907, read: 'Goose Eggs For Ward's Able Artists From Cooksville,' followed by an ecstatic description of a baseball game played in Streetsville, against their local 'Pirates.' In a seven-innings game, the Pirates 'took Cooksville into camp' by scoring fifteen runs, while the team sponsored by Ward's Hotel managed only one.

The excellent description of this ball game gives a picture of just how

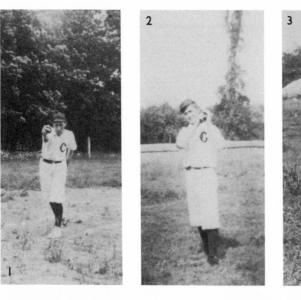

Cooksville Baseball Team, 1910. (Photos: Mississauga Central Library, Cooksville Vol. 1)

1) Gordon Harris, pitcher 2) Murray Brunskill, pitcher 3) Fred Tolman, catcher 4) Harold Sutton, 1st base & pitcher 5) Jack

Livingston, 2nd base 6) Walter Stevens, shortstop 7) Jack
Goldthorpe, left field 8) Harry Tolman, outfielder 9) Herb.
Thompson, outfielder 10) Angus Tolman, Jr.

155

much emotion and joy could be aroused by a home town team, in the earlier days of Toronto Township. It tells of Captain Elder's 'underpaid gladiators' inserting the harpoon into the aspiration of one Cooksville; and of the way McClure, McClintock and Cannon laid their Basswood Bats on to the 'benders' dished up by Wilson, the Cooksville pitcher.

In spite of rain, and a thermometer said to be hovering around the freezing mark, the people sat shivering in the stands with their coat collars up, wishing they had been supplied with ear muffs and fur-lined coats. There was, at the game, a Band of high-priced musicians led by Mr Schofield, a gentleman from Philadelphia, us, who delighted the 'tumultuous multitude' every time there were errors and flukes made on the field, by 'ripping off a few bars of Beethoven's Sonata in Z.' The conductor had to make several gracious bows of acknowledgement to the crowd for their applause.

The Review reporter wrote that fine catches were made by McClure, Bell and McClintock, and only for a fumble in the first inning by the Pirates' first baseman, the visitors would have been shut out. A new umpire, in the person of William Peck, Esquire gave satisfaction to everybody; it was said that, with a favourable wind, Mr Peck's 'strike one!' could be heard down in the Barbertown Woollen Mills. The team line-ups were given, side by side, with all the runs scored by each man; and it was Colwell, Cooksville's centre fielder, who scored the lone run which put Cooksville on the board.

After a loss to Port Credit on the holiday, in 1909, there was great jubilation in the village when the Cooksville team went down to Port Credit and was successful in winning the return match by a score of 11-9. At that time, Harris and Tolman formed the Cooksville battery, with Wilcox and Kingsberry for Port Credit.

It was on the 24th of May, 1910, that a large number of visitors from Toronto spent their holiday in Cooksville and enjoyed the Athletic Sports, sponsored by the Cooksville Baseball Team, on the fair grounds. On that day, two baseball games were played; the first, between Cooksville and Port Credit, was won by Cooksville, 11 to 1. The winning team then had to play Oakville and won this game as well, not quite as easily but still running up a score of eleven runs to Oakville's eight. Cooksville had two pitchers, Roy and Gordon Harris.

The following week, the team went to Oakville for a return match, beating them 9-8. Other teams came to play on the fair grounds, one being the Victorias, of West Toronto. The members of the Cooksville

Baseball Team of 1910 were: Fred Tolman, catcher; Jack Livingston, 2nd base; Herb. Thompson, outfield; Walter Stevens, short stop; Jack Goldthorpe, left field; Harry Tolman outfielder; Dr Harold Sutton, 1st base, and pitcher; Murray Brunskill, pitcher; Gordon Harris, pitcher; and Angus Tolman Jr.

The Victoria Day baseball game with Port Credit, held on the fair grounds the following year, in 1911, was a rather one-sided affair, won by Cooksville by a score of 20-9. One noteworthy feature of this game, however, was a triple play by Cooksville, from a fly hit and two men on bases.

In 1912, *The Brampton Conservator* was commenting on ball games played by the Cooksville 'Leafs,' and a Baseball Tournament with two games was planned for Dominion Day. But the Port Credit team did not arrive and there was only one game held. The weather had been very wet, keeping necessary farm work from being done, and since the holiday weather turned fine many of the farmers were too busily engaged to attend.

'Doc' Sutton, who pitched for Cooksville, did fairly well until the seventh inning, and when he got into trouble Roy Harris took over and finished the game. Walter Livingston was the bright particular star for the local team, both in hitting and fielding; Stevens also played well, but the newspaper reported 'the usual bum plays,' and these were the cause of the Victorias, from West Toronto, trimming the Leafs, 11-9.

As the years passed, the Cooksville baseball boys were still travelling back and forth, playing games with their old rivals from Streetsville, each faithfully recorded and enjoyed by all.

In 1923, the First Annual Field Sports Day, held under the auspices of the Ratepayers' Association, was declared to have been a pleasant and enjoyable event. The baseball programme was begun with a snappy game between the Port Credit Leaguers and the Intermediate Oslers, of Toronto, which resulted in a tied score of 4-4 at the end of nine innings. The tie was not broken, due to the fact that a softball game between the Port Credit and Streetsville High School girls was scheduled for four o'clock and the men's teams gave up the field.

The girls' game was played with vim, in a manner that attracted a large crowd during its progress. The Streetsville girls captured the prize of the 6-pound Box of Chocolates by winning the game, with the score of 14-8.

That these Girls' Softball Games were very popular was shown by the advertisement in *The Port Credit News*, on September 23, 1927, announcing a Tournament to be held at the Cooksville Fall Fair, beginning at one o'clock sharp, on Tuesday, October the fourth. The two winning teams were to play off for a Cup donated by the Agricultural Society.

When Fair Day arrived, the weather was perfect; crowds were drawn from a considerable distance to take in the first day of the Fair and the softball tournament. Cooksville and Streetsville were matched in the opening game, which the latter won by a score of 13-10. The second game, between Brampton and Lakeview was very closely contested, and won by Lakeview, 18-17. The final game, played between the winners of both previous games, was said to be a really snappy contest, which looked as though extra innings might have to be played. However, with one out and leading by one run, the Lakeview players made one of the nicest double plays seen in some time and the game was then all over but the shouting. The very handsome trophy was presented to the Lakeview (St. Nicholas Anglican Church) girls' softball team.

HOCKEY:

In the winter time, around the turn of the century, Cooksville people skated on the creeks and on the ice which formed over the gravel pit. This 12-acre gravel pit provided much industry at the eastern end of the village, supplying gravel for building projects in the city throughout the warmer months, and a smooth ice surface for skating in the winter. There were not many descriptions of hockey games to be found in the newspapers of the time, but boys and young men played pick-up games for their own enjoyment wherever they found the ice.

In February, 1905, however, Cooksville formed a team which went to Streetsville to play an exhibition game against their 'Thistles.' A record crowd turned out to watch, because there was a very warm spirit of competition between Cooksville and Streetsville; and so the Streetsville fans turned up, with full lungs, shouting 'What's the matter with the boys in red and white? They're alright!' to help the Thistles trim the visitors; which they did, in fine style.

This game began at nine o'clock on a Saturday night and started off with a rush, with the play pretty even until the Thistles 'got things working right.' Cooksville's McTaggart, Sutton and Kennedy played a strong, steady game, but the team was too heavy and slow, unable to keep up with the Thistles who were too fast on their skates.

A feature of the first half was the phenomenal rush of Maxwell, the star goalie of the Thistles, who went the full length of the ice himself and landed the puck in the net. After two disputed goals, the game ended in a score of 8-5; Goldthorpe, in the net for Cooksville, stopped many shots and saved the score from being much larger.

For Cooksville, the players were: Goldthorpe, goal; McTaggart, point; Kennedy, cover; Harris, right wing; Sutton, left wing; King, rover; and Beatty, centre. The game was refereed by Mr Waghorne, of Toronto; Umpires were W. Urquhart, and Mr Denison; Timekeeper, W. Teggart.

Following this exhibition game, the Cooksville young men began to think of making a rink on the Agricultural Grounds, which was accomplished as soon as the weather turned cold enough to freeze the ice outdoors. From then on, they practised their game on a proper rink; and in January, 1907, *The Streetsville Review* reported that the Cooksville Juniors had defeated the Streetsville Juniors, in Cooksville, by the score of 8-1.

However, hockey does not appear to have flourished in the early days in Cooksville. Transportation was a big problem in winter, many times impossible, and not much interest appeared in the reports. Cooksville people seemed content to lend all their support to the football and baseball events of summer.

WINTER:
At Valentine's Day, 1907, a Cooksville crowd went up Hurontario Street to enjoy skating on the free rink at Britannia. At that time, also, a large number of the young people found great pleasure in coasting on the high hill that wound its way down the Stavebank Road from Dundas Street. This steep road became very slippery and caused trouble to the people who lived along it; their horses had to be taken more often than usual to the blacksmith to have calks applied to the horses' shoes, to keep them from falling down on the hill. Sleighriding, in 1909, was excellent; aside from this, Dundas Street was in very good condition for the horses pulling the sleighs drawing loads of hay to the city.

Shooting matches were held near the creek in the area called Harris' flats, where Josiah Harris grew vegetables in summer. Turkeys, geese, ducks, chickens and pigeons were the prizes competed for, and some excellent shooting was exhibited. The extreme cold prevailing in January, 1909, had a tendency to spoil the pleasure of the onlookers, but

159

the principal winners that year were: John Fleming, the hotel keeper at Lambton Mills; and Lieutenant B. Gordon, of the village.

Many young people took part in trips on snowshoes, travelling through the fields in the evenings; parties went to as far-distant places as the inns at Erindale and Port Credit, stopping in for hot drinks before returning home. Even up to 1923 this sport was a favourite. Snowshoeing was not always carried on just for pleasure, for if roads became blocked and someone needed assistance, the family could call for help on the telephone and sometimes the doctor would go by snowshoes to a patient's home.

Cooksville men, young and old, enjoyed bowling and playing pool, and contests in these games were arranged from time to time. At one such event held in Harris' Pool Room, between teams from the East and West sides of the bridge over the Cooksville Creek during the winter of 1917, the pool players of the west end defeated the east enders by forty points. Those taking part in this challenge game were:

West enders: R. S. Whaley, T. D. Schiller, Harmon Price, Robert Jamieson, W. C. H. Copeland, and Charles Harris.

East enders: A. C. Crozier, W. Hamilton, Joseph McCurry, D. Stewart, Charles Belford, and John Ward.

Forster's Rink, Hurontario Street, south of railway overpass, 1940s.
(Photo: Mississauga Central Library, Cooksville Vol. 1, #274)

In January, 1923, an outdoor skating rink was assured, with a sheet of ice being completed on the land just east of the Town Hall. Volunteers took three days preparing the ground, and flooding it. It was ready for use by the end of the week, when daylight hours were set for children's skating, and night hours for older skaters. Lights were placed up over the ice surface, and evening Skating Carnivals were held through the winter.

SUMMER:

Summer sports were enjoyed as soon as the ice broke up in the springtime and the days became warm. At the beginning of April each year, with the melting of the ice and consequent overflow of water, suckers appeared in the creeks and every village sportsman got ready with his hook, spear, or net. While the season of migration continued there was a furious onslaught on this member of the fish species. Through the winter months, the hunters had been out in the bush shooting rabbits but, by springtime, everyone enjoyed the sudden change to a fish diet.

June brought warmer days and picnics everywhere in the parks, along the roadsides, and in any little bit of bush where wildflowers grew. People ate their lunches, took a walk to look for different kinds of bugs which had emerged, and followed up by picking some of the marsh marigolds or violets they found. Sometimes they discovered wild berries growing in a field and took these home in honey pails, for jam.

As early as 1892, at the beginning of June, Dundas Street was becoming a favourite run for the Toronto bicyclists, and nearly every Saturday afternoon many of them rode out on their wheels to get the fresh air and have supper at the Cooksville House. Sometimes as many as twenty or thirty of them were served in the dining room on a Saturday. For years, Eldorado Park was well-patronized by picnic parties, and Mr Ward was kept busy looking after their wants. The resort, not far from Cooksville, was becoming more widely known each year. Also, in June, the 'Ole Swimmin' Hole' was popular and enjoyed heartily until the strawberries ripened in the patches and needed picking. Later on, in the 1930s, there was Frank Walterhouse's Pine Grove Park on the east bank of the Credit River, near the Middle Road.

Cooksville people enjoyed all sorts of races, and were especially proud of Dr E. Hopkins' bay gelding 'Jimmie McCarron,' winner of the 2.18 trot at Brampton, in 1920. James Sharpe, of Britannia, bred this fine animal, then said to be worth $7,000. In 1921, 'Jean Bingen,' Dr·

Hopkins' new mare, took the second purse at the Oshawa races. Another horse then becoming well known, owned by Frank Walterhouse, was a three-year-old named 'Patchen Todd.' In February, 1921, the feature of the Mount Clemons track was the establishment of a new record for winter racing by the Canadian entry, 'Jimmie McCarron.'

Cooksville children could watch the horses being trained on the race track at the Cooksville Fair Grounds. On Fair Days this track was very popular, with people watching the horses which came from far distant points to compete with the locals.

Volleyball was being played by the boys of Cooksville and district in 1919, under the leadership of the County Young Men's Christian Association, using the school grounds for these games. At the beginning of October that year, it was reported that the Saturday games had resulted in two games to one for the 'Iroquois' against the 'Algonquins,' and two games to one for the 'Maple Leafs' over the Chinguacousy team. The boys were all in training for the Thanksgiving YMCA Athletic Meet for the boys of Peel County.

At the Field Sports Day held by the Ratepayers on the 24th of May, 1923, Tug-of-War honours went to Joseph Brown's Erindale 'Warriors,' who pulled against the best line-up of Cooksville's Captain, Joseph Allen. Charles Hopkins was awarded the silk umbrella for winning the Fat Man's Race; Walter Harris captured the greased pig, after an exciting chase; in the Tire-Guessing Contest, the tire donated by Clarence Garbutt was won by Arthur Pashak; and Miss Neita Tolman won the pearl necklace as the prettiest lady on the grounds.

A Band from New Toronto furnished the music, and the attendance at this sports day reached the one thousand mark. The Dixie-Cooksville Women's Institute provided refreshments; and the children taking part in the games were treated to free drinking milk by Walter Hayward of the Centre Road, on the Britannia School Farm, who sent two full cans of milk down to the fair grounds. The money from this great affair was used for top-dressing the 6-foot sidewalk along the east side of Hurontario Street, as far up as the school house.

In 1926, tennis courts were built on Bandmaster John Slatter's lot, on Dundas Street; and in 1932, a Badminton and Tennis Club opened near the Town Hall.

* * *

Altogether, over the years, Cooksville people took part in many

community sports activities, most of these enjoyed on their own
Agricultural Fair Grounds. As I walk about the Plazas near Hurontario
and Dundas Street West today, and look over towards Hook Avenue
(Confederation Drive), I sometimes stop and marvel to think of all the
happy events which once were taking place on these particular acres.

Chapter 19: The Railway Station

IT WAS THOUGHT BY MANY, after the destructive fire of 1852, that
Cooksville had been erased from the map, but this was not so. By 1878,
the Credit Valley Railway was built and this made Cooksville, once
again, an important stopping place. At this time, the main line of the
track was laid and ready for use within seven miles of Galt, a distance of
47 miles from Toronto; the north branch was completed to the Forks of
the Credit, 12 miles south of Orangeville.

The formal opening of the Credit Valley Railroad was to take place
on November 14, 1879, and the directors, trustees, and many invited
guests assembled at the Queen Street Station, in Toronto. A special
train of four passenger coaches and the 'Intercolonial Palace Car' which
the Governor General, the Marquess of Lorne, and the Princess Louise

Old Cooksville Station – waiting for the train to take folk to picnic.
(Photo: Mississauga Central Library, Cooksville Vol. 1, #71)

Steam Train. (Photo: Mississauga Central Library, Cooksville Vol. 1)

had been using in their travels in Canada, was attached to the engine, the 'R. W. Elliott.' This engine was a product of Canadian workmanship, built by the Kingston Locomotive and Engine Company, and now stood at the Queen Street Station gaily decorated with evergreens and bunting.

At a quarter past ten o'clock, His Excellency, attended by Captain Harbord, drove up in an open carriage and entered the palace car reserved for their use. The train began moving immediately, and the run to Milton was accomplished in an hour and twenty minutes.

At the two stations along the road, Cooksville and Streetsville, where stops were made, the people turned out in large numbers to greet the Queen's representative and express their appreciation of the new railway. Both stations were decorated with evergreens and bunting; and a song 'This Canada of Ours,' especially composed for the occasion, was sung by the school children. After a few words of thanks, the train continued on its way to Milton, where the people were gathered to meet the first train on the line.

His Excellency made reference to the prosperous farming land through which he had passed, and expressed his pleasure that the people had shown good taste in not destroying some of the beautiful groves he had seen on his journey. He then formally declared the new railway line open, and hoped that the villages scattered along its length would ever increase in prosperity.

Cheers were given for Her Royal Highness the Princess Louise, and the party at once began the return trip to Toronto. The Credit Valley Railway was later to be merged with the Canadian Pacific Railway.

Cooksville's growth was slow but, by 1891, with a population of 500, it was the leading non-incorporated village in Toronto Township. Its CPR Station was situated about three quarters of a mile from the four corners, and Canadian Pacific Railway trains passing through Cooksville in 1891 connected the village with Toronto, Brampton, St. Thomas and other places. Wine from the west end of Cooksville was being shipped out by train; and a big industry in the east end was that of shipping gravel to Toronto for street paving and other purposes. One of the largest and best gravel pits in Canada, with the tracks running within ten yards of it, was located near the railway station. The gravel was taken out by steam shovel, which could sometimes load as many as 100 cars a day. By 1891, thousands of carloads had been shipped and the gravel was just as good as ever.

The Brampton Conservator, November 24, 1890

John Cunningham's new house.
(Photo: Mississauga Central Library, Cooksville Vol. 1, #49)

After the turn of the century, there were bricks being shipped from the Cooksville Brick Yard by train, as well. Coal sheds were erected on the station grounds and shipments of coal were being brought in; and carloads of salt in barrels were being unloaded in 1903. The huge feed store started near the Cooksville Station by H. A. Brown was taken over by John Cunningham and, by 1911, Mr Cunningham was doing a steady business not only in flour and feed, but in Portland cement, cedar posts, fertilizer, and salt.

A change was taking place, probably due to the close proximity of the rapidly-extended limits of the city. From 1909 on, the village was considered to be a desirable suburban residence and many new buildings were erected.

Everything did not always progress smoothly, of course. The Dundas Street crossing of the CPR caused accidents involving horses belonging to farmers travelling the roads with their loads of produce. At the beginning of December, 1909, William Kingdom, a farmer from Islington, was crossing the tracks with his team and a load of maize meal, on his way home about six o'clock, when his wagon was struck by the Goderich train. The wagon was smashed and himself thrown out onto the horses, which ran for some distance before being stopped. Meal was distributed all along the roadway. Mr Kingdom, whose escape was remarkable, had been watching another train stopped at the station, not noticing an oncoming train hidden by tall shrubbery which grew near the crossing.

Two months later, the Railway Commission was consulted on the matter of necessary protection at the crossing and it was proposed that a new station be built. This brought about the cutting down of the shrubbery which interfered with proper vision of the tracks when trains were approaching. Nothing was decided at the time but, in July of 1910, the old station was given a fresh coat of paint inside and out, which improved its appearance.

In December, the news became known that the Canadian Pacific Railway would construct a new line running parallel out of West Toronto to get the best possible connection between that point and London, and a new station would be built just west of the old one, on Dundas Street. Cooksville people had not wanted the station built so far east of the four corners, but the reason given was because of the hill and uneven ground north of Dundas Street. By July, 1912, work had begun on the new station and the concrete foundation was completed; but still there were objections heard regarding its close proximity to the Dundas Street crossing.

The new Cooksville Station was opened for business on a Friday near the end of January, 1913, and was said to have a neat, clean appearance, but much smaller than the old one, and evidently inadequate for any increase in business. The Cooksville residents considered its location inconvenient, besides being a menace to the traffic on Dundas Street.

The old station was purchased by J. Cunningham and moved onto his property, where it was transformed into two dwellings. The Railway Company began purchasing land parallel with the railway line, for the purpose of putting down a double track; and a new sidewalk was put down from the village to the station, in order that pedestrians could walk there without being in danger from automobiles and motorcycles.

In April, 1913, a petition from J. W. Miller and forty-nine others was presented at the Toronto Township Council meeting, asking the Council to take the necessary steps to have a subway constructed by the Canadian Pacific Railway Company under their tracks at the Centre Road, north of Cooksville. The following June, they were assured that the Railway Commission had changed their decision to erect gates and have a watchman on the Centre Road, and would build the subway instead. At the same time, they stated that the Dundas Street crossing would have gates and a watchman by day and night – all to be completed by September 1st, 1914.

Also at this time, the inconvenience due to the walking distance from the village to the station was overcome by W. J. Coulter, who began meeting all trains with his rig, and carrying passengers who desired it to their destination, for a nominal sum.

With the new CPR Station, and the fine residences built along both Dundas and Hurontario Streets, Cooksville had taken on an appearance of urban life rarely seen in the smaller villages. The CPR issued a ten-trip return ticket for $2.25, and also a Business Man's Ticket at a cost of 12 cents return fare which must be used every day. These advantages were bringing Cooksville's claims as a place of residence to the notice of the business men of Toronto. In September, 1915, an electric bell was installed at the Centre Road crossing.

Notwithstanding all efforts to prevent accidents, a wreck occurred near the CPR Station at the end of November, 1916, just before 6 p.m. *The Brampton Conservator* reported that a freight train was moving east out of the yard switch, just west of the station, when a car loaded with

16,000 bricks from the Canadian National Brick Company left the track, owing to a split rail. Running along the ties for some distance, the car overturned crosswise over the tracks. The Goderich train was due in five minutes but was fortunately stopped, along with all other traffic, for several hours. When the auxiliary arrived and attempted to lift the car it broke in two, scattering the bricks, which had then to be removed by hand before traffic could again proceed.

In February, 1921, the gravel pit on Miss Price's farm was acquired by the Railway, where they laid a spur in the field and were said to be starting the building of the subway on Hurontario Street. Both motorists and horse drivers appreciated the installation of the automatic 'danger' and 'stop' signals erected at the Dundas Street crossing in August. The approach of a train was announced by the ringing of a bell on each of the signals, and also by two round 'stop' signals swinging across the tracks, which crossed the road there diagonally. Electric lights, at night, also gave protection. But nothing more was heard of the Centre Road crossing, said to be one of the most dangerous crossings in the province; and once again, the Township Council requested the installation of a subway at the CPR crossing, north of the Cooksville four corners.

In November, 1921, another wreck occurred on the line, this being a freight train derailment near Erindale, which resulted in some local commuters missing a day's work in Toronto. The bus service had been temporarily suspended, owing to the difficulty of driving along Dundas Street. This was at the time while the Highway was being paved.

An effort was made to have an improved CPR train service into the city. The commuters' train left Cooksville at 6.34 a.m., with no train then until 11.06, and another at 11.37 a.m. After the 11.37 train, there was nothing until 5.55 p.m. The public wished to have either the Goderich train or the Detroit train stop, since these went through between 8 and 9 a.m.

The suburban Canadian National Line was regarded as a joke; few people ever thought of travelling that way. There were only three trains daily each way, and travellers were charged 30 cents for a 10-mile ride, with no possibility of buying a return-trip ticket. In addition to this, people had to spend an hour and twenty minutes to reach the centre of the city. The transportation service at Cooksville was bad.

In February, 1922, Mr Whaley, the mail courier, established a bus line to and from the station, thus giving the passengers a regular service which had long been needed. In the year 1924, the Canadian Pacific Railway agent at the Cooksville Station was Mr E. Malpass.

It was not until July 29th, 1926, that the subway under the railroad tracks on the Centre Road, north of Cooksville, was finally opened.

THE RADIAL LINE:

At the beginning of March, 1914, surveyors were engaged in placing stakes along the south side of Dundas Street for a proposed extension of the Toronto to Guelph Radial Line through the village of Cooksville, for which they had been granted the right of way. The following month, a camp was set up on William Pinkney's farm near the CPR Station by the McKenzie Contractors, and operations began toward the completion of this radial line.

There was one objection, from Thomas Rutledge, who complained that his lands were becoming flooded during the heavy rains and his valuable fruit orchard stood in danger of being ruined. The trouble arose because the Railway had not enough culverts to carry the water away; however, inspectors made a list of those necessary, and ordered the Company to put them in.

The Brampton Conservator of June 24, 1915, reported that the line was nearing completion, but it was not until the first of February in 1917 that the first electric car travelled over it, from Lambton to Cooksville.

At the beginning of April, one of the Toronto suburban cars for the new Toronto-Guelph Radial Line was unloaded from two flat cars at the Cooksville Station. The car was of solid steel construction, and nicely decorated and fitted up. Built by the Preston Car Works, it had three compartments. In the rear section were reversible, cushioned seats similar to those for passengers on the railroad coaches, with a lavatory and a steam heater at one end. In the middle was an enclosed section where the conductor stood in control of the side entrances and exit doors, with fare boxes for a pay-as-you-enter system. The front section was a smoker and baggage room, with an enclosed space for the motorman.

Several more coaches were unloaded in readiness for the opening of the line and, on the fifteenth of April, these cars commenced operations, carrying passengers from Lambton to Guelph and return. Platforms had been erected for stops at various points, the one at the Cooksville Station being Stop 31.

Electric Radial Train. (Photo: Mississauga Central Library, Cooksville Vol.1, #57)

The Radial Line ran through Lambton, along Dundas Street to Etobicoke Creek, travelled a little to the north in a curve, crossed the creek, and continued along the south side of Dundas Street to the Station at Cooksville. Its route passed northwards from Cooksville to Meadowvale, Churchville, Huttonville and Norval, to Georgetown. Finally, it passed Limestone and Acton, and continued on to Guelph.

The radial cars were painted dark green, with gold letters and numbers on them. The seats were also green, in plush upholstery. They carried both passengers and freight, and there were five local cars which stopped at Cooksville.

By 1924, forty-two radials were going east and west of Cooksville daily, with double-ender cars being under construction in order to prevent delays in turning. In summer, many people were picked up at the Cooksville Station for picnic trips to Eldorado Park; they could get on the cars and go to Eldorado, on the Credit River, near Brampton, to enjoy boating and swimming. Many Cooksville people long remembered travelling on this line, northwest of Cooksville, to picnic at this summer playground.

In November, 1925, the Guelph Radial had its terminal at Keele

Street and St. Clair Avenue, in Toronto, instead of at Lambton, and its time table was changed. The fare from Cooksville to Toronto was 35 cents, and Cooksville people could travel by the radial to what was known as the West Toronto Junction, do their shopping and return home again, getting off at the Cooksville Station with their bags.

On the 24th of May holiday, in 1928, the radial traffic was heavy. It was estimated that, by five o'clock, 15,000 people had arrived in the village on the radial cars. Later on, however, the automobiles, buses and motor trucks along Dundas Street brought about the cessation of services by the Toronto-Guelph Radial Line.

Chapter 20: Paving the Highways

IN 1905, THE NUMBER of automobiles passing along Dundas Street through Cooksville was increasing daily, and one Monday in August a record was set when upwards of fifty were counted. Five years later, the church-goers were complaining that, especially when they were going to and from church, the joy riders caused such clouds of dust that it covered their clothing and nearly blinded them as they walked along the sidewalks.

The Ontario Motor League had warning signs to beware of speeding put up along Dundas Street, but these did not appear to make any impression on the reckless joy riders, whose 'modern juggernauts raced each other through the village at perhaps 40 to 50 miles an hour, to the imminent danger of everything on the road.' That year, the work of grading the Centre Road and putting on stone for a new road north of Cooksville was begun.

In June of 1912, when the Municipal authorities did not comply with requests to oil Dundas Street, the residents undertook to oil the front of their own premises to protect themselves from the dust created by the continual passage of autos and motorcycles. In winter, snow and ice caused trouble with deliveries by the trucks, and sleighs had to be kept in use.

However, one day during March, 1913, there was so much mud opposite the entrance to the stables at Bowers' Hotel that a large motor truck belonging to the Cosgrove Brewing Company, of Toronto, became embedded in it and could not be extricated until it was attached to the Robert Simpson Company's delivery truck and pulled out. The sudden coming out of the frost put the roads into such terrible condition that stalled autos had to be pulled out by horses daily, one of the worst places being Dundas Street, due to the heavy hauling of the teams pulling loads of bricks from the Brick Yard.

In June, when dust again became a problem, George Bowers distributed five barrels of oil at the corner of Dundas Street and the Centre Road; and in 1914, he asked that a By-law with regard to rigs obstructing the highway be enforced. This law did not come into effect, but one preventing the walks being used in Cooksville by bicycles, motorcycles, and other vehicles was passed.

A good piece of work was done on Dundas Street, east from the Centre Road, in 1915; ditches were put in, and the section was graded, with the centre being filled in with fine stone, covered with gravel, watered, and well rolled in by the steam road roller. It was a great improvement, but people still said that it needed one or two coats of oil to keep down the dust. The Cooksville bridge was repaired and strengthened by the addition of new stringers, and a new three-inch Georgia pine floor put down. A coat of tarvia was then laid down all the way from Cooksville to Summerville, to preserve the road and abate the dust nuisance.

Tall grass and weeds which had been encroaching over the gravel walks of the village were cut down by the road commissioner's men, and residents who had hedges with overhanging branches were asked to top them off. John Leary and John Hopkins made an improvement on a bad stretch of the Centre Road; and the Upper Middle Road (Queensway) was gravelled by the residents on a fifty-fifty plan.

In August, 1921, a new transportation service was inaugurated, by a returned soldier from Toronto, between Cooksville and West Toronto, along the Dundas Highway. The new motor bus had a carrying capacity of twenty passengers, and was much appreciated. A Port Credit-Cooksville Bus Service was also established, under the same management, with regular schedules arranged.

This year of 1921 was the year that the Dundas Highway was being paved, from Summerville westward, and by August the new highway had reached Bethesda Church, at Dixie. Ditches on both sides of the road were opened up, to provide proper drainage; and new 66-foot wide bridges over the creeks were the first of such bridges to be constructed on any provincial highway.

At the Labour Day weekend in September, 1921, the 'Highway Ball' to celebrate the beginning of the paving of Dundas Street through Cooksville was held. The Ball, which took place under the auspices of the Women's Institute, in front of the Cooksville Inn, was enjoyed not only by the merry dancers, but by hundreds of spectators; and a moving picture artist took a series of pictures of the celebration.

Rapid progress was now made in tearing up and grading Dundas Street, with new culverts being put in near Fullwood's Bakery and at the two small bridges to the west, between the Royal Bank corner and the Brick Yard Hill. Both of these small existing bridge structures had to be replaced with the wider 66-foot bridges.

Several local people sent in applications to the Highways Department of Public Works for appointment as speed cops on the Cooksville section of the new highway. At this time, the highway was not lighted; the only lights to be seen on it were the headlights of the motor cars.

An indication of what the new pavement on Dundas Street meant to Cooksville was seen in the erection of several new homes, and a turnover of more than $60,000 worth of real estate in a few weeks. It was estimated that, within three years, Cooksville would have a population of fifteen hundred; already the new school was overcrowded.

Roads – Stone Crusher, c. 1935. (Photo: Region of Peel Archives)

174

Official : Opening

Dundas Street

HIGHWAY

T.O BE HELD AT

COOKSVILLE

SATURDAY

October 1st, 1921

Under auspices

Toronto Township U.F.O. Clubs

Sports

To begin at 1.30 o'clock sharp
Inter Club Tug of War
RACES

100 yard Dash, open for men.	Married Ladies' Race
Sack Race, 1st and 2nd	Single Ladies Race
Three Legged Race, 1st & 2nd	Girls' Race. 12 and under
Boys' Race, 12 and under	Girls' Race, 10 and under
Boys' Race, 10 and under	Girls' Race, 8 and under
Boys' Race, 8 and under	

Speakers

Speeches to begin at 3 o'clock sharp

Hon. F. C. Biggs ....Minister Public Works
Hon. R. H. Grant ....Minister Education
Hon. Manning W. Doherty..........Minister Agriculture
Mr. Herbert Taylor....... U.F.O. Candidate Federal House
Mr. E. A. Orr ....Reeve Toronto Township

Port Credit Brass Band

D. H. McCaugherty, Chairman

The Streetsville Review, September 22, 1921

The abutments under the new bridge over the Cooksville Creek were completed, after which the old structure had to be removed and the creek slightly straightened. The floor of this bridge was then paved with eighteen inches of cement; it had a surface of 66-feet width, by 48-feet length. Dundas Street was concreted from the four corners to the Brick Yard Hill by the end of September, 1921. And after all these works had been completed, work began on the two smaller bridges to the west of the four corners, together with the macadamizing of the two-and-a-half mile section of road to Port Credit.

At the end of September, when the Highway work had reached the Brick Yard Hill, with its eight inches of cement over crushed stone having been laid, and with an asphalt covering to complete the driveway, it was said to be the finest stretch of highway in the province, extending from the end of the Eaton highway, at the Etobicoke Creek.

The official opening of the Dundas Street Highway, this far, was held at Cooksville on Saturday, October 1st, 1921. It began with an old-fashioned sports programme of Tug-of-War, and Races for young and old, followed by speeches by the Honourable F. C. Biggs, Minister of Public Works; Honourable R. H. Grant, Minister of Education; Honourable Manning W. Doherty, Minister of Agriculture; Mr Herbert Taylor, UFO Candidate for the Federal House; and Mr E. A. Orr, Reeve of Toronto Township. Stirring music was provided by the Port Credit Brass Band.

However, the official opening of the highway at Cooksville did not mean that all the work had been completed. The bridge in the village, and the culverts to the west, were still under construction; and surveyors were at work surveying ten feet from property owners on each side of the highway, as required by the Government. The Centre Road was badly torn up, and covered in spots with loose stone six to eight inches deep. Cooksville was practically isolated, as it had been all summer. There was a demand for a motor bus service and, in mid-October, that service was started between the village and West Toronto, with a fare of 30 cents each way.

At least 10,000 yards of earth was removed from the Brick Yard Hill as soon as a steam shovel then working on North Yonge Street could be moved out to the village; but during this time the new Blue Line Bus service had to be discontinued.

Four traffic officers were engaged to regulate traffic over the detour around the new bridge over the Cooksville Creek, two of them working

River Scene at Cooksville bridge. (Photo: Mississauga Central Library, Cooksville Vol. 1, #62)

Filling a Water Tank at Cooksville, Ontario. (Photo: National Archives of Canada; Boyd, John Collection 12 March, 1922; PA 84734)

by day, and the other two by night. On Saturday and Sunday nights several hundred cars were directed around the bridge between the dark hours of evening and midnight. This was Canada's widest highway bridge on provincial or rural roads, it being of the full 66-foot road width. Finally, in November, it was opened, to the satisfaction of people wishing to travel the Highway.

No one found fault with the road work on the new highway, but harsh and bitter criticism was heard regarding the ditches, which were dangerous. Local people were certain that they would cause many accidents, and that pedestrians, as well as motorists and the occupants of horse-drawn vehicles would be injured. It was rumoured that the cost of the construction was anywhere from $45,000 to $70,000 per mile, but the actual cost could not be learned until the next session of the Legislature.

There was an almost continuous stream of traffic over the new bridge, with estimates of 10,000 motorists crossing the Creek on a Sunday, between 1 and 11 p.m., allowing for an average of four persons to a car. This was an average of four cars per minute.

The ten feet on each side of the ditches were to be retained for poles and trees. Thousands of trees had already been set out along some of the mileages along provincial highways, at a cost of $1.25 each.

In mid-November, the new highway was now open from end to end, without any detours or blockades, and it was believed that this newly-paved road would bring hundreds of new residents out to the Cooksville district the next year and each succeeding year. At this time, the Centre Road contractors had completed the foundation work for the Number 10 Highway, on which the top would be laid in the spring.

During November, a large force of men laid 15-inch drain pipe along Dundas Street through the business section of the village but, when winter set in, work had to be temporarily abandoned. The icy periods following heavy rains turned both the Dundas Highway and the Centre Road into a shining mass of ice, dangerous to pedestrians, horses and motorists alike. Motor mishaps were continuous occurrences, with many cars ditched or turned about in various directions. A horse, belonging to Professor Swedelius, while being brought to the Blacksmith Shop to be shod, reached the road from the farm gate, but immediately slipped into a ditch and was so badly cut by its own feet that it had to be destroyed. Many men and women, young and old, fell down in different positions of all shapes on the ice; however, many young people took to the ice on their skates and totally enjoyed the miles of ice, all the way from the Brick Yard Hill to Summerville, and back.

In February, 1922, Cooksville was stated to be the only village or town in the Province of Ontario with two provincial highways running through it, crossing each other at the four corners of Highway No. 5 (Dundas Street), and Highway No. 10 (Hurontario Street).

Mr Whaley placed his motor bus on the job, thus improving Cooksville's bus service. His slogan was 'punctuality and one price only.' Many new cars were now in evidence among village and district people, with sedans replacing open cars. Traffic was heavier, and one Sunday between 2 and 5 p.m., over 6,000 cars passed through Cooksville, but only two horse-drawn vehicles were observed. At this time, a traffic cop was appointed to regulate traffic on the Cooksville section of the Dundas Highway.

In October, 1922, complaints were made that there was no 'Detour' sign at the First Line, either east or west, to save motorists and horse-drawn vehicles an extra two-and-a-half mile drive to and from the Centre Road, which was barred from them at the Dundas Highway. The sign was apparently not considered necessary by either the road contractors or the Department of Highways. The four corners were a very busy scene while the grading, filling, and leveling of the Centre Road was being completed, preparatory to converting it to conform with the Dundas Highway pavement. The old weigh scale, which had been a landmark for over forty years, was torn up in order that the driving width could be extended at the approach to Dundas Street.

Northward, work was progressing between Dundas Street and the CPR tracks, to the point where a new 1,500-foot subway was to be commenced in the spring. There was a need for a 'silent policeman' at the Dundas-Centre Road corners; particularly was it seen as a necessity for safety on Saturdays and Sundays. At this busy intersection, in November, 1923, a truck driven by Eph. Evans, of Streetsville, was damaged by a collision with the huge pole west of King's Hotel, on the northeast corner. Mr Evans was sent flying from the vehicle, but escaped serious injury.

The public was happy to learn that Mr W. J. Fenton, of Niagara Falls, who had started his big 'palatial' bus on a Brampton-Cooksville-Toronto run the year before, and had been obliged to cease operations due to the Centre Road construction, was laying out plans for a new bus schedule. This large bus was able to carry 60 passengers.

Four corners of Hurontario and Dundas Streets, showing 'silent policeman' traffic signal; background; (southeast corner) William Copeland's store, and barn. (Photo: City of Toronto Archives, James Collection, #9158)

On January 11, 1923, a writer in *The Brampton Conservator* asked: 'Is it not reasonable to anticipate that the portion of the Dundas Highway between Cooksville and Toronto will bring about the development of garages, service stations, market stands, and refreshment houses, amusement places, and retail stores of various lines; as well, would not manufacturing industries seek locations for their industries, particularly those in motor accessories, food products, wearing apparel, and other domestic lines?'

That January, more snow fell than had been seen for many years, and the side lines and back roads became impassable. The highway was kept open by the Provincial snow ploughs, though the milk trucks had great trouble navigating with their loads. However, in February, bus service was finally re-established, with three round trips daily. The bus was a splendid new outfit, starting its Cooksville trips from the Brick Yard, and picking up passengers anywhere along the Highway. Return fares were 55 cents, from Cooksville, with commuters' tickets at 50 for $7.00. Still, Centre Road traffic to and from Brampton remained blocked for days, owing to snowfalls and drifts.

In April, 1923, a representative of the Highways Department was interviewed to ascertain what type of silent policeman could be provided at the double-highways corner. A pillar type, with an upright centre reading 'CAUTION,' and with a base displaying red lights at night – two facing each of the four directions – was recommended. Four signs, to be placed 300 yards north, south, east and west of the pillar, reading 'DANGEROUS CROSS ROADS 300 YARDS AHEAD,' were also suggested. The request was promised to be met without delay.

The following month, the Ontario Motor League supplied the Cooksville Ratepayers with ten signs for use within the village, designating speed limits, school, and crossroad approaches. By July, the Centre Road paving to the railway tracks at Port Credit was completed, and work was started north from Dundas Street. Once again, following two collisions between four motor cars at the four corners, a demand for a silent policeman, to be installed at once, was made.

In September, 1923, a two-hour test made with an improvised silent policeman was so satisfactory that Major Kennedy, of Dixie, suggested that a regulation type should be installed. During the test period, this rough-made, wooden creation was photographed, and a picture of it appeared in the illustrated section of *The Toronto Evening Telegram*. But Cooksville people were quick to let it be known that this 'effective, but crude affair,' as *The Telegram* referred to it, had been merely a test job of a couple of hours – and so effective had it been, as a traffic regulator, that a modern equipment would be installed in a few days.

The Brampton Conservator of June 26, 1924, reported, however, that a midnight collision had occurred at the four corners of Cooksville where, it was pointed out that for a year, the Ratepayers' Association had been urging the installation of a silent policeman.

In August, 1924, the Department of Highways stationed a number of men at the principal traffic centres, taking a traffic census of all types of vehicles passing over the highways. It was argued, in Cooksville, that some action must be taken without delay, to regulate traffic at the Dundas-Centre Road intersection, 'before serious accidents bring this forcibly to those responsible for inaction – if nothing more than prominent signs, SLOW DOWN TO 10 MILES AN HOUR, placed 500 feet north, south, east and west of the corners.'

It was asserted that 'Signs should be placed at the approaches to Cooksville, showing COOKSVILLE, and saying REDUCE SPEED TO 20 MILES PER HOUR. This is no longer the backwoods country village of 20 to 30 years ago; it is the busy suburb of a great city, with more traffic passing through it in one hour than passes through the busiest corners of many large cities.'

The Streetsville Review of July 29, 1926, reported that the new subway under the Canadian Pacific Railway tracks on the Centre Road, above Cooksville, was now open. S. A. Commerford, engineer of the Department of Highways, who had been in charge of its construction, gave the word for the removal of the obstructions on the road at precisely 4 p.m. and, within a few minutes, traffic was flowing north and south through the subway. There was, at first, a slight hesitation on the part of the car drivers, despite the absence of the Detour signs which had been displayed for the past three months, but a wave of the hand sent them rapidly north.

Not everyone was happy with the paving of the road north of Cooksville. Farmers complained that they were held up in their threshing. A local thresher for the district was going along the Centre Road, near Britannia, when a traffic cop told him he would have to get off the road. This farmer, Mr Sheard, travelled about, taking his steam-engine, threshing machine, water-tank, tractor and clover thresher with him on his rounds, but he was told that he could not use the Provincial Highway as a route; when he wanted to cross it, he must first cover the pavement with boards.

In one instance, when Mr Sheard had tried to reach a Centre Road farm from the Concession, he said that it required half a day to take his outfit to a crossroad, make a plank cover for the highway, take it around and enter through another man's farm. He said that if he continued to use the highway, the fine would amount to as much as he would get for the threshing. In the meantime, the farmers were at a standstill; the cost of the highway had added about 25 per cent to their taxes, and they asked whether it was fair to expect them to pay for the road, and then put them to so much inconvenience.

A new By-law went into effect at the beginning of April, 1927, by which motorists were allowed to drive at 35 miles per hour. In October, another law was passed to the effect that all horse-drawn rigs and bicycles must carry lights.

In December, 1929, the Cooksville Women's Institute asked for STOP and GO signs at the junction of the Centre Road and Dundas Street; but when the Council investigated the matter, the reply from the Department of Highways was that they were not in favour of having traffic lights; but they were willing to have patrol officers provide more protection, at no extra cost.

In October of 1930, the balmy weather around the village of Cooksville was inducing motorists to stage little picnics along the sides of the roads.

It was not until October 21, 1936, that there appeared in *The Port Credit News*, the following story:

'The automatic traffic control lights installed last week at the intersection of Centre Road and Dundas Street worked rather uncertainly for the first few days, but are now coming along quite well, thank you. Many have unsuccessfully attempted to figure out how the automatic lights work and many an argument has been waged over the subject. Some say it's a 'new-fangled' idea that'll break down when needed most. Others predict they're just what's been needed and will do the job 'just right.'

The only explanation of the secret of the mysterious workings of the red and green lights which seems plausible concerns magnetism, among other things. The initiated claim that when a car passes a box full of complicated machinery set at the side of the road, the metal in the car affects the machinery controlling the lights. They say, 'If you walk past the spot with a crowbar, the lights will turn green for you. Come up and try it some time!'

Chapter 21: The Cooksville Brick Yard

EARLY RECORDS SHOW THAT, in 1871, George Tolman owned and operated a brick yard where bricks were made by hand and dried in the sun. Later, they were taken from the wooden molds and placed inside a kiln, heated and baked by a constantly-burning wood fire underneath. We are told that William Kennedy, of Dixie, built his hotel with bricks manufactured by Mr Tolman.

**

In September, 1912, a Company purchased the McLaughlin family's property at the extreme west end of Cooksville, where there were steep hills and a good supply of the best quality shale. Work was started in December on this farm by the Lyal Company, for the Ontario Brick Company.

The Streetsville Review of December 12, 1912, stated that the railway siding into the brick plant was almost completed and, by the end of the week, a gang of two hundred men would be hard at work getting the factory ready for operation by June 1st, 1913. The plant would have the enormous capacity of producing 300,000 bricks in ten hours; 1,800,000 a week; or, 65,000,000 a year. The amount of hydro-electric power required for that many bricks would be 1,000 horsepower.

The process of manufacturing brick in this plant was by a method known as the 'stiff mud system,' which consisted of taking the blue shale from the pits and grinding it under mullers of ten heavy-duty dry pans, each weighing 36,000 pounds. The material was then run in cup elevators up to a height of fifty feet, emptied over piano-wire screens, and screened to a fineness of powder.

The screens delivered it into shoots, which sent it into heavy-duty machines for mixing clay, called pug mills, where it was thoroughly mixed with water. It was then delivered into two special machines and forced through dies into long columns, after which it was cut into pieces the thickness of brick. These clay bricks were then stacked onto small cars called dinkeys, and passed through a series of tunnels where all of the moisture was taken out of them in about twenty-four hours.

At this point, the bricks were ready for the burning process, in three large continuously-heated kilns of twenty chambers each. This was a new process of burning, which created a saving of 70 per cent in fuel over other types of kilns used at other yards.

The kilns mentioned required fifteen gas producers, with a daily operating capacity of 9,750,000 cubic feet of gas; this was said to be sufficient to supply an entire city the size of Hamilton with artificial gas from ten to twelve days. The contract for this great plant was brought about by Frank A. Elliott, a local boy, who was Canadian Manager of the largest clay-working machinery company in the United States.

To show the capacity this plant had, it was said that if these bricks were laid end to end, one year's supply would reach halfway around the earth. And yet, the general public was not aware, at the time, that such an enormous construction and building operation was in progress, in what was said to be the largest brick plant in the world.

At the beginning of January, 1913, there were about 140 men and 35 to 40 teams of horses working, while a large steam shovel was also in operation on the excavations for the kilns. Large quantities of materials were unloaded from the new CPR siding on the property, and upwards of 300 men were soon daily at work on erecting new buildings. Because there was not enough living accommodation for so many men now at work in Cooksville, many came out from the city daily; the Canadian Pacific Railway Company put on a special car, to stop and let them off at the Company's siding.

By the end of February, 1913, several kilns were ready, a large quantity of machinery was on the ground, and several buildings had been put up. Except for one rain, sleet and wind storm, which did much damage on a Friday night by blowing down one building over the top of a kiln and wrecking it, the weather had continued fair, and considerable progress had been made. Lyal Brothers were making things hum, and the brick yard was a hive of industry. About 400 men were employed on the project, and the pay roll amounted to about $1,500 per day. The plant was to be kept in continuous operation, twelve months of the year.

The Ontario Brick Company now had fifteen new dwellings under contract on their property, and had intentions of building fifty more to provide housing for their regular employees. But they said even that many would be insufficient when the plant was completed, and it would be up to others to supply the extra demand.

There was, in July, a difficulty in obtaining a water supply for the Brick Company. They had dammed up the creek flowing through the property, and a steam pump was being used, but it was feared that it would not be sufficient and a well was excavated in the bottom of the ravine. *The Streetsville Review* reported: 'Should all fail, it may be necessary to lay pipes to the River Credit, at considerable expense, as when the plant is complete, a large amount will be required daily.'

Many Italian workmen had moved into the village, and into the houses provided by the Company. The special CPR train, which had been conveying men from the city was discontinued.

At this time, in the first week of July, 1913, the Brick Company turned out its first shipment of bricks, and within a week, large quantities were being produced daily.

Rumours were flying about that another brick plant would be established next to the Ontario National Brick Company, on the Fisher farm; other rumours maintained that negotiations were ongoing for the purchase of the Sabiston farm, immediately west of it, for another brick plant. *The Streetsville Review* noted that 'If all these proposed plants get going, this village will have to be incorporated and its name changed to Brickville, instead of Cooksville.'

In the village, property changes were numerous, and prosperity seemed to abound everywhere. Nonetheless, there was a great scarcity of houses, and every available house in Cooksville was being used. Bowers' Hotel had been filled with boarders since the previous October, and they were now using the hotel across the road as an annex.

High winds again caused damage in the spring of 1914; three immense chimneys were blown over, and several roofs taken off buildings, causing damages of $15,000. Most of the telephones in the village were out of business, with trees blown across the lines.

Workers at the Brick Yard were interested in sports and, on June 18, 1914, *The Brampton Conservator* described a road race which was run along Dundas Street by workmen from the brick yards, managed by Charles Burrows. The course was from the Brick Yard to the Cooksville Station and back, a distance of three and three-fifth miles. The names of the runners, and their times, were:

E. Lyons – 20 minutes, 4 seconds
E. Ruddock – 21 minutes, 15 seconds
J. Hargreaves – 22 minutes
B. Potts – 23 minutes
I. Taliano – 24 minutes
S. Scrivener – 24 minutes, 15 seconds
S. Beda – 24 minutes, 30 seconds
Stovell, and Larson, also ran.

This was said to have settled the question of who was the Champion Runner at the Ontario National Brick Works.

At the beginning of November, 1914, the Brick Yard closed down, temporarily, with a large stock on hand; again, in October, 1916, it ceased operations during these War years, and many of the employees moved to the city. However, after a considerable number of improvements had been made, the plant was re-opened, with a full force, at the beginning of February, 1917. Work progressed well until, in 1920, due to a shortage of coal, the Company, now named the Shale Brick Company of Canada, had to again lay off a lot of their men, resulting in the closing of the plant.

The ending of World War I was followed by an unemployment situation but, with some changes in the management, the Brick Yard resumed operations, thus helping the unemployed around the Cooksville area. There was a high cost of labour. Building materials showed a marked decline in prices, but the bricklayers, carpenters, and plasterers still demanded wartime wages, and *The Streetsville Review* stated that this condition was responsible for the early closing, once again, of the brick yard.

By the middle of August, 130 men were out of work, some of whom

On 'Brickyard Hill,' overlooking Dundas Highway; left, Mr A. U. Cote's house; right, garage, with chauffeur's quarters above it where Mr Gridelet lived, 1920s. (Photo: Mississauga Central Library, Cooksville School Collection F237)

Cooksville Brick Yard, on Dundas Highway, (east side Mavis Road).
(Photo: Mississauga Central Library, Cooksville School Collection)

Cooksville Brick Company, Dundas Highway. (Photo: Mississauga
Central Library, Cooksville School Collection #238)

left for Western Canada's harvest fields, only to find that they too were already filled with sufficient labour. Circumstances at the Brick Works inflicted serious hardship on many families before spring, and they looked for relief of their problems in the shape of increased road development on the paving of the two highways passing through Cooksville.

The following January, in 1922, men were busily engaged in getting the brick yard plant in shape for a new beginning. Mr Aubrey U. Cote was named General Manager of the Shale Brick Company Limited, Canada, and a number of men were hired to prepare machinery and equipment for a big season's output. The Company published a large attractive calendar with a picture of the plant, underneath which were the words 'The Largest Brick Plant of its Kind in the World,' and an announcement that it would re-open 'full steam ahead.'

On February 2, 1922, they started with a work force of 80 men; the following Monday a considerable number more were taken on, and all were hopeful for a big year's run. A week later, the plant was operating with 120 men, all engaged in turning out several grades of brick in all shades and colours, in many faces, and for all purposes. By April, they were manufacturing an average of 120,000 bricks daily, of superior quality, and in nine or ten varieties.

In the fall, the Brick Yard management leased the Cherry Hill homestead, located just east of the CPR Station, and began fitting it up as a boarding house for their workers. Other premises, near Erindale, were also secured for the same purpose.

Due to the demand for its products, the plant now began to operate during the winter months. In 1922, the Cooksville Company was one of Toronto Township's major industries. Its main plant was a complete unit of its own. It had a waterworks with a capacity of 75,000 gallons a day; on its premises was a complete internal railway system with more than two miles of track, three locomotives, and twenty-six cars, called dinkeys. The site comprised 26 acres of dense, uniform shale, tested to a depth of 300 feet.

The plant now employed 350 men. With the exception of American coal, which supplied gas for the kilns, all of its raw products were found in the vicinity. Straw was obtained from the surrounding farms. Besides bricks, they were now making flooring tile, and hadite blocks.

There were, at this time, thirty-five families living inside the gates on the brick yard grounds, and the priest from St. Patrick's Roman

School Bus at entrance gate Cooksville Shale Brick Company, 1927.
(Photo: Mississauga Central Library, Cooksville School Collection)

Workmen at the Cooksville Brick Yard, 1920s. (Photo: courtesy of Joe
Bandiera)

Catholic Church, located on the southwest corner of Dixie Road and Dundas Street, visited them. He asked the Brick Company to provide a bus to take the children to church on Sundays, as they could not walk that far. Mr Cote agreed, and a bus service was started for them.

Since the Cooksville School on Hurontario Street was over a mile away from their homes, the bus took them to school as well. The driver of the Brick Yard School Bus was Mr Gridelet, who was employed as a chauffeur there and lived over the large garage to the right of Mr Cote's house at the top of the Brick Yard Hill, facing the highway.

Some of the children who rode on this bus were: John Bandiera, his cousin Joe Bandiera, and Ena Bandiera; Frank, Mary, and Albert Franceschini; Yolanda and Sadie Perrin; Flora and Bruno Pavanel; Edward Heron, Ray Bortolatti, Les Riva, Albert Cote, and Genevieve Gridelet.

At the end of January, 1923, the plant closed for its annual repairs, resuming operations the following week, busier than ever. In April, Robert McKay purchased a large new truck with which to haul bricks to Toronto for the Shale Brick Company; and that same week, a car load of cotton in transit took fire on the CPR tracks, near the Brick Yard switch, and was destroyed.

The following month, a large building was erected on the Company's property to accommodate their employees as a boarding house. Jack Richards was the rooming house manager; and Mrs E. F. W. Scott became the cook. The business was continuously developing, and on one day a run of 108,000 bricks was made, constituting a record.

At this time also, at a meeting of the employees, a Football Club was organized, and the following officers were elected:

Honorary President – Mr A. U. Cote
President – Mr Robinson
Vice President – Mr Holland
Chairman – W. E. Martin
Secretary – Mr Potts
Trainer – G. Kitney

These latter three, with E. Edwards, W. Read, and J. Tyler, formed the committee who supervised the activities of the Club.

The Shale Brick Company's football team, on which were some of the best from 'Merry Old England,' played their opening game at Streetsville, in the Peel-Halton League series, which ended in a tie. Their first home game was against Elmbank and, although the visitors won 3-1, the enthusiastic brick yard supporters all agreed that they had a great team to root for.

Building operations continued to grow, and two more cottages were erected on the premises. The Clydesdale horses exhibited at the Canadian National Exhibition, in Toronto, won First Prize and were bought by the T. Eaton Company for $1,100.

In 1923, an entrance to the brick yard pits was made by cutting away the banks west of the main plant entrance. This new entrance was at a short distance north of Dundas Street, up a narrow dirt road, and with a new gate leading into the hadite plant where building blocks were made. This little road, from the nineteen-twenties, where the trucks brought in supplies from other yards, later became a short section of Mavis Road leading north from Dundas Street.

Also, in 1923, an addition to the machine shop was erected; and a seven million dollar order for brick was received, which insured a winter's steady work.

Once again, in 1925, the Brick Company's fine horses netted $550 in prize money from the Toronto and London Exhibitions, and were bought by the T. Eaton Company. That year, Mr Cote left to join his wife and children in France, and J. O. Lefebre, of Montreal, arrived as a resident of Cooksville, to become associated with the Company.

The Streetsville Review reported, in 1927, that the Shale Brick's prized Clydesdale horses had won the R. Y. Eaton Cup for Single Horse, in the Grand Champion Class, as well as First Prize for Pair and Outfit, in Class II, at Toronto.

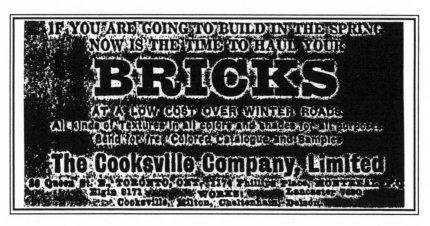

The Streetsville Review, January 10, 1929

At the beginning of March, 1928, the Cooksville Brick Company purchased the Interprovincial Brick Company at Cheltenham, and received a large order for tile from the Royal York Hotel in Toronto.

During the Depression year of 1932, the Brick Yard was idle all winter, but got back into business the following March. Over the next years, it continued to prosper; and in September, 1938, a great Picnic and Party for the Cooksville Company Limited's employees was celebrated at Peel Park (now Croatian Parish Park) on the Credit River, south of Streetsville. A Tug-of-War between the Brick and Block Divisions was the most exciting feature of this day, with the Brick section downing its rivals.

A crowd of nearly three hundred afterwards enjoyed an extensive sports programme run off by a committee convened by Rinaldo Brogna, and consisting of Frank Franceschini, Joe Brogna, Albert Franceschini and Bill Elburgh. Entries in all the races were numerous, with the Men's Three-Legged Race providing the most merriment.

In the softball game, the stars were Jim Harrison, John Bandiera, Albert and Frank Franceschini, Kiper Hopkins, Joe Brogna, and Joe Perrin. The team captained by Frank Franceschini ably disposed of their opponents, under the leadership of Lawrence Watson. Bill Pell acted as umpire-in-chief, and Rinaldo Brogna was official scorer.

On the Tuesday morning of August 16, 1949, a staggering blow to the construction industry in Canada happened when the Cooksville Brick and Tile Company, which produced one-sixth of the nation's output of brick, was put out of operation by a huge fire. The plant, in which 45,000,000 bricks were manufactured annually, was almost entirely destroyed in spite of desperate attempts by Toronto Township's two fire brigades, aided by those of Port Credit and Islington.

The night watchman, George Popovitch, discovered the fire in the Number 3 kiln, and called the fire department; but it spread quickly and destroyed two of the three kilns, thus causing the closing down of two-thirds of the plant's operation. No water could be turned onto the burning kilns, because this would have ruined the structural tile of their chambers.

At first it was believed that the tile would not be hurt; but the dry lumber in the plant provided enough fuel that the flames could be seen for a distance of twenty miles. However, workmen managed to close the valves to the compartments where coal gas was stored in huge tanks, and this kept them from exploding. Two CPR box cars were destroyed, along with their contents of structural tile, as were three of the Company's flat cars. Jim Harrison, the locomotive engineer, made use of the Company's small engine to try and get close enough to move the box cars out, but this was impossible; he could not get within a hundred feet of the burning kilns.

There were three hundred skilled workmen, almost half of the working population of Cooksville, employed in this factory, and most could not resume their positions for many months. Many found employment in the cleaning and re-building of the ruined buildings; but the plant was unable to carry out any work on their contracts for projects, such as that on the Bank of Nova Scotia Building, in Toronto. No cause could be found at the time for this fire, the damages of which were set at five hundred thousand dollars.

Whatever damage it did to the Brick Yard itself, the fire could not dampen the enthusiasm of the players on the Cooksville Brick and Tile softball team. They played their home games on their own ball diamond, located on Dundas Street West, opposite Mason Heights Boulevard, provided for them on the Company's property by Mr A. U. Cote. After reaching the Ontario semi-finals in 1947 and 1948, Cooksville Brick and Tile softball team went all the way in 1949, winning the Intermediate 'C' Championship of Ontario and the Sniderman Trophy.

Danny Masaro, pitcher for Canada Brick and Tile, 1945. (Photo: courtesy of Dan Masaro)

194

The first game was won by Wooler, at Trenton, by a score of 7 to 6; the second game, played at Port Credit, was won by Cooksville Brick and Tile, 7 to 6 in ten innings. With the series tied up, they moved to Oshawa Stadium for the third game, which went twelve innings to a 10-10 tie, the game being called for darkness. This meant that a fourth game had to be played at the same stadium and, this time, Cooksville Brick and Tile took the game and the championship.

Final Score:

	R	H	E
Cooksville Brick and Tile	10	9	1
Wooler...	4	6	6

Cooksville Brick and Tile, Ontario Rural Softball Association Intermediate Champions, 1952-53. (Photo: courtesy of Dan Masaro)
BACK ROW: Pete Gorman, Rino Basso, Buster Duck, Joe Kovalick, Frank Kaszycki, John Culver, Gino Bandiera, Danny Masaro.
FRONT ROW: Bill Scott (publicity), Charlie Yateman, Bob Salmond, Bill Simons (manager and coach), A. U. Cote (president and general manager, Cooksville Co., hon. manager of team), Jean Morin, Armand Jubinville, John Moore, Howard Caton. Front: Johnny Kovalick, bat boy.

Batteries for Cooksville were Culver and Caven; for Wooler, Farr and Radcliffe, with McCall replacing Farr in the sixth inning.

By Toronto Township's Centennial Year, 1950, following the fire the Brick Yard was again in operation as a major industry, with more than 80 per cent of its employees coming from within Toronto Township.

When we lived on Dickson Road in 1950 and the leaves had fallen from the trees, as I washed the dishes in my kitchen sink I could see from my window the lovely white, newly-painted sign across the front of the largest building at the Brick Yard. The sign read BRICK COOKSVILLE TILE, and recalled to my mind the days during the nineteen-twenties when my father, Milford Denison, drove one of the brick yard trucks; he used to go through a little gate, past a small grey wooden hut, and down the narrow, rutted road to the Dundas Highway, on his way to make deliveries or pick up supplies at Milton for the Cooksville Brick Yard.

In 1952-53, the Cooksville Brick and Tile softball team again won the Ontario Rural Softball Association Intermediate Championship, and had their picture taken at the Brick Yard ball park, on Dundas Street West.

Forty-five years later, the familiar old main building, so prominent atop the Brick Yard Hill on Dundas Street West, at Cooksville, familiar for so many years to so many who grew up in the area, disappeared forever, torn down for new developments within the City of Mississauga. However, the Brick Yard Ball Park, put in by Mr Cote, is still in use.

Chapter 22: Cooksville Post Office

THE FIRST POST OFFICE IN YORK, from 1816 to 1827, was in a small log cabin located at Frederick and King Streets, and William Allan was the Postmaster.

In 1820, Jacob Cook received a contract to carry the mail from Ancaster to York, at first on horseback and later by setting up a stagecoach route along Dundas Street. Mr Cook was never the Postmaster, but his network of stages carried the mails throughout this early area of Upper Canada for a period of twenty-eight years.

The 1895 Postal Guide for the whole of Canada listed Cooksville (Peel-o) 1837, 34644, and gave the information that: 'A recent find of this date proves Toronto 1829-1837 was on this site, with Abijah Lewis as Post Master. Another Toronto, previously, 1826-1829 was three miles southwest of Cooksville, with Joseph Carter as Post Master.'

Cooksville Post Office (160) Ontario is today listed in the Post Office Records at Ottawa as having been established prior to 1839, with J. H. Savigny shown as Postmaster up until October 6, 1839.

When the first Loyalists arrived in Upper Canada, once each winter an 'Express,' for the convenience of the army and merchants, travelled from Montreal to Detroit and back, carrying any mail that had accumulated since the close of navigation. The Express consisted of a white man with one or two Indian guides, travelling on snowshoes and carrying axes to clear away bush or fallen trees which stood in their way. Letters mailed from England in November did not arrive until the following spring. In summer, the mail was carried by way of the rivers and lakes.

After the War of 1812, the mail was taken by stagecoach and dropped off at Post Offices, or simply thrown ashore from boats. Post Offices were few and far between, but as a stagecoach approached an inn, the driver would blow his horn loudly to alert the Postmaster; if taken by boat, a carrier would be waiting on the wharf with a horse and wagon, ready to catch the mail bags and take them to the inn or another distribution centre, sometimes the church. A Post Office clerk was there to sort the mail for the district, and forward on the rest.

The Brampton Standard of July 30, 1857, printed a notice that under the Post Office Law of the last Session, newspapers printed and published in Canada and mailed directly from the office of publication would pass free of Canadian Postage. Postage stamps of the value of one half-penny each would be sold to the public at all principal Post Offices, with a discount of 5 per cent upon purchase of not less than 20 stamps; the notice was signed by R. Spence, Post-Master General.

From October 7, 1839 to November 22, 1867, Francis B. Morley was Cooksville's Postmaster, and no one else was put in charge again until John Peaker took over, with the Office then being located in his father's tinsmith shop on Dundas Street. John Peaker held the position from March 1, 1871 until his death in 1873, and Mrs Hannah Peaker carried on in his place until her resignation on November 20, 1877.

In January, 1877, John Weeks, of Cooksville, who for some time had owned and driven the stages running between Brampton and Toronto, sold out to Mr Graham; and in 1878, by an application made to the Post

Old Cooksville Post Office, northeast corner Cook and Dundas
Streets; dwelling at left, Post Office and store at right. (Photo:
Mississauga Central Library, Cooksville Vol.1, #7)

The Streetsville Review, October 5, 1905

Office Department for a change in time, the stages then began leaving at 6 o'clock in the morning instead of 9.30, in order to give enough time for business transactions in the city and enable people to return home on the same day.

T. G. Goulding, a Cooksville merchant, followed the Peakers and operated the Post Office in his general store for six years, from January 1, 1878 until October, 1884.

In 1885, the dwelling with the tinsmith shop on one side of it, owned by William Peaker, was sold to Charles A. Schiller who turned the former tinsmith shop back into a Post Office and took on the duties of Postmaster until his death, at the end of December, 1887. The following year, Sir Melville Parker was appointed to the Office, and oversaw its operation from May 1, 1888 until September 5, 1898, when he resigned.

Sir Melville did not personally act as Postmaster in the village; these duties were looked after by Charles Schiller's widow, Margaret Schiller, who continued to be proprietor of the building. Mrs Schiller ran a small grocery store, where the tinsmith shop had been, and became well-known to all the people of the district as Cooksville's Postmistress.

At the beginning of September, 1896, John Thomson, of Port Credit, auctioned off this valuable store and premises, and Margaret Schiller left Cooksville to live in Toronto with her son Charles. The man who bought the house and the store attached to the east side of it, for cash, was Henry Herbert Shaver, who came there to live, from Dixie; and on October 16, 1898, he was appointed Cooksville's new Postmaster. This Post Office and dwelling, located on the northeast corner of Cook and Dundas Streets, was the white building shown in historical pictures of Cooksville, and recognized as 'Cooksville's Old Post Office.'

The Postmaster's salary at the beginning of February, 1905, was $208.00 annually, and the revenue of the Post Office for that year amounted to $615.85.

Herbert Shaver, besides being Postmaster, was active in business in the village. He advertised in *The Brampton Conservator* of August 26, 1909, stating himself to be a Justice of the Peace, Division Court Clerk and Police Magistrate; he was a Notary Public Commissioner for the Conveyancing of Deeds, Mortgages, Leases, and Wills. He was Agent for the Royal Fire Insurance Company, who sold and rented farms, as well as collecting rents and other monies.

At the beginning of February, 1912, arrangements were made for the removal of the central office of the Bell Telephone Company from the

Post Office to a part of E. Walterhouse's former Revere House hotel, in order that both day and night service could then be maintained. A short time later, a Mail Box was placed at the Cooksville Station to fulfil a long-felt wish by people living in the eastern end of the village, because their distance from the Post Office was so great.

Through December of the same year, there were many cases of Scarlet Fever, and the Post Office building had to be kept under quarantine when Miss T. Black, who lived there, became ill with the disease. The Christmas mail, an unusually heavy one, had to be taken temporarily to the residence of Mr A. E. Tolman until Miss Black could be removed and the Post Office premises thoroughly disinfected, after which the regular business of the Post Office was resumed. It was in the spring of 1914 that Mr Shaver let his plans of building a fine solid red brick residence, with an addition for the Post Office and a private office, be known. By July, Contractor Smith, of Port Credit, had removed all of the old buildings on the property and was making headway in the erection of the new building.

The Streetsville Review of October 15, 1914, described Cooksville's brand new Post Office, which had opened for business on the Wednesday of the week before, located at the corner of Cook Street, as 'a valuable improvement to the requirements of the village.' The Office

House built by Herbert Shaver, at northeast corner Cook and Dundas Streets, 1914; his dwelling at left, and Post Office right. (Photo: Verna Mae Weeks)

was now in the one-storey, solid glazed brick addition to Mr Shaver's home; in area, it was 18 feet wide, by 37 1/2 feet deep. It had a private office in the rear, and was furnished with a solid Georgia pine and maple floor – heated with hot water, and lighted with hydro electric light. The front of the Post Office Department was fitted with an Office Specialty Combination Mail Box System, at a cost of $350.00; and with its two delivery wickets, it presented a very neat and handsome appearance.

The residence adjoining the Post Office was a two-storey, gothic structure, fronting on the corner of two streets (Cook and Dundas), with porticos and verandahs surrounding it. Built of glazed brick, on a concrete foundation 20 by 37 1/2 feet, it was roofed with asbestos slate. Its concrete basement had a seven-foot ceiling, and was divided into several compartments.

There were three rooms and a hall on the ground floor; and five bedrooms, a hall and bathroom upstairs. It was finished with Georgia pine, and dark-stained oak floors downstairs; the second floor in birch. The doors were panelled in double birch. The heating and water system was supplied by a Myers Electric motor with a hot water furnace, and cost $1,100 to install. Like the Post Office, it was lit by hydro electric light. The whole building cost over $7,000, and was certainly one of the finest-equipped and most modern residences in the locality. The house and former Post Office built by Henry Shaver stands today, at 47 Dundas Street West.

In February, 1915, the contract for carrying the mail from the CPR Station and the Cooksville Post Office, for the next four years was awarded to Robert Coulter, who had recently begun carrying passengers to and from the Station. Mr Coulter took the place of H. C. Colwell who, with his father before him, had faithfully fulfilled these duties for the previous thirty-two years.

All went well until the beginning of August, 1917, when Mr Shaver died, at his home in Cooksville. He had been Cooksville's Postmaster up until July 27, 1917. A member of the Methodist Church, and a strong supporter of the Sunday School, he was leader of the Excelsior Bible Class, and the Choir. In addition, he was Chairman of the Laymen's Association and, for many years, the Church's representative at the Annual Conference.

Mr Shaver had always discharged his duties in an honourable and satisfactory manner, not only in the Postal Service but in his community as well. He always took an active part in public affairs, was a member of the Independent Order of Foresters, and a Mason. He was an earnest and consistent Temperance Advocate, being identified with this work.

It was said that, as a Trustee of the Dixie Union Cemetery, he had been instrumental in having those hitherto neglected grounds put in neater condition. When he died, services were held in the Cooksville Methodist Church, and he was buried in Dixie Union Cemetery.

Hugh K. Bowden, who had carried on an excellent drug store business for some years, was next being congratulated on becoming Postmaster, in succession to the late Mr Shaver. As soon as the necessary changes could be effected, the village Post Office was removed east along Dundas Street to the premises of his Cooksville Pharmacy, and opened in the first week of October, 1917.

Considerable improvements were made to the building. The old front of the premises known in earlier times as the Schiller House hotel was taken out, and two plate glass windows, 5 by 6 feet in area, were put in on either side of a centre doorway, with an extra window added for the Post Office Department. The Post Office occupied all of the west side of the premises, and had Combination and Call boxes for the distribution of the mail. The local people continued to be furnished, as before, with ample and efficient service by Mr Bowden, until his death in 1920.

On November 23, 1920, George C. G. Rutledge, a young man and longtime resident of Peel who had taught school at Inglewood for a number of years, moved into Cooksville and took charge of the Post Office. The Pharmacy was continued under the management of Mrs Bowden. In May, 1921, Mr Rutledge bought the Herbert Schaeffer property on the north side of Dundas Street opposite the Methodist Church, and by September, a building under contract by Mr McClure and Mr Galbraith was almost completed. On September 22, 1921, the postal rates to overseas countries, on and after the first of October, were increased to 4 cents per ounce. By this time, William Denison had bought the brick house built by Henry Shaver; and a new Post Office was to be opened in Mr Rutledge's house. Permission had been granted by the Post Office Department regarding the times for removal of mail (between 10 a.m. and 5.30 p.m.) during which hours postal services were to become available. The new Office opened on November 23rd, 1920, the day after Thanksgiving, with mail being dispensed from a special room adjoining Mr Rutledge's residence. Once again, the mail was being received and dispatched from the west end of the village. On

October 20th, many of the village and district people had attended a dance given in the old Post Office building by Postmaster Rutledge, and during the week of November 3rd, this building was occupied by Mr Bailey's new butcher shop, under the management of Mr Halsey.

However, Mr Rutledge, unmarried and living with his parents at thirty-five years of age, had been in poor health for some time and was to remain as Postmaster for only six weeks following this dance. He died at the end of November, 1921. His term as Postmaster had lasted only from November 23, 1920, to November 30, 1921.

The Brampton Conservator of December 8, 1921 commented that when the late Postmaster, Mr Bowden, died there had been no local applicants for the Post Office position and, with the passing of Mr Rutledge again creating a vacancy, there were now no less than six or seven applicants for it. By December 15th, there were ten; and by the time another week had gone by, no less than seventeen applicants for the Postmastership, extending in area from Dixie to Streetsville, had been received.

Petitions began flying about for group favourites, and after a month's time, with no excuse for the delay, and the public not being consulted, people were annoyed. However, they were informed that the Civil Service Commission made the appointments, not the local Members, or patronage boards. While the rumours passed, and the public guessed, Miss Alice Stewart was Acting Postmistress. Mrs Pinkney had been in the Post Office as Assistant for nearly a year. James Crawford was the Rural Mail Carrier; and R. S. Whaley was official Mail Courier between Cooksville Post Office and the Railway Station.

In May, 1922, a number of changes were made, to conform with new International Regulations. The one-cent stamp became straw colour, the red two-cent stamp was replaced with a green one, the new five-cent stamp was a violet shade, and the ten-cent one was blue.

At this time, two Inspectors from the Post Office Department arrived in town and the name of the new Postmaster was announced. On July 17, 1922, William Charles Henry Copeland was approved as Postmaster and, a week later, the Post Office opened in its new quarters in the Copeland Building on the corner of Dundas and Hurontario Streets. Miss Alice Stewart was appointed Assistant.

With Mr Copeland in charge, his four daughters, Violet, Marie, Hazel, and Florence sorted mail in the Office, which was housed in the same building as the Copeland General Store. The following year, Mr

203

Crawford gave up the Rural Mail Route from Cooksville, and it was handled by Mr Whaley.

On February 4, 1926, *The Brampton Conservator* reported that, under Peel Post Office Revenues for the year 1925, Cooksville's amount was the sum of $2,465.64.

In 1927, William Copeland's Store and Post Office Building was moved from the place where it had always stood and deposited forty feet to the east, to make way for the march of progress in the shape of the new British American Oil Company's Filling Station.

Christmas time, 1929, was a particularly busy one for the local Post Office, with Postmaster Copeland taking in 15 bags of mail on Tuesday and 20 bags on Wednesday. Four assistants were required to handle the incoming mail at the wicket.

In 1936, Cooksville Post Office was third in the list of Offices in the County, Brampton being first, and Port Credit second.

On New Year's Day, 1948, Postmaster William C. H. Copeland died while doing some work in the general store he had operated for the past thirty-five years. His son Charles then took over the grocery business, and on January 5, 1948, his eldest daughter, Violet, became Acting Postmaster.

A little later, in 1948, Charles Copeland moved his grocery store from the Post Office into his own new building, located just one door east, in order that mail service could be improved. The building which still housed the Post Office was then leased by the Government and, on September 30th, Miss Violet Copeland, Incumbent, was the new Civil Service appointee, entitled to be called Cooksville's 'Postmaster.' The Post Office now had plenty of space for residents to make out their postcards and address letters, as well as to stop and chat on Saturdays about the happenings of the week.

Miss Violet Marion Copeland is recorded, at Ottawa, as Cooksville's Acting Postmaster from January 5, 1948; and as Postmaster from September 30, 1948 to May 31, 1960, when she resigned.

The home delivery of mail was started at this time, and William Wesley Hawke, OAS, was appointed to the position of Postmaster on July 1, 1960. His Assistant was Mrs William Clark (formerly Hazel Copeland), one of the four sisters who had sorted the mail in their father's grocery store.

The name of the Cooksville Post Office was changed to 'Mississauga, Ontario,' effective July 1, 1968.

Chapter 23: Peel's First Female Lawyer

MARIE COPELAND WAS BORN in the old Copeland homestead, a stone house located on the south side of Burnhamthorpe Road, east of Tomken Road, and first came to Cooksville in 1911 when her father, William Copeland, took over the management of the red brick general store on the southeast corner of Dundas and Hurontario Streets. Marie had one brother, Charles, and four sisters: Violet, Hazel, Florence, and a baby named Lorna Beatrice who died at eleven months, in 1919. She attended the little two-roomed Cooksville School where Hannah Goldthorpe taught, located just north of the Cooksville corners, on the east side of the Centre Road.

Her father was the first constable in the Cooksville area, and Marie decided very early that she wanted to become a lawyer. She was one of the first people to have a vehicle, and drove it to Brampton High School. This school was not far from the Brampton Court House, and she was able to go there to watch the courtroom proceedings, and learn all she could about them, for herself.

In 1933, she graduated from Victoria College and, after finishing

Miss Marie Copeland. (*The Port Credit News*, November 30, 1937)

Osgoode Law School, was articled with the firm of Montgomery, McMaster and Company, of Toronto; and in 1937, Marie L. Copeland became the first Peel-born girl to be called to the bar in the legal profession. For a time, she was associated professionally with Gordon B. Jackson K. C., who owned a law office in Cooksville.

In 1940, Marie Copeland married Edgar Clement in St. John's Anglican Church, Dixie. Edgar, who was born near Wakefield, Yorkshire, England, had been educated first in Lachine, Quebec, and then at the Walkerville Collegiate, in Windsor, Ontario. He had graduated from the University of Western Ontario, and also Osgoode Law School.

The Port Credit Weekly of April 6, 1944, reported that Marie L. Clement BA, and Edgar Clement, BA, had set up practice of law under the firm name of Copeland and Clement, on Shepard Avenue in Cooksville. Edgar had been practising law for some years and, at that time, besides being engaged in post-graduate legal studies at the University of Toronto, was also Secretary of the Yorkshire Society of Ontario.

For years, Marie and her husband operated their own successful practice, and the firm of Copeland and Clement became well-known throughout the whole of Peel County.

In 1991, Mrs Clement still kept the picture taken in 1968 at the reunion of her Osgoode Law School class. She recalled that there had been five women in that class; it was a big class, but there were few women practising law at that time, very few. One of the graduates besides herself was Mrs Margaret Campbell, of the Liberals, who had been a Member for a riding in Toronto, and later a City of Toronto Controller. 'Actually,' Mrs Clement said, 'Margaret Campbell could have been Premier, but the Liberals lost power.'

In her later life, Marie Copeland Clement was asked to take a judgeship, which pleased her immensely; but she said that it would be too hard, at her age. She, who had once helped her sisters sort mail in the Post Office in their father's store in Cooksville, and drove by herself to High School at Brampton to learn about the courtroom, had fulfilled her ambition to become one of Peel County's best lawyers.

This astute, yet compassionate woman said of her father's store, 'It was a hard thing to keep on with the store in those days; the people today don't know much about that. There were a lot of people who couldn't afford to pay their debts, and if they couldn't pay, then they would have to forfeit a piece of property. But creditors are past – we'll forgive their debts.'

Chapter 24: The Churches

WHEN THE FIRST SETTLERS arrived along the Dundas road, they were visited by a missionary or circuit rider about once a year, and they planned on building a chapel; but the War of 1812 intervened and their small log chapel could not be completed until 1816. Built on the north side of Dundas Street, east of the First Line (Cawthra Road), it was agreed that the three Protestant groups (Methodists, Anglicans, and Presbyterians) would use it at different times.

In 1825, when the Reverend John Back was pastor, the circuit covered seven townships, and the membership numbered 350 people. These first pastors would stay about three weeks to minister to their congregations and carry out preaching appointments in each section. In 1837, their first small wooden chapel was replaced by the stone building which still stands today, called the Dixie Union Chapel.

The Methodists later separated from the group and began holding services in the Rechabites Hall, on land which later came to be known as the Cooksville Fair Grounds. In 1844, they built their own church on Agnes Street, in Cooksville; in 1870, the Anglicans moved into their own St. John the Baptist Church, which they built next door to the Union Chapel, in Dixie; and much later, the Presbyterians erected their new brick church, located just north of the Chapel, on the east side of Cawthra Road, in Dixie.

The cemetery surrounding the first small Chapel continued to be used for many years, with Cooksville's early pioneers and their descendants laid to rest there. The earliest grave is said to have belonged to a boy of three years, Philip Harris, the son of Daniel Harris of Cooksville who carved a stone from the field with his small son's name on it, dated 1812.

In 1844, a new frame Church was erected on Agnes Street by the Methodists, and they started a Sunday School. In the cornerstone of this building was placed a little note, dated August, 1844, on which was written: 'Wm. Curtis Stephenson, Cabinet Maker, worked on this Church.' Three years later, the building was coated with roughcast and became familiarly known as the 'lath and plaster Church.'

The Methodist preacher, in 1851, was the Reverend J. Wilson; and Mitchell's 1866 General Directory gave the information that Cooksville had one Church, Wesleyan Methodist, capable of seating 300 people with the Reverend Philps, Pastor.

The first sod was turned for a large brick church in 1886, on the same ground where the old Rechabites Hall was torn down, and the new Methodist Church was dedicated on Christmas Day, 1887. Samuel Emerson Harris bought the old lath and plaster church on Agnes Street and had it moved around the corner and down to the north side of Dundas Street, where he used it to carry on a flour and feed business. His little roughcast home, where he was born in 1857, stood beside it, just east of the building.

Daniel F. Harris, who had watched the moving of the old church building, stated in 1930 when his brother Samuel Emerson died, that Frank McKinney had moved it; and after all the years it was still a firmly-constructed edifice, made of solid timbers, with every appearance of being good for another 100 years. In reality, the lath and plaster church remained standing, and was used as a grocery store, insurance and real estate office, as well as a Township library for another 60 years, before being finally deserted, boarded up, and demolished in the early 1990s. The place where it stood is, at present, a vacant lot just east of Novar Road.

In 1891, though the only church in Cooksville was still the Methodist, those who wished to attend Church of England, Baptist, Presbyterian, or Roman Catholic services could attend these by walking to Dixie, which was considered as rather an inducement than otherwise during the summer months.

The Reverend G. Washington, MA, assisted by the Reverend E. C. Laker, looked after the spiritual welfare of the Methodists of this circuit, which consisted of six stations: Cooksville, Springfield-on-the-Credit, Sheridan, Carmen, Port Credit, and Bethesda. Mr Laker was at the time a probationer, who had succeeded in taking a first-class certificate at the recent examinations. The Reverend Mr Carswell looked after the interests of the Presbyterians, and the Reverend Mr Tracey after those of the Baptists. A note, at this time, stated, 'The Church of England and the Roman Catholic Churches are pretty little structures, and it is seldom that such churches can be met with in the country.'

The Streetsville Review of August 4, 1892, described a Garden Party held on the grounds of the Cooksville Town Hall on July 20th, to raise money for the Methodist Church Organ Fund. A large audience enjoyed a long and varied programme which was not completed until after eleven o'clock. The reason for the lateness of the concert, which was not appreciated, was because the people were late in arriving for the tea; it was the busy season on the farms, and instead of serving tea at 6 p.m., they were forced to delay it until 8 o'clock. The booths were under the care of the Misses Cox, Readman, and Ballon; the Misses Craigie, of Port Credit, were also present to help in the project. The booths raised $25, with total receipts of $80 which, after paying all expenses, almost cleared the Sabbath School of debt.

In November, 1896, when Mrs Margaret Schiller, who had worked not only in the Methodist Sunday School, but as a member and worker in the Sunday School at Dixie, was leaving the village after selling her home and grocery store, she was presented with an address and a purse of money. The congregation met at the Church, and the address which showed plainly the esteem in which she was held by her Presbyterian friends was read to her.

It said, in part: 'While many of us started with little knowledge of Sunday School work, there was among us one who had; and we never looked to you in vain for good advice. We are sure that those whom you have had in charge will in after days be unable to shake off the influence of the lessons taught them in their early years. We recognize in you a liberal mind, desirous of doing good, irrespective of faith or creed, and thus we think that in the community a gap is made not easily to be repaired.' – Signed on behalf of Dixie Presbyterian Sunday School, by J. Craib, Superintendent.

Cooksville had always been noted for its Christmas concerts and entertainments, but the Methodist Sunday School Christmas Tree Concert on Christmas Eve, 1896, was agreed by everyone to be 'the best entertainment ever given in the Town Hall.' There were boys' marching songs, flag and goodnight drills, a tableau and chorus; and the recitations given by the 'babies' of the Sunday School, little Jamesie Schiller and Norman McClelland, fairly brought down the house.

The young men of the Bible Class had decorated the Hall beautifully and, at the close of the programme, Mr and Mrs Santa Claus distributed presents from a monstrous Christmas bell. Mrs George McClelland, a teacher in the Cooksville Sunday School, received from the class a beautiful silver dish, presented to her by Donald D. Schiller and William Pinkney.

A special feature of the Methodist Sunday School Christmas entertainment in 1903, was the contribution by the scholars of gifts to the poor of Toronto, including fowl, vegetables, fruit and groceries, amounting to a goodly sum. The report of John Ezard was most gratifying and the outlook of the School was never brighter; Superintendent Wilmer Dunton and his band of workers were given most deserving credit for the work they were doing in the interests of the young people of Cooksville.

In February, 1904, J. K. Morley, who had just resigned after twelve years of service as secretary at the Methodist Church, was surprised to answer his door and meet two representatives of the officers and teachers of the Sunday School, who presented him with a beautiful marble clock on behalf of all the members.

A gravel walk was constructed for the convenience of all who attended services at the several little Dixie churches, travelling to and fro on foot. This project was all done by gratuitous labour, through the months of December, January, and February of 1905-6.

The Streetsville Review of November 5, 1908, reported that the Cooksville Methodist Ladies' Aid Society was endeavouring to raise a mile of coppers.

Through the next two years, the members of the Dixie Presbyterian Adult Bible Class were holding their meetings and social gatherings in the Pharmacy Hall at Cooksville. On one occasion, a locket and chain was presented to Miss Laura Jamieson as a token of appreciation for the faithful performance of her duties as Organist of their Church. The accompanying letter, from the Managers of the Dixie Presbyterian Church, was written by H. K. Bowden, Secretary.

At the end of January, 1910, the congregation of the Dixie Presbyterian Church decided to build a new church; and at this time, the congregation of St. John's Anglican Church held a limelight exhibition, with a lecture, in the Township Hall.

Throughout February, socials were held by the Ladies' Aid Society of the Presbyterian Church, and the Reverend George P. Duncan contributed to the success of these, their first public ventures, in Pharmacy Hall. The Church secured a fine plot of ground for the location of their new building, in the rear of the Dixie Union Cemetery, a short distance up the First Line (Cawthra Road), and immediately set plans in motion to begin construction in the spring.

The same month of February, the Upper Canada Bible Society held its Annual Meeting in the Methodist Church at Cooksville, at which the Reverend W. E. Hazzard, District Secretary, gave a fine address illustrated with lantern slides.

When March weather permitted the work to begin, in 1910, ten teams with about fifteen men were busily engaged in drawing gravel from William Pinkney's pit for the new Presbyterian Church. In April, tenders were let, and a description placed in *The Brampton Conservator* gave full details on the plans for the new brick building. The paper stated that Herbert G. Paull, of Toronto, would be the architect. The concrete foundation was to be 40 x 60 feet, with a tower on the southwest corner fitted up in modern style. The basement would have a vestry, kitchen, pantry, commodious schoolroom, and a store and fuel room with two furnaces therein. The ground floor was to have a front vestibule, and two rear vestibules with entrances to the basement from each; there would be a balcony on the front vestibule, with an entrance from the tower.

The floor of the new church was to be inclined, with three aisles, and seating, in circular form, capable of accommodating 300 people. The whole church was to be wired for electric light and when completed, by October, would be a credit to the congregation and an ornament to the locality. The total cost of the building was set at between eight and nine thousand dollars.

On July 23, 1910, at 2.30 p.m., the cornerstone of the Dixie Presbyterian Church was laid, by His Honour Lieutenant Governor Gibson; and on August 4th, John Wanless, of Toronto, presented for its tower a 200-pound steel alloy bell.

At Harvest Thanksgiving, the Church was profusely decorated with an assortment of fruit, flowers and vegetables; a notable feature of the day was a branch of a raspberry vine with a second crop of ripe raspberries on it, which came from the garden of Mr Rea, on the Middle Road. Following the service, the whole contribution, including a special collection of $12.25, was forwarded to the Hospital for Sick Children, in Toronto.

The Brampton Conservator of August 19, 1915, stated that the Methodist Church was the only church in the village of Cooksville, although the clergy of other denominations visited their parishioners regularly.

In June, the Methodist Sunday School picnic at High Park, in Toronto, was a huge success. The quoit pits were in constant use all day;

and the volleyball court was well-patronized, although the game was new to the Cooksville district. There was a programme of sports under the leadership of Frank Beckwith, Secretary of the Peel County YMCA. Races were held; group games for boys and girls which were usually used at the YMCA included Relays by Teams. They played Cap Hustle, Dead Man's Flag, Step-Over, and Leap Frog Relays; Cross Tag, in pairs; Hook Arm Tag, Circle Tag, Ostrich Tag, Oriental or Hindoo Tag, Slap Jack, Swatum, London Bridge, Nuts and May, and many other games. It was a glorious day.

Following Saturday's great picnic, the Cooksville Sunday School held its regular session on Sunday morning. The basement schoolroom was delightfully cool, and the attendance good, in spite of the strenuous day at the picnic. The YMCA Secretary spoke to the classes on some lessons from the picnic, comparing the Christian life to a Long Race and a Relay Race. He said, 'This is a busy fruit district, but time is found for play, work, and worship.'

In October, 1921, the Young People's Society elected Principal Dyer, of the Public School, President of the Society for the ensuing year. Others elected were: Treasurer, Douglas Rowbotham; Secretary, Miss Ella Pardy. Conveners of Committees: Miss Anita Tolman, Miss Bessie Johnston, Miss D. Thurston, and H. Long.

The next October, in 1922, eight large bales of clothing were shipped to the far north by the Ladies' Aid Society of Cooksville Methodist Church, to people who had suffered from fires. The Bethesda congregation at Dixie supplied $130 in cash; and Sheridan sent more than $60. At this time, also, the first meeting of the Women's Missionary Society, recently organized, was held at the parsonage.

During the summer of 1923, a Monster Garden Party, under the auspices of the Bible Class, was held on the Cooksville Fair Grounds, with the proceeds in aid of the Church Building Fund, following a storm which did severe damage to the Church. A baseball game was played at 6 p.m., after which an attractive programme was presented. The Howard Park Methodist Church Orchestra, of Toronto, provided music; and local people joined in with their talents. James Esplin, Comedian; Angus Tolman, Baritone, and Miss Pearl Quinnell, Soprano, accompanied by Miss Ethel Braithwaite; Mercer Garbutt, Saxophonist; Gordon B. Jackson, Tenor Soloist; and Miss Gladys Stewart, Elocutionist, all added to the fun and entertainment.

At the beginning of June, 1925, the Cooksville Methodist Church

Cooksville United Church, Dundas Street. (Photo: courtesy of the Copeland family)

was crowded to the doors for a special Jubilee service, with a big 100-voice choir drawn from the local and surrounding churches singing magnificent anthems. Originally the centre of the settlement circuit, over one hundred years before, Cooksville Methodist Church had been the centre of activity since its beginning. The brick Church, erected thirty-five years before, still had over 350 members in the district; the oldest members, in 1925, were Mrs H. Langdon, aged ninety-nine years; and two brothers, Daniel F. and Samuel Emerson Harris. The Pastor was the Reverend Bell Smith.

During that year of 1925, after much discussion, Methodists, Congregationalists, and some Presbyterians, joined together to form the United Church of Canada; and Cooksville Methodist Church thenceforth became Cooksville United Church.

In May, 1927, at the Annual Meeting of the Cooksville United Church, the following officers were elected:

Session – L. D. Sanderson, P. A. Christie, W. Irwin, T. E. Brown, S. Patchett, P. Pardy, C. H. Bradford, Mrs Duff, and Miss Readman.

Stewards – W. Irwin, L. D. Sanderson, Mr Dulmage, P. A. Christie, Rev. J. E. Bailey, George Dyer, Sam Harris, Rupert Pickett, and John Ezard.

Representatives to Presbytery – L. D. Sanderson, and Orange L. Lawrence.

The Cooksville congregation numbered 103, with a Sunday School membership of 150. Approximately $1,400 had been raised in Cooksville during the previous year.

A number of special services were held. On the Sunday following the Annual Meeting, the Reverend S. J. T. Fortner, of Streetsville, occupied the pulpit, while a choir composed of the mothers of the congregation supplied the music.

In October, 1944, Cooksville United Church celebrated its 100th Anniversary, commemorating the work of Cooksville's two churches, the first lath and plaster (roughcast) Church on Agnes Street, and the brick Church erected in 1887. The Pastor in the Anniversary Year was the Reverend A. E. Owen.

In 1957, the congregation of Cooksville United Church moved to their new site, located south of King Street West, on Mimosa Row.

Chapter 25: Rosemount Farm

UNDER THE PATENT dated December 9, 1807, for Lot 20 on the South Side of Dundas Street, William Barber was granted all two hundred acres, which were later owned by William Blackley. In 1834, Mr Blackley sold one hundred acres to an innkeeper named Stanous Daniell, for 100 pounds sterling. This property was inherited by James Daniell, and in *The Streetsville Review* of October 7, 1854, James Daniell's son William placed an advertisement stating that the farm was To Let.

On January 18, 1859, William Daniell became the owner; and in the year 1871, John Callanan came down from Streetsville and bought the whole hundred acres.

William A. Callanan was born on January 20, 1880, in a log cabin on the north side of Dundas Street and two weeks later, when his mother died, he was taken across the road to live in the homestead owned by his grandfather. In his later years, Mr Callanan, who was the last Callanan to live in the farmhouse, always remembered it as 'the old house,' and that it had fourteen rooms, with an outside kitchen extending out at one side; the rest of the house was encircled by a three-sided verandah. The beams of the house were hand-hewn, eight inches square, and the rooms were large, with wide hallways; its front door was surprisingly wide, as

Original Callanan Farmhouse, Dundas Highway, 1918. (Photo: Mary Anne Kelly)

Callanan Farm, Dundas Street West, looking south (now Huron Park), 1926; ploughed (fallow) field is where the baseball diamond is now. (Photo: Mary Anne Kelly)

William A. Callanan,
Callanan Farm in Cooksville.
(Photo: Mary Anne Kelly)

Beatrice Watson (Callanan)
visiting Callanan Farm, in
1918. (Photo: Mary Anne
Kelly)

compared with those of any other houses he had known.

John Callanan's grandson William continued to live in the old house, and to carry on in farming. In 1924, he and his wife, Beatrice Watson, were operating the Rosemount Farm, with plans under way for building a new house on the property. Mrs Callanan, who had been a bookkeeper at the St. Lawrence Starch Company, kept a wonderful Household Book in which she wrote faithful accounts of all events which took place, and from this book we are able to record the following information about people who once lived and worked on the Rosemount Farm, at Rural Route No. 2, Cooksville, Ontario.

* * *

ROSEMOUNT FARM:

1924
 – Sold Milk and Cream to Credit View Dairy

1924-25
 – Had Cattle, Horses, Swine, Poultry
 – Grew Tree Fruits, Small Fruits, and Strawberries
       Butter Beans, Green Beans, Vegetables, Onions, and Potatoes
       Flowers, Dahlias, Gladiolas
 – also, Cream, Milk, Alsike (clover) and Hay

1925
 – Had Pigs (Swine)
 – Poultry: sold nest eggs, for setting as well as eating
       sold 15 hens, at 21 cents a pound, $14.49
       also, old hens and roosters, $20.75
 – Traded 1 Horse for 2 Cows
 – Sold Butter, Apples (Greenings, Spies, Sweets),
       Black Currants, Raspberries, Strawberries and Cherries,
       Butter Beans, Potatoes and Onions

1925
 – Working on Farm, 5 Men (James Gaitland, George Britton,
       Cyril Boyes, William Kennedy, Wilfred Miller)

1925-26
 – Milk, Buttermilk and Cream sold to Credit View Dairy

1926
 – Names of Calves and Cows (bought and sold): Spot, Star, Wild Cow,
       Black Heifer, Vera, Daisy, Mousy Calf, Blossom, Kelly and Beauty
 – Name of Horse: Charlie

217

Callanan Farm Cattle coming up the hillside, where today the path
leads up to Lions Garden on Dundas Street West, above Huron Park.
(Photo: Mary Anne Kelly)

- Gave Thos. Mashinter 25 Bu. of Oats for use of Ross Binder,
    (threshing tool)
- Were serving Meals to threshers on the Farm
1928
- Apr. 21, sold 8-lb. Hen at 20 cents a lb., $1.60
    1 old Hen, 5 lbs. for $1.00
    2 young Roosters for $2.00
- Crops Grown: Hay, Barley
- Vegetables: Corn, Turnips, Carrots, Beets, Cucumbers, Lettuce,
    Beans and Potatoes
- Fruit: Black Currants, Raspberries, Plums
1928-29
- Inventory
    10 Cows, 2 Horses, 2 Calves, 2 Heifers, 30 Hens
    Land: 50 acres
    2 Houses (Homestead and New House)
    Buildings: Barn, Hen House, Milk House

BUILDING THE HOUSE:

- Started 1924
- In March and April, George Beamish delivered 782 blocks.
- In May, the Cooksville Brick Co. delivered 8,000 bricks, and 10 loads of sand and gravel, and by May 30, William Kelly was sawing logs for the house.
- Through July, J. H. Pinchin delivered 12 bags of cement; George Devlin put in a water system; and five more loads of sand and gravel were obtained, by means of a horse deal instead of cash.
- In August, 2 kegs of Nails were obtained from the St. Lawrence Starch Co.
- In September, tile was bought for a manhole cistern and Joe Lolato put in a drain; Robinson and Simpkins did the carpenter work, using lumber delivered by William E. Savage. The walls were lathed and plastered with lime and cement, also using a 24-pound bag of hair, bought from Thomson Bros. The plastering was done by G. G. Haddon.
- At the beginning of December, J. A. Walker began the painting; and J. E. Higgins installed the furnace for $165.00.
- The payments by Feb. 1925, amounted to $3,121.24.
- On March 31st, the account book stated that 'Tree Fruits were given on account, $6.00, and Vegetables, $11.65, to Hartwick and Haddon; 1 Barrel of Apples, $3.00, to the Bricklayer; and 1 Barrel of Apples to L. Robinson, for putting on Tar Paper.'
- The final item, on November 29, 1926, 1 gal. of Spar Varnish, purchased for the Floors, $5.82.

ROSEMOUNT TOURIST HOME:

Now that the new house was finished, in the spring of 1925, the Callanans decided to start the new Rosemount Tourist Home Business, and the first requirement purchased for this, on August 25th, was a new Cot and Mattress, for the sum of seven dollars.

The next articles, meticulously written down by Mrs Callanan, in her Household Account book were: frying pan, 70 cents; mirror, 15 cents; a quart of white enamel, 35 cents; white paint, 50 cents; and 7 pounds of Galvanized tin, 98 cents, was needed for some unspecified purpose.

It was also considered wise to obtain, for opening day, 2 Pennants for 50 cents, 2 Flags for 50 cents, and 4 Flags for $1.20.

Rosemount Tourist Lodge, with sign on house; Mr and Mrs Callanan sitting on the steps. (Photo: Mary Anne Kelly)

During September, there were added the following; 2 1/2 yards of Oilcloth, $1.25; 3 prs. Towels at 55 cents each, and 3 Tea Towels at 33 cents each.

For the kitchen: an Egg Turner, 6 cents; Skewers, 20 cents; Flour Sifter, 27 cents; Glasses, 30 cents; Rolling Pin, 30 cents; Chloride of Lime, 15 cents. A Hinge and Catch, at 40 cents, were needed for the Screen Door.

Near the end of September, a Bed Spring for a Double Bed was bought for $4.90; 5 yards of 60-inch sheeting (for single beds), $1.95; 2 yards of Tea Towelling, 66 cents.

A new Clothes Line was bought for 35 cents; 8 Clothes Hooks, 10 cents, and 6 Hangers, 24 cents, were also needed.

For the dining room table, Mrs Callanan bought a new Centrepiece for 30 cents, and a Call Bell for 19 cents.

Finally, a Road Map was bought for 50 cents, and the Piano was tuned for $5.00, making a total outlay to date, of $36.54.

Expenses for the beginning of the actual operation of the business consisted of Food, bought from Alex O'Brien's Grocery Store:

Steak, at 25 cents a lb; Sausage, at 25 cents a lb; Bacon, at 40 cents a lb; and Roasts of Beef, at 70 cents to $1.00 each.

Bread cost 11 cents per loaf; Eggs, 45 cents a dozen; Cream was 5 cents, and 100 Paper Napkins, 25 cents.

Other needs were: Fly Tox, 40 cents; Fly Pads, 10 cents; Tacks, 10 cents; Ink, 15 cents; Phone, 10 cents; and 1 gal. of Gasoline, 30 cents. In September, 4 more gallons of Gasoline cost $1.20.

The total Expenses for August and September, 1925, amounted to $51.48.

The Receipts for the Rosemount Tourist Home, for Rooms and Meals, during this period can be read today, recorded faithfully in this remarkable little household book:

Suppers were served at 50 cents each; Breakfasts at 50 cents each.

2 Rooms (5 people), $10.00

1 Room (1 person), $1.50

1 Room (3 people) and 3 Breakfasts, $4.50

Young Boy's Breakfast, 25 cents

1 Single Room (2 boys), $1.00

Chicken Dinners were served at $1.00 each

– 8 Breakfasts were served on one morning, and 6 Suppers on one day.

Through August and September, up to October 3rd, the total receipts for Meals, $62.75; and Rooms, $89.90, amounted to $152.65.

Tips, noted down for August and September, were: from Mr Garrett, 50 cents, and from John Cestone, 50 cents, a total of $1.00.

The Rosemount Tourist Camp collected a total of $3.00, for 2 cars and 6 people.

Sales to Tourists, from the Rosemount Farm, still being kept in complete operation by William Callanan, amounted to:

3 quarts of Milk, at 12 cents each;

3 eggs, at 10 cents, and 1/2 dozen eggs, at 30 cents;

1 basket of Plums, at 50 cents; and 1 pint of Milk, at 7 cents.

Altogether, the Farm collected a total of $1.33. The Receipts for the 1925 season of the Rosemount Tourist Business added up to a total of $165.65.

Expenses of House, plus Advertisement and Equipment bought, was $88.02, leaving the Net Profit of $68.63.

Thus was this new business on Callanan's farm well begun, with the neat books being kept by Mrs Callanan, in her fine clear writing.

The Rosemount Tourist Home re-opened on April 30th, 1926, with the serving of a dinner for 'Dr Hart, 50 cents,' and continued to progress successfully. People who called there were made welcome, and served with every nicety of life that the Callanans themselves could provide.

One pound of Tea cost 75 cents, and apples were readily available on the farm; and it was a treat to call in for Tea and Apple Pie, or for one of Mrs Callanan's Steak Dinners. From Mead's Butcher Shop, she bought 5-lb. Sirloin Roasts for $1.00, a 6-lb. Picnic Ham for $1.50, and a 4-lb. Roast of Pork for $1.00.

In 1926, the Rosemount joined the Canadian Tourist Club, and erected a sign at their front gate. This sign was kept illuminated at night, at first by a gate light using coal oil.

At the end of August, Mr Ewing came and wired the gate light for $10.50, and put into it 2 coloured bulbs and 1 white bulb, for $1.75.

Everything to make guests feel special was provided; the table had good linen, with a silence cloth underneath.

That year, George Middleton and Jack Kelly came to board at the Rosemount Farm.

When the fruit was ready, in August, fruit jars and rubber rings were bought, along with 100 lbs. of Sugar, $6.70, for preserving. The prices set down under Household Expenses, on August 31, 1926, were: 40 quarts raspberries, $8.00; 6-quart basket cherries, 25 cents, 11-quart basket, 50 cents; 6-quart basket black currants, $1.00, an 11-quart basket, $2.00; 10 quarts raspberries, $2.00; and 5 6-quart baskets cherries, $1.00.

Another boarder, Leonard Hall, arrived in June, 1927, and during 1927 and 1928, the Callanans had tourists in the homestead house, and in the new house rooms, as well.

A new Bed Spring and Mattress, a Bedspread, more Towels and Sheeting were ordered; a new Mirror for a Dresser was also needed. A new Ironing Cord cost 40 cents, and a Mangle was purchased for $2.00, from V. C. Hector.

Tips, Mrs Callanan faithfully noted down, alongside the names of the people who left them:

Mr and Mrs Martin, 25 cents;
Mrs Heaney, 25 cents;
Mr Weichel, $1.00;
Mr Reynmuth, 50 cents;
Mrs Martin, 25 cents;
Mrs Trenholm, 25 cents;

Mrs Andrews, 10 cents (to make even money);

Mr and Mrs Naskrit, 75 cents.

Total, for July and August, $4.60.

Every purchase and every payment remains carefully written down, to show us, today, the prices of yesterday. A Wick for the Oil Stove cost 45 cents; Coal for the Stove was $72.18; a Visitors' Book, from Grand and Toy, cost $4.00; and 5 gallons of Coal Oil was $1.25.

Seven Eggs, from their own farm, were valued at 5 cents each, with 'Dad' collecting the 35 cents.

In 1928, Dr McFadden, from Cooksville, made house calls at $1.00 per visit, and received $2.00 for the medicine.

Dr Frawley, and Dr Emmett, were also practising at that time; and the Callanan family visited Dr Dudgeon, the dentist at Port Credit.

Regarding clothing, a man could buy a good Grey Suit for $25.00, and a Snap Brim Hat for $4.00. A woman's Black Velvet Hat was $8.00. Silk Stockings were $2.50 a pair, and enough Georgette to make a pretty dress cost $2.71. Twenty-four Yards of Gingham, for 6 House Dresses, cost $4.32; and Mrs Callanan could buy 9 Yards of Flannelette to make Nightgowns for $2.52. New Shoes ranged in price from $5.00 to $7.50, and in 1929, people went to the shoemaker to have new soles put on them for one dollar.

On May 14, 1929, the Bell Telephone Company installed, for $2.00, a telephone in the Rosemount Tourist Home, and the charge of $1.85 for service up to June 30 brought the total amount to $3.85.

Later, when a new baby arrived at the Callanan home she was wrapped in a Wool Shawl, purchased for $4.50; her gowns were sewn of Nainsook, a lovely light material, at 50 cents a yard, with Embroidered Flouncings and yards of Lace. Her knitted Bonnets were tied with Pink Rosettes, and she had White Pullovers, and a pair of little White Moccasins.

In August, Mr Holland came and re-modelled a crib to a cot, for which he was paid $5.00. The little cot was lined with 4 yards of Pink Sateen, and two Blankets were bought, 'Clown' and 'Teddy Bear,' for 98 cents.

Rena Burlin came to Rosemount Tourist Lodge to do Cleaning and Scrubbing; and later on, Caroline came.

Wall Paper, along with 2 lbs. of Wallpaper Paste and 1 lb. of Glue Sizing, were bought for three upstairs bedrooms, at $9.52; and 7 1/2

Yards of Marquisette, for making the Sun Room Curtains, cost $1.05.

In 1930, the price of a Stamp for a letter was duly noted in the Household Book as being 2 cents; and a child's Haircut was 25 cents.

Amid all the miscellaneous expenses of operating this family-owned Tourist Home, the Church was never forgotten. The nearest Roman Catholic Church, at the time, was in Port Credit, on the Lakeshore Road, and the Callanans were faithful in attendance. Carefully recorded were their contributions, as 'Church (Pew 10, Plate 10, Candle 10, Paper 5) – 35 cents.'

Through the Depression days, Rosemount Farm continued in operation, with Feed for the Chickens obtained at Copeland's, in Cooksville: 100 lbs. Scratch, $1.59; 100 lbs. Laying Mash, $1.69; 400 lbs. Maize Meal, $5.40; Oyster Shell, 40 cents; and 50 lbs. of Oats (from their own farm) 60 cents. At that time, Eggs were selling for 30 cents a dozen.

The farm was still in business, collecting Milk cheques from the Dairy; and they were advertising in *The Toronto Globe* and *The Toronto Evening Telegram*.

After World War II, some of the prices recorded by Mrs Callanan, in 1949, were as follows:

Taxi Ride home from Port Credit, $1.00
Curtains, $7.50
Shampoo and set, $1.25
Bus to the City, 65 cents
Board for Son, $8 per week
Telephone Call, 5 cents
Basin Plug, 5 cents
Dish Cloths, 2 for 10 cents
Cleaning, pink wool dress, 96 cents
Theatre, 35 cents.
Canada Bread, 14 cents a loaf
Cooksville Dairy Milk, 18 cents a quart
1 lb. Butter, 74 cents
1/2 lb. Bacon, 41 cents
6 qt. Basket Peaches 85 cents; Grapes, 69 cents
1 Basket Carrots, 20 cents; Corn, 40 cents
Eggs, 50 cents a dozen.

From *Recipes For What Ails You,* in the Rosemount Tourist Home
Household Book:

Fruited Oatmeal Muffins (for Blood Building Diets)
Ingredients for 12 Muffins

3 T. Sugar	1 Egg
1 t. Salt	1 c. Milk
3 t. Baking Powder	1/4 c. Oil, melted Margarine or Butter
1 c. Flour	1/2 c. Seedless Raisins
1 c. Rolled Oats (quick cooking)	

Sift sugar, salt, baking powder and flour together twice, in large
bowl. Stir in rolled oats.

Break egg into small bowl and beat well; add milk to egg, then the
oil.

Stir raisins into the flour mixture.

Grease muffin tins.

Make a well in centre of flour mixture; pour in liquid mixture, into
the well, all at once.

Stir just enough to combine dry and wet ingredients. The batter
should have a rough appearance.

Fill greased tins 2/3 full.

Bake 400 degrees (F) – 25 to 30 minutes.

* * *

William Callanan kept the Rosemount Tourist Home house, which
he himself had built, but the 'old house' was sold.

The Port Credit News of October 28, 1936, reported that: 'Mr W. A.
Callanan held a clearing auction sale on his farm on the Dundas
Highway, on Thursday. In spite of the rain, there was a large attendance.
Around 4 o'clock a count was made and it was estimated that there were
nearly a hundred cars and trucks parked around the farm. W. A. Russell
was the Auctioneer.'

* * *

In 1961, thirty-three acres of Rosemount Farm were sold to form
part of Huron Park. Today, William Callanan's Rosemount house still
stands, at 840 Dundas Street West, beside the Lions Garden; the
pioneer homestead house, next door, on its right, was demolished in the

The new house on Rosemount Farm (today, 840 Dundas Street West). (Photo: Mary Anne Kelly)

Swimming in the creek which still flows through Huron Park. (Photo: Mary Anne Kelly)

summer of 1975, and in its place at the top of the hill overlooking Huron Park, at 880 Dundas Street West, there stands today a modern, high-rise building.

Chapter 26: The Doctors

IN SMITH'S CANADIAN GAZETTEER of 1846, there is one physician and surgeon listed in the village of Cooksville, in Canada West; and in the 1850-51 Directory for the Home District, his name is given as W. P. Crewe, MD and JP. Dr William Pool Crewe came to Canada from Newcastle under Lyme, England, and bought 100 acres of Lot 14, on the south side of Dundas Street, for three hundred pounds sterling. On this site he built Stafford House, a 15-room building in which he used five of the rooms as surgical suites. He made long house calls, travelling on foot, on horseback, or by horse-drawn buggy or sleigh. Patients came to him from many parts of Canada West and, for a time, Stafford House was known as a temporary hospital. Dr Crewe died in 1861 at the age of sixty-four, and was buried in the Dixie Union Cemetery.

The W. H. Smith Register of 1851 lists the name of Dr G. C. Cotter, as Professional Man, at Cooksville; and on June 3rd, 1854, in *The Streetsville Review*, Edwy. Ogden Jr. was advertising his services as a Physician and Surgeon, at Cooksville, CW (Canada West).

Dr John Ogden was the Cooksville area's doctor during 1873; and in 1891, Dr R. K. Anderson arrived in Cooksville to be appointed Medical Health Officer for Toronto Township. Dr Anderson was a graduate of the Medical Department of Victoria University, and a Member of the College of Physicians and Surgeons of Ontario. His office and residence, located on the Centre Road, south of the Cooksville four corners, was said to be a 'pretty structure.'

At this time, Dr Wilkinson, Dentist, began visiting Cooksville on the second and fourth Friday of each month, with his office located in King's Hotel. He kept this office until January, 1890, when his practice was taken over by Dr W. J. Laker, of Toronto. Two years later, in 1892, Dr T. T. Harris, a Dental Surgeon from Oakville, began making visits to the same Cooksville House hotel.

In 1892, Dr Silverthorn MD was taking care of patients at Port Credit, and when Mrs Schiller's youngest son fell over a box in her store, a news item in the paper stated that he had been treated by Dr Silverthorn.

Dr Marshall Sutton's house, Centre Road, south of Dundas Street.
(Photo: Mississauga Central Library, Cooksville Vol. 1, #42)

It was in February of the following year, 1893, that Marshall Sutton
MD arrived to move into the house on the Centre Road and take over the
practice of Dr Anderson. Dr Sutton was born in Clandeboye, Middlesex
County in 1851, and graduated in 1878 from the Toronto Medical
School. He took several graduate degrees abroad, and afterward
practised in North Dakota before coming to Cooksville. Dr Sutton
became well-known for miles around, as he travelled about by horse and
buggy, or by sleigh in wintertime. He kept two valuable horses, and a
quantity of hay and oats in a small barn on his property, near the road.

Dr Marshall Sutton was Township Medical Officer for many years,
and was also appointed Coroner for Peel County. His two sons, Arthur
and Harold, both graduated in Medicine. Dr Arthur B. Sutton became
Port Credit's doctor, while Dr Harold C. Sutton, his younger brother,
went overseas as a Lieutenant in the Royal Army Medical Corps, during
World War I.

In 1914, Dr Edgar J. Leary was appointed Medical Officer of Health
at a salary of $50, replacing Dr Sutton and opening an office in part of

the residence of H. K. Bowden, adjoining the Cooksville Pharmacy. Throughout the spring of that year, Dr Leary reported a number of contagious diseases, at least one of which was diphtheria. At the beginning of September, 1915, Dr Leary also left Cooksville to take up duties in a Military Hospital overseas.

During the War years, in 1916, Dr Marshall Sutton was injured in a serious runaway accident. As he was driving east on the back line (Burnhamthorpe Road), while coming down the hill towards the Centre Road, his horse started to run and kick. The doctor tried to control it but he was thrown into the ditch at the corner, and the horse broke away from the buggy and ran down to the village. Some neighbours who saw the accident hurried to his aid, and he was taken out from under the buggy and conveyed to his home. His son, Dr Arthur, was called and said that as far as could be found, his father had several ribs broken and his left arm injured.

Although he seemed to have recovered from his injuries, and was able to go about the village again, three months later, in November, Dr Sutton died. He had practised his profession in Cooksville for twenty-three years, and was said to be intimately identified with most of the resident families in the district, all of whom held him in high esteem. His parents had been of United Empire Loyalist stock, and Dr Marshall Sutton was buried in the little cemetery close by the Dixie Union Chapel.

Dr Austin H. McFadden, from Toronto, opened his medical office in May of 1917, when he leased the premises in the rear of the old Revere House. The following September, he leased the fine new residence which had been erected by the late Mr H. H. Shaver, on the corner of Cook Street.

* * *

On November 19, 1918, *The Brampton Conservator* reported that Cooksville was in the front rank when it came to celebrating the signing of the armistice, and the end of World War I. The women of the village were the first to celebrate, when the news came; at five o'clock in the morning they were on the corner, singing patriotic songs, and the crowd grew, with everyone joining in. At six o'clock, copies of *The Conservator Extra* that had been printed to spread the good news were being eagerly seized and read; and all day long, the people kept up the celebration, without any signs of ceasing or slackening.

Telephones were kept ringing, arranging for a big gathering of the citizens of the whole district, that night. By the evening, everyone who could get there from any part of the Township had arrived, and the vigour and enthusiasm became greater than ever. Reeve D. H. McCaugherty was there with the members of the Township Council and, from the balcony of George Bowers' Cooksville Hotel, addresses were delivered to the crowd.

The balcony was beautifully illuminated, and had never before looked so attractive. A choir had been gathered to lead in the singing of hymns and patriotic songs. Those who addressed the crowds were Messrs. Hamilton and Terry, of Lorne Park and Clarkson; the Reverend H. V. Thompson and J. L. Ross, of Erindale; D. E. Hughes, of Port Credit; and S. Charters, MP of Brampton.

The Editor of the paper wrote: 'Cooksville saw a sight and heard words that will sink deep in the hearts of those who heard the speakers, for every address bore much weight on the duty of citizens in regard to the future of Canada.'

* * *

After the War, Dr Harold Sutton returned from overseas and took up the medical profession in the premises where his father had formerly lived. He had grown up in Cooksville, and Cooksville people thought it natural for him to come and take his father's place. Dr Harold did not have a horse and buggy; he owned a small coupe car in which he drove about the village making house calls. Dr Sutton's office had been one of the first to have a telephone wire connected, since the year 1902, and whenever an urgent call came in by telephone, Dr Harold would now drive out from his home to care for the sick person.

In 1922, Dr Girvin, a dentist from Toronto, began visiting dental patients on Mondays and Saturdays; and the following year, Dr Wilson, another dentist, arrived and announced that he would become a resident practitioner in Cooksville.

Dr McFadden remained in the office on the corner of Cook Street and, like Dr Sutton, he too made house calls. Even before the nineteen-twenties Cooksville was able to sustain two physicians, and Dr McFadden had his own practice, which did not interfere with that of Dr Sutton. He later lived in a beautiful stone house erected on land east of the Cooksville Creek, near Littlejohn Lane.

He was a good doctor who, in the days when back roads in winter

Dr A. H. McFadden's house, Dundas Street, east of Cooksville
Creek. (Photo: Mississauga Central Library, Cooksville Vol.1, #46)

were often covered in deep snow and uncleared for long periods, was
ready to answer an urgent call by travelling on snowshoes. He was one
who did much work for the public good of the community, as well. A
news item which appeared in *The Brampton Conservator* on July 23,
1923, gives some insight as to how he had progressed over the years, in
his relations with the people throughout the district: 'Dr McFadden
gave a number of the little lads of the village a rare treat last Friday
afternoon, indulging them to the sight of a Ball Game at the Island,
between the Toronto and Newark teams. Maybe the kiddies didn't enjoy
it – Just ask them!'

In September, 1925, Dr Harold Sutton's new red brick house, built
on the site of the old frame house on the Centre Road, was nearing
completion; and when it was finished, he made certain that there was
also a small frame garage, for his car, built on the left side of his
property, very close to the road. Dr Harold continued to tend the sick
people of Cooksville for many years.

However, Toronto Township lost one of its most outstanding citizens
when Dr A. H. McFadden died, in April of 1930, at the very young age
of forty-nine years. A native of Millbrook, Ontario; and a graduate of
the University of Toronto, he had lived in Cooksville for twelve years.

Dr A. H. McFadden.
(*The Port Credit News*,
April 11, 1930)

He was held in such high regard by all who knew him that his funeral, conducted from his family home, was one of the largest ever held in the history of Peel County. Traffic officers from the Provincial Police Department were on duty, and stopped all traffic on the Dundas Highway while the long cortege was wending its way to the Dixie Union Cemetery; it was reported that over a hundred and fifty vehicles were in the procession.

Chapter 27: The Bush Pilot

DURING WORLD WAR I, by the end of the summer of 1917, planes and engines for the training of pilots were arriving at Canadian flying fields, but when winter came and the snow was eighteen inches deep, these small Curtiss flying machines, being equipped only with landing wheels, were unable to land. The aerodromes at Camp Borden and Deseronto had to be closed and, from November, 1917 until April, 1918 the 42nd and 43rd wings of the Royal Flying Corps were sent south to Texas for their training.

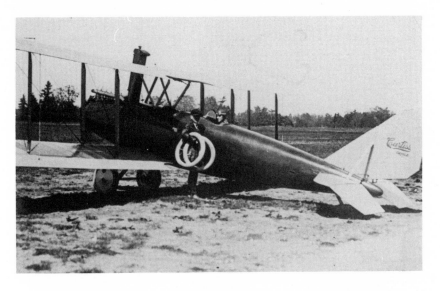

Curtiss Aeroplane at Long Branch Aerodrome, 1919. (Photo: Harold Hare Collection)

While this was going on, skis were being fitted to the planes in Canada, and proved so successful that flying courses could be resumed; and in the spring, when the two wings of the Royal Flying Corps returned from Fort Worth, young Clarence Schiller returned to Leaside Camp, in Toronto, with them. Thus it was that, in *The Streetsville Review* of April 11, 1918, there appeared, under the Cooksville News heading, the following story:

'This vicinity was awakened on Saturday morning from its time-wonted lethargy by the loud roar and humming of the engine of an aeroplane flying close to the earth.

'The dauntless aviator performed many a daring stunt for the benefit of the populace, dipping low between trees, skimming over the tops of buildings and wires – ascending to the clouds and dropping straight down in a nose dive, until one would think he was due for destruction, so close would he come to earth before elevating his plane and quickly ascending.

'The skilful pilot in charge was an old Cooksville boy, Lieut. Clarence Schiller, who is not yet 18. He has just returned from completing his pilot's course in Texas, and came out here from Leaside Camp to let the boys see what fun there is in the service.

233

Cooksville School, 1908 – Teachers: Miss Moffatt, Mr Brown.
(Photo: Region of Peel Archives, N367-23)

FRONT ROW: Irene Hodge, Maggie Martin, Phoebe Martin, Lillian
Park, Violet Harris, Viola Harris, Nell Stewart, unknown, Lily
Ellingham, Cecil Burrows, Leslie Burrows, Willy Law, Billy Mead,
Allan Mead, Melville Donnelly, Mabel McCauley, Susie McCauley.
2ND ROW: Osley Gummerson, Connie Stewart, Susie Brown, Jennie
Fieldhouse, Ina Heslop, Neita Tolman, Alice Stewart, Mary Brown,
Gladys Sherwood, Edith Green.
3RD ROW: Fred Green, Frank Birkett, Harold Gummerson, John
McCauley, Dudley Stewart, Charlie McCauley, Angus Tolman,
Oliver Harris, Walter Livingston, Vic Schiller, Fred Brunskill, Rena
Moore, Arthur Irwin, Bob Kee, **Duke Schiller**, Lloyd Moore, Percy
McKay, Harold Burrell, Arthur Currie, Archie Burrell, Leslie
Hopkins, Eleanor Barsotti, Louie Park, Jenny Livingston, Lily
Harris, Charlotte Ellingham.
TOP ROW: Frank Dolson, Nellie Donnelly, Minnie Goldthorpe,
Ethel Hodge, Margaret Donnelly, Mabel Birkett, Martha Thomas,
Miss Moffatt, Mr Brown, Carol Goodison, Mabel Clark, Gussie
Sherwood, Leatha Stewart, Jessie Fieldhouse, Maggie Curran,
Maggie Kee, Ethel Harris, Lola Irwin, Myrtle McKay, Harry
Tolman.

'He is one of the eldest sons of Donald Schiller, who formerly lived here, and now resides in Toronto.'

* * *

Following the end of World War I, on August 25th of 1919, Lieutenant C. A. (Duke) Schiller took part in the International Air Races between Toronto and New York, sponsored by the first Canadian National Exhibition held following the end of the war. Two contests were held, the Canadian race from Toronto to Mineola, New York, and back, and the American race following the same course but in the opposite direction, from New York to Toronto.

Twelve Canadian planes took part, among them the one being flown by Lieutenant Schiller. His Royal Highness, the Prince of Wales, opened the CNE that year, and was present when the Canadian flyers took off.

The weather was bad, with a high crosswind blowing; the worst section of the race was an area around Albany, where the high wires and tall city buildings posed a serious threat, causing many planes to crash while trying to make a landing. A letter, sent from the United States President to the Prince of Wales was unable to be delivered, and had to be delivered by post. One Canadian flyer carried a bag of air mail during the race, filled with letters bearing one-dollar stamps and the words: 'The First International Air Service, August, 1919, Toronto, Canada.' There was a large number of these letters, but the name of the airman who carried them was not disclosed.

The winner of the race was Major Schroeder, an American, who arrived back in Toronto on the 26th, after covering the round trip distance of approximately 1,142 air miles in 9 hours and 35 minutes.

Duke Schiller was not the winner, but he was happy to take part in this event. He loved to fly; indeed, it was said by many that he lived to fly. This young man who had attended classes in the little two-room Cooksville School on the Centre Road, north of Dundas Street, was to become a legend in the records of Canadian Aviation.

It was the year following the first World War that the Ontario Provincial Air Service was formed, and the men who were its original members were those young pilots of the Royal Flying Corps who had trained and served in the Great War. The original list included: G. A. (Tommy) Thompson, J. R. Ross, C. S. (Jack) Caldwell, J. Clark Ruse, C. J. (Doc) Clayton, Fred J. Stevenson, Pat J. Moloney, Ed. Burton, Terry Tully, Leonard J. Tripp, Harold Foley, R. Carter Guest, Jack Leach, and C. A. (Duke) Schiller.

235

The new Air Service began on May 23, 1924, with its base at Sudbury. They started late in the year in that first flying season, using Curtiss HS2L flying boats, called 'H-Boats.' On September 2, 1924, Duke Schiller flew an H-Boat in the Northern Ontario skies for 7 hours and 35 minutes.

These new planes had been obtained from the United States surplus stocks between the years 1921 and 1924. They were clumsy and lumbering, yet impressive-looking, and at that time they were considered to be immense. They were bi-planes, with a wingspan of 74 feet, and from the rear of their rudders to the tips of their hulls, they had a length of 38 feet. They measured 14 1/2 feet high, and were powered by a 12-cylinder, 360 horsepower engine called the Liberty. Their propellers were made of wood, and their engines had to be cranked by mechanics.

The plane could carry 700 pounds, and its 153 gallons of gasoline had a range of 300 miles. Its two cockpits carried the pilot and his mechanic, who made the necessary repairs whenever the plane made a forced landing. The only method of communicating with this plane was by sending telegraph messages, back and forth, to the railway stations along the way, and asking the agents if they had seen an aeroplane passing by.

Two bases were established, at Sudbury and Sioux Lookout, with a total of 13 flying-boats, 16 licensed pilots, and 19 licensed air engineers. In 1924, 2,595 flying hours were counted, spanning 170,000 air miles. During that season, a total of 597 forest fires were reported from the air.

The longest day's flying time was recorded on July 5, by C. J. Clayton, with 10 hours and 40 minutes spent on the forest fire patrol. In 1925, J. O. Leach flew 9 hours and 30 minutes; and T. B. Tully had the best weekly time, with 49 hours and 5 minutes. In 1926, C. A. (Duke) Schiller broke both of these records with a flying time of 12 hours and 10 minutes, on August 4th; and he was credited with 52 hours and 15 minutes as his time during one week.

In May, 1927, after Charles Lindbergh made the first flight across the Atlantic Ocean, the Carling Brewery Company at London, Ontario, offered a prize for the first Canadian to fly from London, Ontario to London, England. Duke Schiller travelled, with his mechanic Phil Wood, to Newfoundland, in a Stinson-Detroiter monoplane named the Royal Windsor, with the intention of trying for the prize. However, when Terry Tully and Jim Medcalf, two pilots who had set out on the

'Royal Windsor' aeroplane.
(Photo: courtesy of Bush Pilot
Heritage Museum, Sault Ste.
Marie)

The aeroplane which carried the first shipment of Christie's Biscuits
by Canadian air freight from Toronto to Windsor. (*The Streetsville
Review*, May 24, 1928)

Air Express Inaugurated. A new air route gives bi-weekly express
service in each direction between Toronto, Ottawa, Montreal, and the
steamship off Rimouski. (*The Streetsville Review*, May 31, 1928)

How planes will speed up delivery of letters; map shows how air mail will reach Toronto from Rimouski, and how much time and distance will be saved by the air route over the rail route. The time shown is the actual running time. (*The Streetsville Review*, May 17, 1928)

1) Shows how letters will be stamped 2) Postmaster Lemon, of Toronto 3) Steamer Empress of Scotland which brought the mail from the Old Country – mail was dropped off at the Rimouski dock, and taken by truck to the landing field there 4) Transcontinental Airways plane which brought mail from Rimouski to Montreal 5) 'Duke' Schiller, who will now pilot the Transcontinental plane on the airmail first leg 6) Canadian Airways Company plane, which will make the hop from Montreal to Toronto 7) H. S. Quigley, president of Canadian Airways 8) Louis Couture, president of Transcontinental Airways 9) Hon. P. J. Veniot, Postmaster-General at Ottawa, who had charge of the arrangements

day before, were unheard from and considered lost over the Atlantic, Duke Schiller re-considered the idea and changed his mind.

The first attempted east–to–west crossing of the Atlantic was made in 1928, in a Junkers plane called the Bremen. When this plane crash-landed on Greenly Island, in the Strait of Belle Isle, two Fairchild aircraft equipped with skis were sent from Lake Ste. Agnes, Quebec, to fly seven hundred miles to the rescue of the three men in the Junkers. The first Fairchild, piloted by Duke Schiller, carried Dr Louis Couisinier, through blinding snowstorms, to give whatever aid they could.

On this rescue mission, Lieutenant Schiller brought back to the Seven Islands base, Captain James Fitzmaurice, the second pilot of the Bremen, and the doctor. The relief plane was met by a representative of Christie Brown & Company Limited, and Mr Stewart of the Clarke Trading Company, who offered the occupants refreshments of hot coffee and Christie's biscuits, which were very much appreciated.

The Bremen Junkers aeroplane was taken to the United States, and renovated; and it can be seen today at the Ford Aeronautical Display, in the Museum at Dearborn, Michigan.

In 1929, the Northern Aerial Minerals Explorations Company was hiring pilots, with its base established at Sioux Lookout, Ontario, and Duke Schiller was hired for work on mining explorations. In August of that summer, the Loening Amphibian G-CATM, piloted by him, with Jack Humble as his assistant, ran out of gasoline near the Arctic Coast, between Baker Lake and Wager Inlet. Their passenger was Tom Creighton, a prospector, who had lived all his life in the north; he was said to be the founder of Flin Flon, and had been many years in The Pas.

After a full week of searching, the plane was located near Packashan Lake and, upon being refuelled, was flown back to Baker Lake by Duke Schiller. There were many gales and blizzards, and scarcely any shelter for an aircraft, which had to be landed on rocky shores and kept constantly anchored. When October came, and the northland became frozen over, the mining planes returned south.

The next stage in C. A. (Duke) Schiller's adventurous life began with the carrying of mail, freight, and passengers in Quebec and New Brunswick. Fairchild monoplanes were used, and were operated by Canadian Transcontinental Airways. Powered by Pratt and Whitney Wasp engines, these were the first engines to be used in commercial work in Canada.

Left, Duke Schiller; right, Al Torey. (Photo: courtesy of Barb Tindall)

Duke Schiller. (Photo: courtesy of Barb Tindall)

Planes delivered letters from Rimouski to Toronto, saving sixteen hours over train connections. The route gave twice-weekly express service, from the steamship off Rimouski; and on the Air Mail's first leg, the pilot of the Transcontinental plane was Duke Schiller who picked up the mail from the steamship 'Empress of Scotland' and carried it to Montreal.

Many rescue missions and other works in the northern bush lands were accomplished by Duke Schiller. In the records of the Canadian Bush Plane Heritage Centre, at Sault Ste. Marie, Ontario, Duke Schiller's employment rolls show that he was stationed at Sioux Lookout Air Base in 1937. At that time, he was the pilot of a Hamilton (CF-OAJ); his engineer was Knobby Clarke. During the years of World War II, Duke Schiller was ferrying planes across the Atlantic Ocean.

* * *

On March 18, 1943, *The Port Credit Weekly* reported the following: 'Captain Clarence Alvin (Duke) Schiller, the pioneer Canadian northland pilot and famed mercy flyer, died Sunday, in a ferry command crash at Bermuda, the Royal Air Force Ferry Command revealed today ... since the dawn of commercial aviation in this country, his name has been a legend among the airmen of North America.... Duke Schiller is a nephew of the late Mrs W. McKee, Centre Road, Cooksville, and also of the late Mr J. Bell, and was known by many in the Cooksville district.'

Chapter 28: Loyal Orange Lodge 1181

ON JULY THE TWELFTH, 1690, the Protestant forces of William of Orange, the new King of England, defeated the Roman Catholic troops of King James at the Battle of the Boyne, and after that day the 'Glorious Twelfth' was always celebrated as a holiday by the Protestants to emphasize their loyalty to the Crown. A secret society was formed with the object of maintaining Protestant succession to the British throne, and for the support of the Protestant religion in Great Britain and her colonies; and in 1861, the first Orange Hall in Toronto Township was erected on a corner of Lot 9, on the Lakeshore Road.

Up until 1864 members from Cooksville went down to meetings in this Hall, being taken there by William Kennedy, of Dixie, in his heavy

241

lumber wagon. A warrant for Loyal Orange Lodge 81 was granted in
1864, and Joseph Wright was elected Master of this first Cooksville
Lodge. Two years later, Mr Wright was succeeded by John C. Price,
who wore the heavy red merino robe and small tasseled cap which
belonged to his rank.

Mitchell's Gazetteer of 1866, under the Village of Cooksville, stated
that 'An Orange Lodge is held in the village, No. 1181, every
Wednesday on or before the full moon;' and by 1867, there were very
few villages which did not have a small building where Orange meetings
could be held. In 1885, Cooksville's Lodge moved to William Snowden's
house; and after a year, to the frame public hall which later became
known as Bowden's Hall.

At the beginning of December, 1909, Bro. J. B. Guthrey was
unanimously re-elected Worthy Master for the fourth time, and the
following officers were installed: Bros. John McKee, DM; John E. Bell
Sr., Chap.; H. K. Bowden, Recording Secretary; Robert McKee,
Treasurer; Wm. Snowden, Director of Ceremonies; and Robert Hall,
Lecturer.

Committee: Bros. Henry Gilmore, Wm. Bell, Sam Richey, R.
Crawford, and H. Richardson.

Tilers: Bros. W. William, and J. Buchanan. Auditors: Bros. George
Bowers, and Joseph Gilmore.

The Annual Ball took place in 1910 in the Township Hall; and at the
beginning of June, nine candidates received the Royal Arch degree.
Bros. Jas. and Jno. Elliott, Jas. Bonham and Thos. Wood, of Streetsville
Lodge, assisted the officers of Cooksville Lodge in the ceremony, which
occupied most of the night. The arduous duties of the evening were
happily enjoyed, even by the candidates who passed the ordeal quite
satisfactorily, convinced that they were much elevated thereby. The
destination of that year's celebration of the 12th of July was
unanimously decided to be Tottenham.

The Cooksville Orange Lodge was popular, and on July 9th, 1914, at
its Annual Garden Party held on the Cooksville Fair Grounds, almost
one thousand persons were in attendance. In addition to the residents of
Cooksville, many came from Port Credit, Dixie, Erindale, Streetsville,
and Brampton. The Port Credit Band played patriotic music and, at the
conclusion of the entertainments on the fair grounds, a large number of
young people stayed on for the dance in the Town Hall. The Lodge,
already one of the largest and most prosperous in the county, was in a

very healthy condition, and the ample proceeds from the Garden Party provided enough money to allow the members to travel to Shelburne for the Annual Celebration.

Each year, garden parties held by the Orangemen raised money for the celebrations, and it was said that the entire population of Toronto Township came out to enjoy themselves. In 1915, the members, accompanied by the Port Credit Brass Band, travelled on the morning CPR train to Brampton, with Jas. Guthrey as Master, and H. K. Bowden, Secretary.

At the beginning of January, 1917, John C. Price, a Charter Member of LOL 1181, died. Mr Price had been Worthy Master for almost fifteen years, with great acceptance by all members.

In February, a committee was appointed to negotiate for a new Banner to be carried in the next 12th of July parade, the old Banner having served its usefulness for the past twenty-five years. At the end of that month, a concert under the auspices of the Lodge was held in the completely packed Town Hall. Talented Scottish entertainers, the Laurie Brothers and Sister, made their first appearance, delighting everyone with their singing and dancing. Miss Emma Thompson read stories and recited; Duncan Cowan's excellent singing, and neat and natty appearance caught the crowd, who gave him two encores. Mrs Westlick was the accompanist for the evening; and the Lodge received a good surplus for their new Banner.

Cooksville LOL 1181 grew more and more popular, and the feeling that animated the Cooksville Orangemen was stated succinctly in *The Brampton Conservator*: 'There is no reason why the guilt and treason should ever be forgot. This was the feeling that animated Cooksville LOL 1181, when annually on the Fifth of November, the date of the never-to-be-forgotten Gunpowder Plot, the members and their wives and friends gathered to celebrate one of the most famous events in English history.'

In the Township Hall at Cooksville, three hundred people sat down to a fowl supper that was meant to live in the annals of the Lodge as one of the best ever. 'Such a spread! Fowl cooked as the good housewives of the neighbourhood know how to cook it; salads of the good Irish spud, and other ornamental but less tasty vegetables; jellies, celery, pie, cake, and fruit in the greatest abundance, with the best tea and coffee in which to drink the toasts.' James Guthrey, County Master, called on Deputy Grand Master Grey, of Toronto, to take the chair after the

Orange Parade, Cooksville, on Dundas Street, c. 1922. (Photo:
Region of Peel Archives 86.0051M, H166-4)

Dundas Street, Orange Parade, (another view) c. 1922. (Photo:
Mississauga Central Library, Cooksville Vol. 1, #33)

guests had done full justice to the artistic cooking of the ladies, and the speech-making was of the kind that thrill loyal Orangemen.

Past Deputy Master Powers spoke on the significance of the Fifth of November, of the coming of William of Orange, the Gunpowder Plot, and the crossing of the Boyne. He spoke of these as the great and momentous dates in the history of the British Empire, saying that from the events which took place on those dates, the British Empire had achieved its greatness. With earnest appeal, Mr Powers begged his hearers to remember that they were living in critical times, and that it behooved all loyal Orangemen and all loyal citizens to stand staunchly by their principles, and to cement their loyalty by taking a firm stand on behalf of King, Country, and Flag.

Other speakers were Major Kennedy, MPP, and S. Charters, MP, and after the speech-making there was singing of popular and patriotic airs, under the direction of Bert King. Mrs Stewart also gave a clever rendition of 'The Courtship of Saunders McGlashan.' The patriotic decorations of the Hall, the glowing lights and prettily decorated tables made a scene which brought many hearty compliments to the committee in charge.

In 1925, the Loyal Orange members were told they must leave their old Hall, which made them feel badly. The Orangemen used the upstairs of the frame building which had once been the public hall connected with the old Schiller House hotel, while an Insurance Company also shared the same hall. However, the building had been sold to William Copeland and was about to be torn down, and at that time, the Lodge began holding their meetings in the Public School. Faced with the necessity of finding new quarters for their Lodge room, the Orangemen bought a lot on Agnes Street from Mr Morris, of Erindale, and began making plans to erect a new Hall.

Cooksville made history, in 1925, by celebrating the Glorious Twelfth in splendid fashion. For the first time, L.O.L. 1181 was host to about 4,500 visitors on the fair grounds, with twenty-two Lodges present, seven of these being Ladies' Lodges. The weatherman smiled and everyone had a really good time. All Orange Lodges held a big Annual Parade on the Twelfth of July, the only real requisites required to distinguish it from other parades being 'King Billy,' riding on a white horse, and orange sashes worn by the marchers. The horses could not really always be white, but for the most part they were.

Lodge members marching in Cooksville's first great parade were

The Annual County Meeting

—OF—

THE LOYAL ORANGE ASSOCIATION

of the County of Peel will be held in the Methodist Church, Cooksville, on Tuesday, February 3rd, at 2 p.m. All officers and members requested to attend.

ROBT. SHAW,
County Master.

W. H. McKENNA,
Rec.-Sec.

The Brampton Conservator, January 29, 1925

from: Sandhill 184; Brampton 5; Brampton 10; Union Streetsville 263; Bolton 146; Caledon 293; Campbell's Cross 76; Port Credit 163; Brampton Young Britons; Huttonville 211; Castle Dawson 2799; Credit Valley (Streetsville) YB 142; and Cooksville 1181. There were also ladies from the True Blues, Caledon East; LOBA Harmony, Port Credit; LOBA Jeanie Gordon, Streetsville; LOBA Cooksville; LOBA Tullamore; LOBA Brampton.

The 1925 parade of the numerous lodges, lodge bands, and brass bands, from the fair grounds to the CPR Station and back, was a brilliant spectacle, and the route of the march through the village was lined all along the way with visitors. Huttonville Lodge won the prize for best dress; Queen Alexandra Brampton was the pick of the Lady Lodges. Brampton's Brass Band was awarded First Prize; Scarlet Plains Lodge, West Toronto, had the best Flute Band. Sand Hill Lodge out-pulled the others in a Tug-of-War contest.

In 1926, the Orangemen left the school to hold their meetings in the Town Hall. In 1927, their old frame Orange Hall was torn down, with a part of it being left and moved a little to the south, to be used by Mr Copeland as a storehouse and garage. The same year, a new chapter was written in the history of Orangeism when the Cooksville LOL 1181 passed a resolution to begin work on their new Hall.

The Lodge was in flourishing condition, and on July 12th, at the parade in Guelph, Arthur Herd was accorded the credit of winning First Prize in appearance. The members wore white trousers, white shoes, dark coats, and light straw hats; and they were accompanied by the Bugle Band of the 17th Canadian Troop of Boy Scouts.

For the Annual Banquet in November, that year, those who had prepared the feast sent out invitations, and gave their services as a gift to the new Hall. Tables were set the length and breadth of the Township Hall, which was gaily decked with Union Jacks for the occasion. Masses of red and white asters decorated the tables, with an orange ribbon running down the centre of each.

Following the dinner, Past County Master James Guthrey made the new Hall the subject of his address. 'We want funds,' he said; 'you will find me at the little table on the west side of the Hall, while the dance is in progress.'

So successful was this appeal that Brother Guthrey had the honour of handing over to the treasurer of the Building Fund $300 in cold hard cash from donors, before they left the Hall. He received a 'Bravo! Bro.

Guthrey!' for that made a grand total of $1,465 in funds on hand.

After dinner, the speech-makers were Reverend H. V. Thompson, of Erindale; Reverend E. Harden, of Cooksville; and Robert Crawford. Colonel Kennedy recalled pioneer days in the southern part of Peel County, when times were hard and desolate. 'But,' he said, 'the same spirit that kept the Orange alive three hundred years ago was in the people who settled not only in the south, but in the entire area of Peel.'

Robert Crawford had a dozen of his best stories; and George Duck came up from Port Credit to sing. Miss Carmen Scott, of Brampton, furnished several readings; and Lex Schrag played the flute. Sandy Rankin, also from Port Credit, sent his audience into gales with his Scotch songs and monologues and completely won over the crowd until they didn't want to let him go. Mrs Arnott McClure, in magnificent voice, sang four times; and Mrs McMichael and Mrs Schrag were the accompanists for the evening.

That evening, the Lodge Brothers had set the tables, served and cleared them themselves, though when dish-washing time came, the ladies washed while the men wiped the dishes dry. The proceeds of the evening's entertainment amounted to one hundred dollars, and was also donated to the Building Fund.

Other suppers and concerts were held to raise money; and on July 12th, 1928, the Cooksville Lodge hosted another remarkably fine church parade, held on a Sunday evening when many local and visiting lodges marched with them to the Dixie Presbyterian Church. Over two hundred brethren and sisters lined up for the long hot walk. They kept the line wonderfully well in spite of the intense heat, and of the fact that many of the marchers had already taken part in the afternoon parade at Brampton.

Cooksville Young Britons were ahead, the Union Jack being carried by Fred House, followed by the New Toronto Scouts' Trumpet Band. The young lads carried their flags, with the colour bearers being: King's Colours – Eddie Bowyer, and Cub Allen Ferguson; Troop Colours – Tom Lucas, and George Thwaites, There were twenty-four lads in the parade, and their Scoutmaster was A. E. Bowyer.

When the parade arrived at the Church, it was a pleasant surprise for the marchers to find that their comfort had been planned by having seats placed outside on the lawn. The Reverend G. C. Lamont's pulpit and seat had been set up on a large truck, with the organ and choir placed at the foot of the pulpit. With the beauty of the surroundings, the green trees on three sides of the enclosed area, and the beautiful Church on the fourth side, it was a place conducive to worship.

The choir sang two anthems, and the Reverend Mr Lamont took the words of St. Paul, 'I am a debtor' for his text. He pointed out that every human person in the world is a debtor to someone, and that the Orange Order was discharging that debt in a very beautiful manner in its care of the little inmates of the orphanage at Newmarket. He said that this was not an act of charity, but an expression of brotherly responsibility toward those not so favoured in life.... 'The world is inclined today to pay more attention to its debt to mankind, more in favour of considering the obligations of brotherhood than formerly.'

By November, the commodious first storey of the new Orange Hall on Agnes Street was completed, at a cost of $5,000 – $3,800 of which had already been paid.

In July, 1929, the village of Cooksville was thronged with cars, the sidewalks crowded with men and women anxious to take part in the Annual Parade of the Orange Order. Fully two thousand people waited patiently until, after leaving the Orange Hall and marching south on Hurontario Street, the procession turned westward along Dundas Street, towards the United Church. Those who found it impossible to get into the Church sat down in the cooler outdoor air with all the decorum of those inside.

Cooksville Loyal Orange Lodge 1181 Hall, on Agnes Street, today. (Photo: Verna Mae Weeks)

The Orange Young Britons' Fife and Drum Band furnished the music and led the procession, under the leadership of James Nixon, and Fred House was in charge of the Union Jack. At the head of a long line of members from the Brampton, Huttonville, Streetsville, Queen Alexandra, Port Credit, and Islington Lodges, walked George Plant of Brampton, wearing his black collar, his face lit up by his satisfaction in the surging Orangemen behind him.

Delightful music was provided by the Church choir, with Miss Lois Tolman at the organ. The Reverend C. Sinclair Jones, preaching in his new charge for the first time, made a warm impression on his future congregation in his address to the Orange Order on the subject of Patriotism and Religion. He said: 'Orangemen and women are bound to honour their Sovereign ... to observe the law of the land ... and to live so as to bring no disgrace on the great family to which you belong.'

A very successful Garden Party was held in July of 1929, on the fair grounds; and on October 16, 1930, it was announced that the Cooksville Orangemen had cleared their Hall of debt. On November 5th, 1930, they burned the mortgage at their Annual Supper.

Chapter 29: The Cooksville Women's Institute

AT FIRST, Peel County's Institutes started out with no women members and were called Farmers' Institutes but later on, speakers from the Department of Agriculture addressed the women, with a woman speaking on subjects of interest to farmers' wives, while the men had meetings when outstanding speakers spoke to them on agricultural pursuits. In the evenings, joint meetings were held, and then topics which interested both were discussed.

In 1901, the first Peel Women's Institute was organized at a meeting in Brampton. At the beginning of January, 1903, *The Streetsville Review* printed a programme for both the Farmers' and the Women's Institutes, to be held on January the thirteenth. On that day, the Cooksville Farmers met at the afternoon session, when W. S. Fraser spoke to them about the Bacon Hog, and F. A. Sheppard discussed the Growing of Fruit Trees, Grafting and Pruning. During the same afternoon, the women were advised, by Miss Ida Hunter, about the Selection and Preparation of Foods. A paper was read by Miss Marshall, and a report of the year's work was given by Mrs Hunter.

In the evening, both Institutes were addressed on the subjects of Farm Bookkeeping, The Education of our Girls, A Plea for the Boy, and What Farmers Need. The meeting closed with the singing of music by a choir. Such was the beginning of the Cooksville Women's Institute.

As the years passed, other meetings provided advice on growing clovers, the feeding of cattle, marketing the grain on the farm by feeding it to the cattle and thus adding to the fertility of the farm. For the men, there was also stock judging, and other short courses with new and enlightening ideas as well.

In April, 1926, the Cooksville Women's Institute held a meeting at the home of Mrs W. Harris, with an attendance of forty-five, presided over by Mrs A. H. McFadden, and Mrs Sheather, Secretary. Their objective was to make a donation to the Peel Memorial Hospital, and nurses of the Victorian Order of Nurses spoke on their activities and service to the community. Mrs J. C. Patterson, their President, gave valuable information from the nurse's standpoint.

A splendid debate was then held on the subject that 'Life in the Country is Better than Life in the Town,' the affirmative being taken by Mrs Johnston Pinkney and Mrs Bert Oakes; negative by Mrs H. Mitchell and Miss Muriel Sheather. The negative side managed to refute the arguments of the affirmative, after which a very pleasant half-hour was spent over the tea cups. The ladies were served delicious tea, bread and butter, and cake, demonstrating the very happy spirit which animated their branch.

In September, the Cooksville Women's Institute assisted at the School Fair by conducting a booth and serving luncheon to adults, with the proceeds of the booth going towards paying the balance of $75 on a new Victrola which had been placed in the School. In response to a request from the Hospital for Sick Children, in Toronto, the Institute had a Fruit Shower in December.

The beginning of May, 1927, saw the Institute with a membership of sixty, and an average attendance of thirty-four. The receipts for the year, through September, 1926 to May, 1927 were $349.29; expenditures, $276.76.

During the new year, flowers were sent to all sick members; a Bale of Flannelette was cut up and sent to the Sick Children's Hospital; also, a Shower of Fruit was taken to the Peel Memorial Hospital, at Brampton. Donations were given to the School Fair, the Brampton rest room, and the Canadian Red Cross. A Bale of Clothing and Reading Material was sent to Northern Ontario, which was much appreciated.

A Nutrition Course, conducted by the Peel home demonstrator, Miss K. McIntosh, was enjoyed by all members, along with other valuable information given them. The Cooksville Institute extended a hearty invitation to all of the ladies to attend their Annual Picnic on June 28th, with sports for young and old.

The combined Institutes of Toronto Township intended having a Refreshment Booth at the Jubilee Celebration on the Fair Grounds on Saturday, July the second, and looked to the people to patronize them well, as the proceeds were to be used in the community.

In October, 1927, a Pumpkin Pie Contest was held at the home of Mrs Wylie, with the winners being Mrs John Cunningham, Mrs W. Maxwell, and Mrs Corbett. The proceeds from the Cooksville Fair Booth amounted to $73.81, and arrangements were made to supply milk for a baby for one month.

Officers elected for 1927-28 were as follows:

President – Mrs Stanley Patchett
Vice Presidents – Mrs John Cunningham, Mrs George Laver
Secretary-Treasurer – Mrs H. R. D. Woodall
Assistant – Mrs A. Baker
Directors – Mrs A. H. McFadden, Mrs C. Hopkins, Mrs C. Cliff,
    Mrs G. Ardill, Mrs E. Harris
District Director – Mrs S. Patchett
Flower Committee – Mrs L.R. Whiting, Mrs R. Whaley,
    Mrs J. Woodall
Refreshments – Miss Sophia Johnston, Mrs F. Taylor, Mrs C. Belford.
Social Service – Mrs C. Turpel, Mrs Squires, Mrs C. Harris
Auditors – Mrs Whiting, Mrs Cunningham
Pianist – Mrs A. H. McFadden

The following June, 1928, the Cooksville Women's Institute made a great venture and held their first Garden Party. Over five hundred persons attended, and the programme put on by Ye Old Tyme Village Quartette and Mr Harry Bennett was of a quality that Cooksville people liked and appreciated.

Three booths were set up on the grounds, two near the Town Hall, and one at the far side. They were brightly lighted by electricity, and hung with gold and mauve garlands of fluttering tissue that presented a lovely appearance under the lights. The ladies wore gold and mauve bands around their heads; most of them were dressed in white, and the effect was declared to be wonderfully attractive.

Mrs Cunningham's booth bore a bewildering supply of homemade baking, lovely cakes and pastry, attracting the male portion of the attendance. There was a booth with hot dogs, chocolate bars, peanuts, and ice cream cones; and with a Fish Pond and balloons for the little folk, nothing had been left undone to make the Garden Party a success.

The Institute put on a programme on a stage set up and brightly illuminated, being well provided with footlights. Lots of flags and bunting made it very cheery. The lovely flowered dresses of the ladies in the quartette, with their many old-fashioned flounces over hoop skirts, and their Dolly Varden hats trimmed with flowers, and wide brims turned down at one side, gave touches of colour which provided a contrast to the dark grey of the men. The programme was vivid, and the ladies were congratulated on their efforts by being heartily encored, in anticipation of another such programme for next year.

In September, 1928, the new season was announced, to be started on the 22nd, with a rummage sale of clothing in the Township Hall. This sale was the first of its kind to be held in Cooksville, and afternoon tea was served. The money was for the purpose of assisting the Sidewalk Fund.

The schedule, following the special business of each meeting, was planned as follows:

1928, October 9 – Speaker, Mrs R. B. Colloton, District President, and a Biscuit Baking contest (4 tea biscuits)

November 6 – Euchre

December 4 – Christmas Gifts for the Social Welfare Box

1929, January 8 – Malton Institute visiting and a Candy Contest

February 5 – Valentine Party

March 4 – Speaker, Mrs W. H. Greene, St. Patrick Tea

April 3 – Election of Officers

May 7 – Speaker from the Department, on Interior Decorating

That year, the Officers elected were:

President – Mrs J. Cunningham

1st Vice-President – Mrs G. Laver

2nd Vice-President – Mrs F. Taylor

Secretary-Treasurer – Mrs H. R. D. Woodall

Assistant – Mrs A. Baker

District Director – Mrs J. Cunningham

Branch Directors – Mrs A. H. McFadden, Mrs C. Hopkins, Mrs H. Cliff, Mrs E. Harris, Mrs H. Wilson

Refreshment – Mrs S. Johnstone, Mrs J. Allen, Mrs G. Hadlow
Flower Committee – Mrs C. Turpel, Mrs Wylie, Mrs R. Whaley
Social Service – Mrs C. Hopkins, Mrs Brown, Mrs G. Turner
Press Reporter – Mrs A. Baker
Representative for the League of Nations – Mrs W. Maxwell

The Brampton Conservator of May 30, 1929, reported on the Silver
Jubilee of the Peel Women's Institute, and the occasion of its 25th
Anniversary was marked with a function in the Orange Hall, at
Brampton. At this banquet, a cheque of $1,000 was presented as a gift to
the Board of Governors of Peel Memorial Hospital.

It was the Women's Institute that gave Peel County its School Nurse.
Clinics were held and, for one year, the Institute bore the entire cost of a
nurse. After this, the work was undertaken in such a way that the cost
would be partly paid by the School Boards. One nurse was permitted to
look after only a certain number of schools, and this was the beginning of
the Peel School Nurse System, as it was being conducted in the year 1929.

THE LIBRARY:

There had been, in 1904 and for some years following, a free Public
Library in the village; it was a branch of the Streetsville Public Library,
and had a couple of hundred books. In March, 1904, *The Streetsville
Review* stated that the Library had a membership of about 80, which
was steadily increasing; however, later on this membership gradually
dwindled and no other reports were given.

Thus it was that, at the beginning of May, in 1930, the Cooksville
Women's Institute held a meeting in the Orange Hall and made plans to
form a Public Library. A committee was appointed, in charge of Mrs W.
Harris.

The Cooksville ladies began collecting books. They appreciated all
donations, which were left at the homes of Mrs A. Baker, Mrs Ida
McFadden, Mrs H. Wilson, and Mrs W. Harris. The Library was given
the use of Mr Harris' empty store on Dundas Street, through the winter
months, for paying only the cost of the electric light.

On Saturday, February 7th, 1931, the Cooksville Women's Institute
opened the new Cooksville Public Library, in one side of Gordon
Harris' Real Estate Office building. A good selection of books had been
placed on the shelves and were ready for borrowing, with the Library to
be open on Friday evenings from 7 to 9 p.m. A little note appeared in
the local paper saying, 'Everybody welcome to come and join.'

'Cooksville Public Library Association' lending library, left side of G. M. Harris' Building (first Methodist Church) – north side of Dundas Street, east of Novar Road. (Photo: Mississauga Central Library, Cooksville Vol. 1)

Through March, the Institute asked every one of its members to donate two books, to be sent or brought to the library on a Friday evening, or left at the home of a committee member. In April, the new Library moved, and opened in P. Christie's Drug Store next door to the Real Estate Office, after which books became available to the public at all times.

Over the years, money was raised by the Cooksville Library Board in various ways; such as the Euchre, held in March, 1934, at Mrs W. R. Harris' home.

In 1948, the Cooksville Branch of the Toronto Township Library opened, once again in the building on Dundas Street West, where

Gordon Harris had long operated his successful real estate and insurance business.

In 1957, a new Toronto Township Central Library system was established and, in 1963, a new building was erected in Cooksville, on the southeast corner of what is now Confederation Drive and Dundas Street West.

At that time, in a large landscaped area close to the Central Library Building, there were to be found the Municipal Building, the Police Court, and the Board of Education Office Building.

Chapter 30: The Cherry Hill House

THE PICTORIAL ATLAS OF PEEL, 1877 gives us a beautiful picture of the Cherry Hill home of Joseph and Jane Silverthorn, located on a slight hill overlooking Dundas Street, between the First Line (Cawthra Road)

RESIDENCE OF JOSEPH SILVERTHORN, CHERRY HILL, COOKSVILLE.

(Photo: Pictorial Atlas of Peel, 1877)

256

and the CPR Cooksville Station. The reason for its name is said to be the fact that, when the Silverthorn family arrived in Canada by way of Queenston Heights, they brought with them the first little cherry trees to be grown in Cooksville.

The Brampton Conservator of December 24, 1908, reported that Augusta C. Silverthorn died on December 18th at her residence, Cherry Hill, Cooksville, at the age of seventy-three years. Shortly afterwards, an advertisement by Auctioneer John Thomson, of Port Credit, listed the following articles from the Silverthorn Estate, for sale:

Furniture from: 2 Drawing Rooms;
                     1 Sitting Room;
                     2 Dining Rooms;
                     Downstairs Hall, Upstairs Hall;
                     6 Bedrooms;
                     Kitchen, Pantry, and Store Room.
Also: a Bay Horse, and Rigs;
                     Covered Buggy Phaeton;
                     One-Horse Wagon;
                     Cutter, complete with Harness;
                     Saddle, Bridle;
                     Goat Robes, and a Buffalo Robe;
                     – and other Articles too Numerous to Mention.

The furniture itself was not discussed, merely left to the imagination of those who wished to attend the sale. For such a large house, there were no doubt many persons who did avail themselves of a wish to purchase beautiful things, or at least to view them.

Following the auction sales of those days it seemed usual to pass on a little information regarding the disposal of the goods, and who the buyers of the property were; however, in this case nothing else appeared for some time afterwards. At the beginning of September, 1912, a garden party was held on the Cherry Hill grounds for the benefit of St. Patrick's Roman Catholic Church, located on the southwest corner of Dundas Street and the Dixie Road.

Following this garden party, a sensational accident took place on the Centre Road, near Port Credit, in the vicinity of the Craigie home, by what is now Mineola Road. Two horse-drawn carriages owned by Miss O'Brien of 'Shandon Lodge,' Dixie, were racing abreast down the Centre Road, with passengers wishing to board the electric cars at Port Credit. It was a Wednesday evening, about eleven o'clock, and very dark. Mr and Mrs John Wolfe were returning home, at the same time, after attending the wedding of Miss Beamish at Port Credit. In the centre of the narrow roadway, all three rigs collided and upset, their occupants being thrown out willynilly, in a state of utter confusion.

William Morrison, one of Miss O'Brien's coachmen, was considerably hurt and cut; both of her carriages were wrecked, with one of the horses seriously injured. Remarkably, under the circumstances, Mr and Mrs Wolfe escaped without much hurt, nor much damage done to their carriage; but their new harness was broken to pieces. While all this disaster was taking place, George Bowers, owner of the Cooksville Inn, happened on the scene and rendered assistance. He picked up the injured and badly shaken parties in his car, and conveyed them to their different destinations. The horses and carriages were all left at the place where the accident happened, until daylight of the following day.

Six years after this account of the aftermath of the garden party, an advertisement appeared in the Streetsville newspaper, announcing that the Cherry Hill Tea Gardens were open every day in the year. Their situation was given as being just east of the CPR tracks on Dundas Street, fourteen miles from Yonge Street. The account mentioned that Cherry Hill Farm had been founded in 1807 by Joseph Silverthorn, 'who came from Wales and built the first dwelling house of logs, a stone's throw back of the present house.' At this time, in 1918, the house was said to be then owned by 'the Great Grandson,' and that it contained many of the furnishings which had been used in the log house, and restored to use.

The gist of the advertisement was to the effect that the Tea Gardens was an excellent trip out from Yonge Street, for Motoring and Sleighing Parties, for Skating and Dancing, for Corn Roasts and Chicken Dinners. Special arrangements could be made for private parties. Also, guests could view the house for a nominal fee to the guide; otherwise, the entire Cherry Hill grounds were free to guests.

It was in mid–September of 1922 that the Cooksville Shale Brick Company leased the Cherry Hill homestead house and fitted it up for a boarding house. Bricks were in demand, with not enough houses for rent in Cooksville and, since the Company wanted to remain open during the winter, they made such repairs and alterations to the house as were needed for such a purpose. Transportation was not good through the winter time, and while their employees occupied the house the Company conveyed them in their trucks, to and from the Brick Yard.

258

The Brampton Conservator, April 24, 1924

When the boarding house was no longer needed, the house remained empty for a short while, but in April, 1924 it was once again opened and improved, to become a highway inn. Under the new name of Cherry Hill Tavern, it had a booth and entrance at its east side, and was being operated by the same management as that of the Old Mill Tea Room, by the Humber River.

At the beginning of July in 1924, the editor of *The Brampton Conservator* drove down to visit the Cherry Hill Tavern, on a Saturday evening, and wrote his comments in the newspaper. He told of his pleasant surprise and pleasure upon being escorted through the house, saying that 'this grand old home of 117 years' standing is admirably furnished for this purpose.'

In the entrance hall, the walls were apparently adorned with the same wall paper which had been placed on them seventy-five years before, and looked as if they had been done only yesterday. In the corner of the entrance hall was a Chickering piano, in rosewood, said to be the first one imported into Canada. In another room, stood a player piano. The dining room where the dinners and suppers were then served was tastefully decorated in attractive colours, and there were in it some very valuable pieces of antique furniture and furnishings; the same could be said of the lounge.

The old homestead was being operated, under its new name, by Mr Gibbs and Mrs Charles, who were at that time highly pleased with the success of their venture. Reservations for parties for evening dinners and dancing were being taken for nearly every night of the week. The editor stated that the only fault he could see in it was its limited accommodation; 'Were it ten times larger, it would still be small to meet the coming business.'

For some time, the Cherry Hill Tavern prospered; but later days came which saw the formerly splendid house in sad condition, still standing on the slight hill overlooking Dundas Street. Memory brings it back to mind as a rectangular, large frame building, surrounded and overgrown with scraggly trees, with shrubs grown wild, and weedy patches everywhere. Its formerly white-painted boards were washed pale grey and bare by the rains and snows of weather; its window panes seemed like blank dark eyes, staring out from between the limbs and branches, wherever they could be seen at all. Still, it remained, the old Cherry Hill house, in its old familiar place.

* * *

In 1975, the Cherry Hill house was moved to a new location a little further north, to 680 Silvercreek Boulevard, where it was restored as the Cherry Hill House Restaurant.

Today, the place where the old homestead once stood on the slight hill overlooking Dundas Street, west of Cawthra Road, has been covered by tall apartment buildings, and Dundas Street itself has become the slight hill from which we may now look down upon the place where the old homestead stood.

Chapter 31: Franze Drive

AT THE FIRST OF SEPTEMBER, 1921, John Stewart sold his property on Dundas Street, together with the adjacent land, to Santo Franze for a sum stated to be fifteen thousand dollars. On these fourteen acres, located next to Adam Brunskill's home and just west of the CPR Cooksville Station, Mr Franze operated a market garden where he grew mainly lettuce, asparagus and grapes. He sold the grapes and other fruits which grew on the property at a Fruit Market he built himself on the front of his lot; other produce he took to the Farmers' Market in West Toronto, near Jane and Dundas Streets. He also delivered vegetables to stores in Cooksville, like the store on the corner of Cook Street when it was owned by McCords, and later by the Carload Groceteria.

The business prospered; and in the large yard around their home, set well back in from the road, the family held many picnics and barbeques, with all of their own family, some of the neighbours, and the priest coming. Aunts, uncles, cousins, and grandparents, all came out from the city in their old-fashioned cars, which they parked in the yard alongside the shed and near the fence.

Outdoor barbeque on Santo Franze's farm, before 1930. (Photo: courtesy of Anthony Franze)

CENTRE: Reverend Father
LEFT: Joe Amedeo, Roy Amedeo, Grandfather Palumbo, Lena Palumbo, Florence Amedeo, Flo Amedeo, Christine Amedeo, Lena Amedeo, Agostine Amedeo, Lillian, Mrs Groves (friend of the family)
RIGHT: Grandfather Santo Franze, Lena Franze, T. Naso, M. Palumbo, Tony Franze, T. Palumbo, N. Naso, M. Pirri, Grandmother Palumbo, Grandmother Franze.

They had a large stone fireplace built, with a spit, and Mr Halsey, the butcher at the time, would dress a cow or a pig for them and they would barbeque it; sometimes there were a hundred or more people present at a time. Everyone contributed to the cost of the feast, and all enjoyed themselves. Anthony Franze, today, remembers that they would put on a huge pot filled with gallons of water, get it boiling, and throw in a large cheesecloth bag of coffee and boil it; he says, 'Oh, it smelled so good you could have just jumped right into the pot!' He has many happy recollections of those picnics.

It was during the month of December, in the 1930s, that one day when Mrs Franze and the children went away to the city to a wedding and Mr Franze had to stay at home to look after the greenhouse, a disaster happened. At that time, he was growing tomatoes, water cress, lettuce, and other vegetables in his big greenhouse, and could not go away and leave it for fear of the crop being ruined by the cold, if the heat went down.

Lena Franze, who went to live in Cooksville when she was a very small girl, recalls that when they were coming home from the wedding there was a big snowstorm going on, and the house caught fire. Her father was asleep at the time, but they managed to wake him up and

Second house built by Santo Franze, 1930s. (Photo: Verna Mae Weeks)

rescue him. They saved some of the furniture by throwing it out into the snow; they owned a player piano, and they saved that, she doesn't know how.

The farmhouse was lost, but they built a second one of cement blocks covered with stucco, and with glassed-in sunrooms on the sides. The new house stood out closer to the road than the old one had been.

After the fire, when Mr Franze could not handle the market stand any longer, he leased it to Phil Palumbo, who turned it into an Ice Cream and Refreshment Booth.

West of Hurontario Street, on the north side of the Dundas Highway over towards Cook Street, there was a very old roughcast building which had been an old Cooksville landmark dating back to a hundred years before, and which had been bought by Mr and Mrs J. E. Smith in 1927, from Mrs Annie Wylie. In this building, the Smiths conducted a Clothing and Dry Goods Store for five years, and in 1932 they decided to replace their old store with a large new solid brick building.

One morning in July of 1932, the editor of *The Port Credit News* went up to Cooksville, arriving just in time to see the old building fall, under the hands of the wreckers. The wrecking operation started on Monday, and it was expected that by Wednesday the foundation work of the new store would be under way. Mr Sam Benskey, a contractor from Toronto, had been awarded the contract to tear down the old roughcast building and build the new one, which was to be a two-storey structure with two

J. E. SMITH Dry Goods Store

COOKSVILLE

BARGAINS FOR ALL

LADIES' SILK STOCKINGS, pair	10c
MEN'S ALL WOOL SWEATERS, each	$1.95
GIRLS' SILK and WOOL STOCKINGS, pair	25c
LADIES' WAISTS, each	49c
ALL KINDS OF GIRLS' DRESSES, from 6 to 11 years	85c

The Port Credit News, September 27, 1933

263

stores, each 26 feet by 46 feet, and modern in every respect.

When the building was completed, there was Smith's Dry Goods on one side; and on the other side was a fruit store operated by Albert Spoto. At the end of August, 1932, the stores which housed the Dry Goods and the Fruit Market received a new coat of paint; Julius Smith and Albert Spoto (Lena Franze's husband) were reported to be responsible for the painting job.

Albert and Lena Spoto were able to keep the fruit store going only about six months, from June until January. In those times, they just couldn't make a go of it; Albert worked at the Brick Yard for awhile, and later at the Ford Plant, in Oakville. The fruit store had been leased and, when they left, it became McClintock's Drug Store.

The market garden farm on Dundas Street was later sold for a subdivision, with a street running up the centre of it; and when Santo Franze asked the developers if they would name the new street after him, they did. And that is how the street that runs north from Dundas Street West to the train tracks, just west of the overpass at Cawthra Road, got its name – Franze Drive.

Chapter 32: People of the Past

THE BONHOMME FAMILY:

Albert E. Bonhomme came to Canada from South Shields, in the north of England, in 1912; and by 1914, he had built a small cabin on his own property on Dundas Street. Mrs Bonhomme arrived a short time later, and they were married on August 16, 1915. Their life was pretty rough in that small house, in the beginning, but they managed.

Albert was a carpenter by trade, and kept improving the house; in the fall of 1923, he erected a new addition to it to fill the needs of his growing family. Together he and his wife raised five children, named: Mary, Monica, Joe, Mildred, and Leo. It is interesting to note that, in those days, married women were never called by their first names except by family and close friends. Their daughter Mildred recalls today that although her mother's name was Elizabeth, and Mr Bonhomme called her Jenny, Mildred never heard her mother ever called anything but Mrs Bonhomme, by others.

Their home was located just west of Hook Avenue, where there is now a small plaza. There were two other houses on the southwest corner

The Bonhomme Family –
L TO R: Mary, Mrs
Bonhomme, Joe, Mr
Bonhomme;
FRONT: baby Mildred, and
Monica. (Photo: Miss
Mildred Bonhomme)

Mary Bonhomme in the
garden. (Photo: Miss Mildred
Bonhomme)

Mary Bonhomme, sitting on grass at southwest corner Dundas and Hurontario Streets; background, Cooksville Hotel, c. 1922. (Photo: Miss Mildred Bonhomme)

Albert Bonhomme, at his home, immediately west of Hook Avenue (Confederation Drive), looking east along Dundas Street. (Photo: Miss Mildred Bonhomme)

of Hook Avenue; in the first house was the Harper family, who owned a small plant at the rear of their property for the manufacture of oars, paddles, and custom woodwork. The Harpers came in to play cards quite often in the winter evenings; later, they moved to the Centre Road, and the Bonhommes missed them. In the second house lived Mr and Mrs Trdak. Mr Trdak worked at the Cooksville Brick Yard, and later on, in 1940, it was Mrs Trdak who opened a new dry goods store on Dundas Street, near the four corners.

Mrs Bonhomme and her children picked berries, beans, tomatoes, or whatever was in season, for Miss Edith Miller, who ran a farm which took in the whole block from Argyle Road as far as Orchard Road, and from Dundas Street right down to the lane by the fair grounds. Her greenhouses were on the west side of her land, and she had fruits, trees, and all kinds of vegetables. Miss Miller was good to her workers and the Bonhommes were always well supplied from her garden; needless to say, Mrs Bonhomme took great pride in her cellar shelves, stocked for the winter with all kinds of canning and preserves.

Mildred remembers that after the berries were picked for the day, Miss Miller would say: 'All right, kids, go home and get washed and ready; you can come to Toronto with me.' She used to sell her berries to the Toronto General Hospital and the Sick Children's Hospital, and delivered them herself in an open-sided truck with wire mesh panels, very like the old Eaton's and Simpson's delivery trucks of that time.

After the berries were disposed of, she would buy each of the children an ice cream cone. That was a great treat. After a hard day's work on the land, Mildred wonders today how she could have been bothered with a bunch of kids in the truck with her, all the way to Toronto and back.

It was through Miss Miller that Mrs Bonhomme met her good friends the Harrisons, of Toronto; and when, in 1926, she became ill and had to stay in hospital, they took Joe and Mildred and cared for them for over a year. Miss Miller herself kept Mary; Monica went to Brampton, to Rose Donnelly, and Leo, the baby, was cared for by Rose's sister, Nellie Sullivan. These were very hard days for Mr and Mrs Bonhomme, having no relations in this country; but kind friends, and friends of friends, stepped in to help them.

When Mrs Bonhomme was well again, Albert Bonhomme built a store on the property in front of their home on Dundas Street. This store stood on the exact location of where, today, there is a Tim Horton's

Donuts Shop, at 144 Dundas Street West; the Bonhomme home was directly behind their store.

As for Miss Miller, an announcement which appeared in *The Port Credit News* of August 9, 1933, stated that Miss F. E. Miller and Mr James A. Smith had established a new floral and nursery business in the community. Greenhouses had been erected on the Dundas Highway, at the west end of Cooksville, to supply cut flowers, pot plants, and nursery stock; design work for all occasions could be executed at short notice. A cordial invitation was extended to everyone to visit the greenhouses any time by The Cooksville Floral Company.

While Albert Bonhomme continued to work at his trade of carpentering, Mrs Bonhomme ran the store. At first, she sold ice cream and tobacco, and refreshments, later adding canned goods; in the 1930s, it became a small grocery store and customers came to shop there from

---

ANNOUNCEMENT

Miss F. E. Miller and Mr. Jas. A. Smith announce that they have established a floral and nursery business in this community.

- Greenhouses have been erected on Dundas Highway, at the west end of Cooksville.

Cut flowers, pot plants and nursery stock will be grown and supplied in season and design work for all occasions executed at short notice.

A cordial invitation is extended to everyone to visit our greenhouses at any time.

The Cooksville Floral Co.

Dundas St. West,
Cooksville.

Phone 43 Daytime
Phone 43W or 57 Nights

The Port Credit News, August 9, 1933

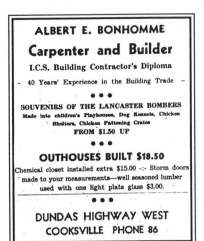
The Port Credit Weekly,
October 25, 1945

the Cooksville Brick Yard. Many of the workmen at the Brick Yard were foreign-born, and did not speak English well; and when Mrs Bonhomme discovered that they had difficulty in buying work clothes, she had a counter put in across one side of the store. She then stocked shelves behind this counter with work clothes, like overalls, shirts, and work socks.

She had a telephone installed, and phoned orders in for them to Eaton's and Simpson's Department Stores, in Toronto. She kept the

Bonhomme Store on Dundas Street, west of Hook Avenue; Bobby
Eddy with dog Collie, c.1941. (Photo: Miss Mildred Bonhomme)

269

catalogues on the counter, and helped the workmen to study them. At first, she called in the orders for them but, later on they would call in their own, while she stood and listened to make sure they got the order numbers right.

The Bonhomme Store was well-known to all the passers-by along Dundas Street, just west of Hook Avenue, a street now developed and changed into a main Mississauga street named Confederation Drive. Mrs Bonhomme passed away in May of 1948; Mr Bonhomme, in 1963.

PHILIP PARDY:

Philip Pardy was born in England, and had only two years of regular schooling, from the age of five to seven years, when he left school and was put to work as a sort of human scarecrow in the neighbouring farm fields, to keep the rooks away from the wheat. Later on, he tended sheep and drove horses until, at the age of thirteen, he was apprenticed to a shoemaker for seven years.

When the time of his apprenticeship was over and he became a qualified shoemaker at the age of twenty-one, he and another young

Pardy Harness Shop, north side Dundas Street, half block west of Hurontario Street; Mr Pardy standing at extreme left. (Photo: Mississauga Central Library, Cooksville School Collection F 106)

fellow were recommended to the Commissioner of the London Police by the local minister's daughter, and they both went to London and joined the Force. For three-and-a-half years, he walked a beat as a London bobby.

Mr Pardy liked to recall that when he was young, he was an active football player and played in many games; and he told of an experience he once had while he was a member of the London Police Force. During his time there, he went on a visit to Westminster Abbey and was shown around by the beadle, who conducted him on a tour of the famous old Church. In Mr Pardy's own words, he 'stole a march on the beadle' by streaking back and taking a seat in the great Coronation Chair, one of the few people in the world, he said, who had attained that honour.

After leaving the Police Force, he came to Canada and first settled in Oakville, in 1875, meaning to set himself up as a shoemaker. However, he soon learned that the better-paying trade was that of harness-making, and he learned to make harnesses from Henry Gullidge, at Oakville. Later on, in 1888, he moved to Cooksville, where he was to remain as a continuous resident and harness maker for over forty years. His Harness Shop stood on the spot where, today, there is a large parking lot belonging to the Bombay Palace Restaurant, at 35 Dundas Street West.

Mr Pardy became a member of the Cooksville Methodist Church, and always took a keen interest in religious affairs; he sang in the choir, and was on the Board of Managers for many years. An ardent student of

28 YEARS IN BUSINESS

Philip Pardy

HARNESS MAKER

Twenty-eight years in continuous business in Cooksville is the best evidence of good work and satisfactory prices.

See me at the old stand, Dundas Street.

COOKSVILLE

The Brampton Conservator, August 19, 1915

Philip Pardy at his work bench. (*The Port Credit News*, February, 1932)

the Bible, he was able to quote many passages without reference to it; he used these passages throughout his daily life, and oftentimes friends called into his shop to discuss the affairs of the day and get his thoughts on them, in relation to Bible teachings.

He was friendly and kind to the children of the neighbourhood, and was always willing to let them visit and watch him as he sat at his work bench in front of his window, which faced out onto Dundas Street. He would tell many stories of things and places he had seen in the world, and if a child's shoe strap came loose, he could be depended upon to mend it on the spot in order that the little person would not trip over it and fall down. He was well-liked by all who knew him.

Mr Pardy owned some property on the Centre Road, where he grew potatoes and fine crops of corn; and once, in 1913, a tree there was blown across the Hydro line to Port Credit, which shut off all the lights. In 1917, two large willow trees in front of his Harness Shop on Dundas Street were cut down by the Hydro linesmen; these were ancient landmarks of immense proportions, being in height seventy-five feet tall, and upwards of five feet in diameter.

At the beginning of October, in 1922, Mr Pardy took a week's vacation to visit his son, who lived at Bobcaygeon, and he returned home feeling happy to have landed three nice lunges one afternoon, whose total weight was twenty-five pounds.

On January 15, 1925, *The Brampton Conservator* published a little note stating that Mr Pardy had installed electric lights in his Harness Shop. And the following December, everyone was interested to read that he was now having Santa Claus install a radio for him – it was hoped that the radio would not interfere with his regular church work.

When he was eighty years old, Mr Pardy was still going strong and celebrated his birthday in his shop, busily at work repairing a collar. He was still proud to be working from ten to twelve hours a day, and continuing to mend a few pairs of shoes, along with his other work. With his smooth skin and ruddy English complexion he could persuade almost anyone to think of him as a man twenty years younger than his age.

He talked of the changes from horse-drawn vehicles to the modern automobiles and trucks passing by his window; he said that during the night, from about three o'clock until seven in the morning, there would be the sounds of wagons rattling and horses' hooves clip-clopping along Dundas Street, and then all would be quiet again except for a few small rigs, once in a while, until four o'clock in the afternoon when the same farm vehicles returned.

In the 1930s, he would sometimes sit quite still, with his work in his hands, looking out at the hundreds of cars rushing past his door during an ordinary day, marvelling at the changes from the old days. He would recall the first automobile which appeared in the section of Dundas Street; it was a funny, open machine, run by an engine that used coal, and which belched black smoke.

On February 18, 1934, Mr Pardy celebrated his eighty-third birthday. When *The Port Credit News* editor visited him to wish him well on his birthday, he found him at his work bench, still practising his craft, but by this time the leatherworking business was not so much in demand. 'The motor car has killed the business,' Mr Pardy said. 'Even the farmers don't order much new harness, just repairing the old; but if it wasn't for the farmers, there would be no more saddlery business.'

Even so, Mr Pardy found little idle time on his hands. 'I have as much as I can do,' he said. 'I have good health. I have never got rich, but neither have I been poor. I always had enough to eat and plenty of work, because I always do the best possible job for a reasonable price, making a fair profit. Many people kill their own business by trying to grasp everything for themselves.'

Philip Pardy died in February, 1935. A service was held at his home on Dundas Street, and another in the Cooksville United Church, conducted by the Reverend C. Jones. Mr Pardy was buried at the United Church cemetery on the hill at Erindale.

JAMES K. MORLEY:

James King Morley was the son of Francis B. Morley, the Postmaster and owner of the Cooksville House hotel; his uncle, John Morley, was Cooksville's tailor.

Francis B. Morley left Lakeneath, County of Sussex, England, in 1834 with his father and mother, four brothers and one sister, and settled in the clearing where Dundas Street crossed the Centre Road. It was but a rough and stony tract of land, at a time when settlers were still clearing homesteads. The settlement, however, was already marked on the map as the village of Cooksville, with stores and a stage route to connect it with other parts of Upper Canada.

The entire Morley family had musical talents, and performed on violin, guitar and piano in days when a musical education was almost unheard of. William Morley, their father, was listed as a Music Master, and taught his sons; Francis (called Frank) was a genial performer, who not only bought the hotel but provided entertainment for his guests.

Frank's son James King Morley, who liked to be called 'J. K.,' followed in his father's footsteps, developing his musical gifts at an early age. For years, he was a member of what in 1885 was known as one of the best bands west of Toronto, the Cooksville Brass Band, which travelled about over the whole district. At first, J. K. played the snare drum, then became efficient on the tenor horn; later still, he took as his choice the E-flat Bass.

As a young man, and for many years, J. K. Morley was in business as a painter and decorator, taking on such contracts as painting the hotels of Cooksville. In April, 1903, he painted and decorated the King's Hotel; and in February, 1907, when the Revere House was secured by the Sterling Bank branch, he did such a fine job of decorating it, he was complimented in the newspaper as having made a decided improvement to the corners.

In June, 1907, he moved into the apartments upstairs above Bowden's Pharmacy. That year, as Secretary of the Cooksville Fall Fair, he arranged for the advertising, describing its new grandstand and the attractions scheduled to be held in front of it. He was an energetic and obliging secretary, ably assisted by the equally popular Colour Sergeant Schiller. He was ever the active man of the day, answering the many requests of all persons looking for information, making out entry tickets, and keeping the operations of the Fair in constant motion.

When the Annual Meetings of the Cooksville Fair Association were held in the Town Hall, he was busily working on the prize lists, entry forms, and all particulars; and at the Annual Banquets, then held in Bowers' Hotel, he contributed speeches, music and singing for the entertainment. When Fair Day arrived, in 1913, the Hall was filled with the music of gramophones and pianos. The next year, 1914, there were Hurdle Races, with the officers of the cavalry troop of the Governor General's Horse Guards; these proved a wonderful success, and Colonel Sanford Smith's horse 'Silver Buckle' was the winner of the main race.

By 1926, J. K. Morley had been Secretary of the Fair for twenty-four years. He served as the Township Auditor for seventeen years; and as a Conservative, he was Chairman of the Cooksville Ward of the Township for eight years. He became a member of the Independent Order of Foresters, and served as Chief Ranger for many years. Although he was

J. K. MORLEY

UNDERTAKING AND EMBALMING

Representative at Cooksville of Munro & English, Streetsville

Call him by phone any time of the day or night and
he will be promptly at your service.

The Brampton Conservator, August 19, 1915

Mr J. K. Morley's home on Dundas Street, west of Hurontario.
(Photo: Mississauga Central Library, Cooksville Vol. 1, #307)

himself the son of a hotel keeper, J. K. Morley was a Worthy Associate of the Grand Lodge of the Sons of Temperance; and even through all the days of bitterness, he stood on many platforms to support establishments which refrained from the sale of liquor.

The Morley family had belonged to the Church of England since first coming to the country, and their service to St. Peter's Erindale and St. John's Dixie was part of the history of the area; but James K. Morley was also actively connected with the Methodist Sunday School in Cooksville for twelve years.

By 1915, he had become associated with the Funeral Home of Munro & English, at Streetsville, and was advertising himself as their representative in Undertaking and Embalming, at Cooksville. He had his undertaking business at his apartments in the upstairs section of Bowden's Pharmacy.

In May, 1916, he bought the Transatlantic Home, with the attached store, on the lot on Dundas Street; the property had once been owned by A. W. Aikens, of the vineyard, and there, in 1899, A. C. Pettit had carried on an undertaking business. The house had been later occupied by Dr Reginald Murray, who was an appointed Veterinary Inspector for the Dominion Government and, after Dr Murray died, in 1915, Mr Morley made considerable repairs to the house and fitted up the store for his own undertaking business. In July, 1916, Mr and Mrs Morley moved into their new home and settled in very comfortably there.

J. K. Morley still found himself able, after the death of H. H. Shaver in 1917, to take over the position of Clerk of the Second Division Court.

By 1920, when there was talk of a new Band being formed, it was recalled that, of the far-famed 1885 Cooksville Brass Band, only three of the players were still living in the village, the rest having passed away, or moved somewhere else. Those who remained were Messrs. J. K. Morley, William Weeks, and Joseph Goldthorpe.

Mr Morley was a member of Loyal Orange Lodge No. 1181; as well, he was an honoured Past Master of Riverpark Masonic Lodge, AF and AM, No. 356, Streetsville, in which he was particularly interested. When the Annual Supper and Concert was held for the first time in Cooksville's new Orange Hall on Agnes Street, five Past Masters were seated at the head table, all of whom wore their Past Masters' jewels – James Guthrey, J. K. Morley, Joseph Allen, John Ward, and John McKee.

Following the passing of his wife, in 1921, Mr Morley remained in

Mr James K. Morley.
(*The Brampton Conservator*,
January 13, 1926)

his home on Dundas Street, still retaining a few of the quaint and
charming relics of the pioneer life of Peel County. He kept a chair,
dating back two hundred years, which had come to Canada with his
family; the old Family Bible, purchased in 1846 and bearing on its
pages, in the old-fashioned handwriting of the time, the records of
births, marriages and deaths of the older members of the Morley family.

James King Morley died at the beginning of June, in 1939.

THE WOLFE FAMILY:

With other Pennsylvania Dutch families, the Wolfe family came to
Canada and settled on a farm northwest of the village of Cooksville, in
that rural route area of Dundas Street, just east of the tollgate which
separated Cooksville from Erindale. Lot 22 NDS was first obtained from
the Crown by Thomas Williams in 1807, and in February, 1835, John
Wolfe bought seventy acres of it for 150 pounds sterling. At the time of
the Mackenzie Rebellion, in 1837, he was stationed at Port Credit, and
each evening returned to his home through the bush with nothing more
to guide him than the marks blazed on the sides of the trees.

His son, also named John Wolfe, was born there in 1846, and lived all

278

his life in the same log house on this farm; at the age of eighty-four years, he told that he had never lived anywhere else. He remembered his father working the farm with oxen and, one day as he watched him breaking in a new team, he saw his father's foot become tangled up in one of the chains and the oxen dragging him all around the field.

Once, as a boy, when he and his father were going to Streetsville, the key (wooden pin) in the yoke holding the oxen together became broken; but his father simply stepped down and cut a limb off a hawthorn tree at the side of the road and made another wooden key. His father planted a small tree near the window of their log house to shade it from the sun and, as John Wolfe grew, so did the tree; it was Mr Wolfe who outlasted the tree, and finally lived to see its stump, now old and grey, sticking up from the ground on the lawn near the house.

When he grew up, Mr Wolfe teamed loads of squared logs and staves for barrels down to the banks of the Credit River, where they were tied together into rafts, to be delivered to various places along Lake Ontario. He rolled the staves from the roadway into the Credit River. He recalled that once his grandfather's team backed too close to the river, and in went all the logs, wagon and team, together; and his grandfather was left standing on the bank, holding only the whip in his hand.

In his youth, fall wheat and barley were what they grew for the cash crops; they took the wheat to be ground into flour at Streetsville, and hauled the flour to Port Credit to be shipped. He had two older brothers, Samuel and George, and they took loads of wood to Toronto, to sell them at the market. They had to be there at daylight and stay all day long, until the lamps were lighted; and they received only $5.50 for two big loads of wood.

Mr Wolfe remembered that in the early days, Indians were frequent visitors at the Wolfe home. They peddled wicker baskets and axe handles of their own make; and an Indian woman named Polly came to help his mother make maple sugar.

The family farm stretched northward from Dundas Street to the Burnhamthorpe Road, and there was a lane, called the Wolfe Lane. George Wolfe, born in 1840, met his death in 1902, as he walked down this road to the railway crossing, where he was struck by a CPR train and killed. Samuel Wolfe, born in 1835, lived, after his marriage, on the adjoining farm on the western side of the Wolfe Lane. Samuel Wolfe was a supporter of the Orange Order, and was a charter member of the Cooksville Lodge of the Ancient Order of United Workmen.

Everybody in the southern section of Toronto Township knew and liked Sam Wolfe and his wife, the former Sarah Rogers, and this was one reason why two hundred men and women travelled to their home on a Saturday in September of 1920. The other, more direct, reason was the fact that a frame for a new bank barn was ready to be raised, and the neighbours near and far wished to have a part in the work and festivities of the day.

The barn was to be 42 x 60 feet in area, and have good stabling underneath the whole building. The stone work had already been built by Fox & Sodden, and the framework by the Messrs. McKinney, of Streetsville. All the mortises had been cut, the holes bored, and the pegs and nails set out all ready for the visitors when they arrived. Mr McKinney directed operations, and the sides of the barn were soon raised up by the large number of hands. By six o'clock, everything was in place, all tightly-joined together, without any accident or mishap of any kind.

It was after this that what the visitors considered the 'real work' began. While the barn was being raised, tables had been set up on the front lawn, and a feast said to be fine enough to do honour to a king laid out by Mrs Wolfe and many other willing and charming wives, who had come with their husbands for the barn raising. In all, about two hundred persons were served, after which, in response to an invitation to join in a game of football, one Cooksville lady voiced the feelings of many when she said, 'How could I, after such a supper?' Before leaving, the neighbours all congratulated Mr and Mrs Wolfe, and expressed the hope that their barns might be full and plenteous with all manner of stores, and that health and happiness would continue to be their lot. Samuel Wolfe, at the age of seventy-four, died on January 27, 1910; he left his widow, and three sons: Joseph, Samuel Jr., and Harry.

In 1929, John Wolfe, the remaining brother of the three, at the age of eighty-four was still living in their father's original homestead house on what was then called the Wolfe Road. His wife, formerly Sarah Patterson, had died in 1924, but he had three sons still living: Ollie, of Cooksville; Albert, of Streetsville; and John, at home with him.

John Wolfe had never entered into political life but was, for twenty years, Tax Collector of Toronto Township. Today, the old Wolfe Lane is now Wolfedale Road, in Mississauga.

TURPEL'S MARKET:

Charles Turpel married Mildred Rutledge, of Cooksville, in 1910 and they moved to a small farm which fronted on the north side of the Dundas Highway, a short distance east of the Centre Road. On this farm, they had an orchard and a good plot of ground for growing vegetables and, as did many other people of the time, they opened a little stand near their house to sell their produce. They put out baskets of apples, plums, cherries, strawberries, and whatever vegetables they grew, in season.

After the highway was paved and numbers of people began driving out from the city in their cars, passing through Cooksville, the great thing was to have refreshments ready for them; and Charlie Turpel put up an ice cream stand to sell ice cream cones. Later, he turned this into a refreshment booth, and sold chocolate bars as well. He improved the stand where he displayed his market garden goods, and set out flowers in pots for the city people to buy and take home with them.

The market bearing their name grew, until the Turpels themselves could not supply enough produce to satisfy their customers. They began to buy from the larger farms in the township, such as Richard Guthrie Sr.'s farm at Dixie, and Austin Robinson's farm closer down to the Lakeshore Road; these farmers supplied Turpel's Market with asparagus, cherries, strawberries and raspberries, as well as other vegetables. One person who knew the Market well, from before he started school in the late 1920s, was young Richard Guthrie, whose mother worked there occasionally during the busy periods.

The Women's Institute began having Bake Sales at Turpel's Market at the end of April, 1929, and invited everyone to come. Mr Guthrie recalls that Pete King worked and boarded there, and drove a Model A Ford truck around to pick up the extra fruit and produce during the early 1930s.

The Market was open from spring until fall, and each weekend many carloads of people arrived, parking their cars by the sides of the highway and buying the fruits and vegetables now spread out, not only on the lawn but all over the sidewalk as well. The place seemed like a county fair, with all the accompanying hubbub.

Charles Turpel bought a 1937 Ford V8 two-ton truck and began driving to West Toronto to sell local produce and pick up other fruits and vegetables for re-sale. Since the highway was quite narrow then, with only two lanes, the Market seemed to create a roadblock and

The Port Credit News, June 3, 1927

Cooksville Market. (Photo: Region of Peel Archives, 81.3398M N166-3)

became a real menace for cars trying to get through Cooksville. People going out on a summer evening had to be very careful on their walks past the market, to avoid setting a foot down in one of the baskets of peaches or tomatoes, or to keep themselves from tripping over a big squash which had been knocked, or had rolled, off a pile of them near the corner of the lot.

Turpel's Market, known by people from out of town as 'the Cooksville Market,' was well-patronized by everyone driving along Dundas Street. However, when the road was finally widened to four lanes the Market had to be closed, and the building which had been erected beside Turpel's home was rented out to other people, for other uses.

Chapter 33: The Storm

ON MONDAY, JUNE 25, 1923, the polling booth for Cooksville, in the Provincial Election, was located in the Township Hall. The workers at the polls spent an enjoyable day, dealing with the routine work in the most friendly way, with no undue party feelings or prejudices seemingly entered into by anyone coming into the Hall. Everything went forward quietly, with less than sixty per cent of the electors coming to cast their ballots, the usual Conservative victory being anticipated in Cooksville.

The polling officers in charge of the voting that day were P. G. Lamphier, Returning Officer, and D. McKendry, Polling Clerk; their cars stood parked near the wall of the building, awaiting the completion of the counting of the ballots. It was a typical voting day in Cooksville, with the polls due to be closed at six o'clock.

At about ten minutes before the hour of six, black clouds could be seen in the sky, followed about five minutes later by sheets of hail and winds like those of a cyclone, which caused everyone in the Hall to scatter and make a mad dash for home. While it lasted, people cowered in their homes, all concern about election results forgotten. After the worst was over, the winds were estimated to have reached a velocity of seventy to eighty miles an hour. The oldest Cooksville inhabitants all agreed that never before had the village and district been visited by such a storm.

One of the oldest landmarks in the village, a huge pine tree with a three-foot trunk, which had stood for scores of years by the front porch

Methodist Church, after the storm, 1923. (Photo: Mississauga
Central Library, Cooksville Album 1)

of the Township Hall, was one of the first things to go; snapped off at its
base, it went crashing down along the roof of the Hall, on top of the
election officers' cars. Mr Lamphier's car body and rear tires were a total
wreck; Mr McKendry's top and windshield were demolished.

The entire right front half of the Methodist Church, and fully two-
thirds of the east side of its roof, were seen, with the return of daylight,
to be removed. Most of the gable of brick work at the front of the
church fell inwards, carrying both the floor of the church and the
ceiling of the basement down upon the basement floor, leaving them
lying in floods of water carried in by the winds. The furnace, chairs,
and benches were crushed to debris. One section of the roof landed in
the berry patch of Robert Hopkins, barely escaping his house; and the
west section landed on the kitchen of Gabriel Ellingham's house, cutting
it completely in two, and wrecking it.

To the east, on Burnhamthorpe Road, Mrs Ellis' home was destroyed. Mrs Ellis herself fainted from the effects of having part of her house removed. Her son picked her up to carry her to shelter, and had only moved a few feet when the chimney came crashing down on the spot where she had fallen. Robert Sherwood's new house, in the process of being erected, was also destroyed; and Thomas McCarthy's drive shed was flattened by the wind.

Charles Lawrence's huge barn, on Hook Avenue, was blown completely down off its eight-foot foundation, as was Mr W. F. B. Rubidge's garage, on the Centre Road; all were destroyed. Other buildings reported to be damaged were the barns owned by Harry Wolfe, William Cooper, and Robert Davidson. The whole district was littered with debris, and thousands of dollars' worth of damage done. Roumegous' Winery had the east end of the roof blown off. The roughcast house adjoining his brick residence was struck by lightning and damaged.

Telephone service was badly interrupted, and several phones were still out of commission days later. The highway, between Ogden (Novar) Street and the Brick Yard, was blocked by eighteen of the sixty-foot poles blown down; these cut off the telephone communications westward.

East of the bridge over the Cooksville Creek, two huge cottonwood trees, blown down in front of Miss Price's property on the highway, tore down hydro wires, thus cutting off lights in all houses and business places at the east end of the village. All traffic going eastward was completely blocked until the trees could be cut up and removed.

In both Pinkney's and Cliffe's groves, huge pines and beechwoods were uprooted and broken. Orchards suffered great havoc, as well, where trees were also uprooted, and all plum trees were stripped of fruit; those on the farms of Leslie Pallett, George May, Rupert Pickett, Joseph Page, and John E. Bell were badly hit. Scarcely any yard or orchard escaped the terrific gales, accompanied by lightning and downpours of rain. Charles Turpel's loss in tomatoes and melons, due to hail, was heavy.

The loss from damages could not be readily calculated, but was thought to add up to an amount of six figures; worse, there was no insurance against wind damage. The Township Council had been scheduled to meet in the Council Chambers on the following Saturday, to transact considerable business, but owing to the destruction, and no lights, the meeting had to be postponed.

On Thursday, June 28th, *The Brampton Conservator*, regarding the election, which no one in Cooksville had even been able to think about, offered congratulations to the winner, and likewise to the defeated. It stated: 'It was a real wild black night, and whether it came as a celebration of Drury's outgoing, or Ferguson's incoming, it will live long in the memory of young and old, being the worst, and we hope the last, to visit Cooksville and district.'

On July 16, 1923, the Honourable G. Howard Ferguson was sworn in as Premier of Ontario.

Chapter 34: The Volunteer Fire Brigade

AT THE BEGINNING OF JUNE, 1936, after an unsuccessful appeal to the Township Council, the Cooksville Business Men's Association bought their own fire engine, at Woodstock. The members of the committee who made the actual purchase were Paul Sayers, Ed. Moisey, Jack Braithwaite, and George Bowers. The truck was old, but they considered it sufficient for their purpose; and the first thing they bought for it was a new siren, at a cost of forty dollars.

The reason for buying the fire truck was because, when a fire started in Cooksville, a call had to be put in to the Port Credit Fire Brigade, and by the time these volunteer firemen could assemble and drive the three miles to Cooksville, the fire had usually made too much headway to be quelled. With fire fighting equipment always ready at the four corners, Cooksville volunteers could get to the site of a fire quickly and could probably, with only the 100 gallons of chemical on the truck, put an end to it before it razed a building to the ground.

A volunteer brigade was formed by the business men of the village, which was no problem. The difficulty was in the raising of the money to pay for the new machine; the Business Men's Association had already put up quite a sum, and therefore decided to hold a public subscription to pay off the balance.

The truck itself, which was said to be probably the first of such apparatus in Peel County purchased by other than a municipality, arrived on a Tuesday morning in June. The sight of a fire engine all their own attracted a crowd, to comment on it and criticize. Some people declared it, on sight, to be too small; but others strongly expressed the opinion that 'She's a dandy!'

Cooksville's First Fire Truck, 1926. (Photo: Lex Schrag (*The Evening Telegram*), Mississauga Central Library Collection)
L TO R: B. I. Bickle Sr., who delivered the machine; William Lennard, Jack Braithwaite, G.W. Henderson, and James Halsey, of the Business Men's Association.

The Business Men agreed that it would not, perhaps, stop a three-alarm fire; still, they had great faith in their ability to arrive at the fires 'in short order,' and they intended to do just that.

The following week, *The Port Credit News* reported that, since no fires had yet occurred, the Cooksville volunteer firemen had taken the new truck out for a practice run, and pointed the hose at an imaginary target. They did not make use of the chemicals because of their high cost, but each man familiarized himself with the proper procedure in case they received a call.

The call came in mid-July, in the shape of a grass fire in a field on the farm of M. Johnston, of Britannia. Just to make sure the run was properly accomplished, Charles Copeland, one of the Business Men, drove his car along behind the truck, in order to push it ahead faster. A tractor and buckets of water were used to draw a furrow around the burning grass, and two hay stacks and the fencing were saved. Many of the Cooksville firemen were dressed in gala attire, as they had been in the midst of getting ready to attend the Orange Parade, at Brampton.

The following month, they were put to the test when a chicken house, 50 by 14 feet in area, owned by Frank Brogna, of Cooksville, was partly destroyed by fire at around 9.30 p.m. Through the quick action of the Cooksville Volunteer Fire Brigade, the loss was not as heavy as it might have been. Three tanks of chemicals had to be used before the fire was checked; however, the firemen were successful in rescuing all the fowl.

Cooksville people were proud of their new Fire Brigade. That week, a writer signing himself only as 'Dick' submitted to *The Port Credit News*, of August 19th, 1936, the following parody of a well-known poem:

'The boy stood on the burning roof
When all but he had fled.
The flames, the smoke, and dirty soot
Went whirling round his head.
Yet beautiful and brave he stood
And never called for aid.
Because he heard the siren
Of the Cooksville Fire Brigade.'

Chapter 35: 1st Cooksville Scouts and Guides

IN JANUARY, 1930, a movement to establish a Troop of Boy Scouts in Cooksville came to a standstill because, although a splendid troop headquarters was available and a group of the best citizens stood ready to back up the organization, Provincial Headquarters insisted that someone must first be found to take active leadership of the Troop before organizing the boys. Accordingly, J. M. Vale and Gordon B. Jackson asked for suggestions from citizens who might know of suitable leaders.

In February, the Annual Conference of Scoutmasters was held in St. Catharines, when representatives of troops and associations from all over Ontario gathered to discuss the many problems that confronted the leaders of boys and young men. Toronto sent a bus load of representatives, and among them were Lakeview's Reverend A. H. Ferry and Port Credit's veteran Scouter S. M. Hayes. Three hundred and forty men and women debated, discussed, and listened, for the good of

288

Scouting in Ontario. A Model Troop Meeting, an Ideal Scout Headquarters, and a Proper Court of Honour were demonstrated, and talks were given on the Troop Committee and its functions, what it should and should not do.

Following this conference, by April 11, 1930, a newly-formed Scout Troop at Cooksville was getting away to a good start, with S. A. Herd acting as Scoutmaster. The Patrol Leaders, Don Woodall and Arnold Varley, were being trained so that everything would be in good order when a large number of boys started to study the Scout work.

An illustrated lecture was held in the Orange Hall on April 15th, under the auspices of the new Troop, in charge of Scoutmaster Arthur Herd. Field Secretary E. T. Jones showed pictures of the Jamboree held in the Old Country the summer before, when Boy Scouts from all over the British Empire were represented.

On November 9, 1930, the 1st Cooksville Troop of Boy Scouts attended service in Cooksville United Church. They met at the Orange Hall and paraded to the church under the leadership of Scoutmaster Arthur Herd. Assistant Scoutmaster Charles Merritt carried the Scout flag and, during the service, two Scouts, Eric Jones and Allan Christie, placed a wreath on a cross in the church. The Reverend C. Sinclair Jones preached the sermon, which was most appropriate for the day, and took as his text: 'Ye are not your own, ye are bought with a price.' Many families attended the service.

At the beginning of November, the 1st Cooksville Troop received their Charter; and their regular meeting on Friday, November 14, took the form of a Social Evening, to which the parents of the boys were invited. The boys opened the programme by singing 'The Land of the Maples,' followed by 'All the Girl Guides Love a Boy Scout.'

Piano selection – Donald Woodall
Reading – Leslie Riva
Recitation – J. Jamieson, Jr.
Piano Selection – Arnold Varley
Reading – Clarence Hepton.

Mr J. M. Vale, of Port Credit, presented the Charter to Mr G. B. Jackson, Chairman of the Cooksville Scout Committee. Mr Frank Irwin, Commissioner of Boy Scouts, gave a very interesting and instructive address.

A pleasant surprise of the evening to the Scouts was the presenting of the Union Jack and staff, complete, donated by the Cooksville

Women's Institute. The President, Mrs J. Cunningham, gave a short address in making the presentation, expressing the Institute's good wishes and interest in the Scout movement. Mr Gordon B. Jackson received the Flag on behalf of the boys, thanking the ladies for their interest, and presenting it to Scoutmaster Arthur Herd.

The following month, on December 12, 1930, the 1st Cooksville Troop Girl Guides was organized, and held its first enrollment in February, 1931. The following Guides passed the Tenderfoot Test and received their badges from Captain L. Merritt, assisted by Lieutenant Trachsler:

Doris Kitney, Ena Allen, Pauline Trachsler, Gladys Kitney, Hilda Varley, Kathleen Harrison, and Vina Bailey. They were introduced by Patrol Leaders Eleanor McKay and Doris Kitney.

At that meeting, the Cooksville Guides expressed their deep regret at the death of Mrs Parsons, Grand Organizer, of Ontario.

On February 15th, the 1st Cooksville Troop Boy Scouts and 1st Cooksville Girl Guides joined with the Port Credit Scouts and attended church service at Middle Road School. The Scout Committee thanked Messrs. Braithwaite, Allen, and Irwin for providing transportation for the boys and girls.

At the beginning of March, Doris McKee and Genevieve Gridelet were enrolled in Guides. At the first of May, the 1st Cooksville Scout Troop dedicated their flag and colours, with the Reverend Sinclair Jones, their Chaplain, and a large number of Scouts, Cubs, and Guides in attendance.

In June, 1931, two Girl Guides, Pauline Trachsler and Doris Kitney, passed the Second Class Test; and Lillie Merritt and Mary Trachsler received their Captain's and Lieutenant's Warrant Pins.

The Scouts and Guides together held a Masquerade, in November, 1931, to which they invited the Troops and Companies from Port Credit and Lorne Park. The party was a big success and everyone had a splendid time, with programme as follows: General Post, Dance, Grand March, Ham and Eggs, Blindman's Buff, Dance, Musical Chairs, Dance (Duke of York), Bob-apple, and Forfeits.

The winners of the Grand March costumes were:
Brownie (fancy) – Jean Varley, Cooksville
Cub (fancy) – R. Boyd, Port Credit
Guide (original) – Olive Miles, Cooksville
Guide (comic) – Patricia Kemerer, Port Credit

Scout (original) – D. Woodall, Cooksville
Scout (comic) – R. Knott, Port Credit
Guide (fancy) – Verna Brown, Port Credit
Best Pair – Edna Kee and John Miles, Cooksville
Fancy Scout – H. Warner, Port Credit

It was a difficult task for the judges to decide the winners, as the costumes were all so good.

At a December meeting of the Scouts, in 1931, Clarence Hepton got his Tenderfoot Badge. Five Cubs received their Star Test Badges: C. Harris, Friend Garbutt, Bob Roffey, Everett Hepton, and Austin Hepton. Afterwards, games were played and a sing song enjoyed.

That December, the Guides held a Social and invited their parents. Evelyn Garbutt and Mary McDonald were enrolled. The Company sold candy, and had songs and recitations around the campfire. The following Badges were presented:

Year Star Badges – Eleanor McKay, Pauline Trachsler,
Kathleen Harrison, Doris McKee, Hilda Varley, Jean
Goldthorpe, Mary Trachsler
2nd Class Badge – Kathleen Harrison
Thrift Badge   – Kathleen Harrison, Doris McKee
Cyclist Badge – Doris McKee, Pauline Trachsler
Homemaker and Laundress Badge – Doris McKee
Child Nurse Badge, Domestic Service Badge, Friend to Animals,
and Pathfinder Badge – all were won by Pauline Trachsler,
Doris McKee, and Kathleen Harrison.

April of 1932 saw meetings being held in the Town Hall, led by the Guides' new Captain, Miss Mary Trachsler. On one Friday evening, the full Company had a very busy time, when everybody was ordering tickets to sell for the Concert and Dance to be held on April 29th, in the Cooksville Town Hall, under the auspices of the Girl Guides. The entertainment was to be put on by a well-known Company from Toronto, with admission fees set at 25 cents for Adults, Children 15 cents.

After the excitement over the tickets had subsided, they had a Relay race, and an Observation game. Both were won by the Honesty Patrol and, as a result, their Monkey climbed a step up the ladder. They were then in the lead, with the Poppy Patrol second; however, it was hoped that the Violets would waken with the coming of spring. After the games, the girls spent some time on their Wicker Work, and learned some new songs.

In December, the 1st Cooksville Scouts had Inspection Night, which included Scout work and games. Dr Brayley inspected the boys for their First Aid; and the Crow Patrol won the Silver Cup.

In April, 1933, the Scout Troop went on a long Hike with Port Credit, Long Branch, and Toronto Scouts.

The following year, in January of 1934, the Guides were holding their meetings in the school, with Mrs H. R. Miles having charge of the Company, assisted by Mrs Herd. The Scouts presented Mr Herd, their retiring Scoutmaster, with a picture of Lord Baden-Powell, Founder of the Boys Scouts Association, after which Donald Woodall, Troop Leader, read a suitable address.

In April, 1934, the Guides went to a Rally in Toronto; and the Brownies were now having meetings in the Town Hall. At the beginning of November, that year, an English Girl Guide came to visit them at their meeting and showed them new games. Jean and Bertha McKay passed Tenderfoot, and on November 30, they were made Guides.

In February, 1935, sixteen Guides of the Cooksville Company, their Captain, Mrs Miles, and Lieutenant, Mrs A. Herd, visited the Streetsville Company on a Friday evening. Mr Jack Walterhouse lent his truck, and Mr C. Garbutt drove the Guides to Streetsville. On the way, they sang Guide songs and, on arriving at the Sunday School of Streetsville United Church, were made very welcome by the Captain and the Lieutenant of that Company, as well as by the Guides. Games and competitions were enjoyed, and later a hot supper was served. Everyone agreed that it was a real evening of fun, and the Cooksville Company thanked Mr Walterhouse and Mr Garbutt for assisting them with transportation.

At a meeting in April, Jean Goldthorpe, Bessie Kee, Betty Goldthorpe, Pauline Trachsler, and Patsy Herd received their First Year Service Stars. In May, Hilda Varley received her 4-Year Service Star; Vera and Mildred Varley, each, their 3-Year Service Stars. In December, the Guides were still meeting in the school, when Margaret Goldthorpe and Faith Roy passed Tenderfoot Tests.

At the Field Day for Guides, held in Port Credit at the beginning of June, 1936, Cooksville won the Silver Cup. That summer, twenty Guides with their Captain, Mrs Miles, and Lieutenant, Mrs Herd, went to Centre Island; Mr Thomas drove them to the Toronto docks in his truck. At the end of October, 1936, the 1st Cooksville Girl Guides received their new Scarves of red, yellow and green plaid. They closed their meeting with the Guide Prayer and Taps, followed by the 'Electric Squeeze,' before leaving for home.

Over the years, the Scouts, Guides, Cubs, and Brownies of Cooksville went on hikes, held meetings in the open, studied Morse Code, learned Knots, played baseball, and went swimming in the old Cooksville Swimming Hole; they held Wiener Roasts on the property behind Mrs Price's home, with big bonfires and plenty of wieners and buns, and marshmallows for toasting; they received instruction in First Aid, given by Dr L. G. Brayley; they marched in Church and Armistice Day Parades; they held Apple Days, and Do-Nut Days, and ran Booths at the Cooksville Fall Fair.

For five years, Scouts and Guides were putting on concerts, selling light bulbs, chocolate bars and other articles, and seeking donations for the construction of a Hut to be used by all of the 1st Cooksville Scouts, Guides, Cubs and Brownies, but there was a general apathy towards this project until, by 1950, the part-time facilities available for meetings were sufficient to allow only a small number of the children of the growing community to take part. Up until then, the United Church had sponsored the group, and paid rent on a small building on the fair grounds for their meetings.

However, at the beginning of May, Group Committee Chairman James A. Smith was assured that members of the Toronto Township Council, Cooksville Agricultural Society, Cooksville Business Men's

The Port Credit Weekly, May 18, 1950

1) Scout, Gordon McKendry 2) Cub, Albert Russell 3) Guide, Betty Cantelon 4) Brownie, Beverly Scriver. (*The Port Credit Weekly*, May 18, 1950)

'The Cooksville Boy Scout and Girl Guide Hut' nearing completion.
(*The Port Credit Weekly*, June 21, 1951

Association, the Police Department, the Fire Brigade, Cooksville schools
and local industry would act as patrons of the Fund and a new building
would be erected on land donated by the Cooksville Agricultural
Society, located behind the Municipal Hall.

The objective of the Fund, to be raised by subscription, was $6,000,
and by the middle of June, 1951, the building to be known as 'The
Cooksville Boy Scout and Girl Guide Hut,' was well under way.

* * *

Today, there is a 1st Cooksville Scouts Hall, located at 80 King Street
West.

Chapter 36: News and Views

Items of interest to Cooksville people, taken from *The Brampton Times, The
Brampton Conservator, The Streetsville Review, The Port Credit News,* and *The Port
Credit Weekly:*

October 28, 1848
STRAYED – From Romain's Grist Mill, near Cooksville, on the 1st
October last, a brown cow, with horns rather crooked, long tail, and a
white stripe on her right hind leg.

Any person giving information or delivering her to Robert Chisholm, Cooksville, or to the subscriber, will be suitably rewarded.
    – Peter Chisholm.

January 26, 1877
Mr John Weeks, of Cooksville, who has for some time owned and driven the stages running between here and Toronto has sold out to Mr Graham, who will commence driving on February 1st.

March 10, 1877
Cooksville has become quite an important village of late. We have two weekly papers, *The Tattler* and *The Hornet*, published in the village, and although Cooksville is looked upon as such a quiet dull little place, I doubt if any other village in the county can sport two weekly newspapers.

May 19, 1892
Mr Charles Schiller, of Cooksville, was Mouth Organ Soloist at the Temperance Meeting in Streetsville.

June 19, 1892
Dundas Street is becoming a favourite run for the bicyclists of Toronto. Often during the week, and nearly every Saturday afternoon, many wheel here for supper and Cooksville ozone.
    Thirty dined at the Cooksville House on Saturday.

June 3, 1898
The Morley House has undergone repairs and painting, which makes it more and more attractive. It is no unusual thing to see one hundred cyclists sit down to dinner in this modern, respectable and well-equipped hostelry. Frank Morley runs a good house.

July 8, 1898
Miss Maud Readman, of Cooksville, now gives lessons on piano and organ.

February 23, 1899
Mr J. C. Eaton, Toronto, who was passing through this village on Saturday last with his gasoline carriage, stopped at the Morley House for the day.

May 19, 1899
Eaton's and Simpson's delivering to Cooksville; they visit three times weekly, and monopolize the business.

May 3, 1900
Mrs Mary Harding, who for many years kept the toll gate between Cooksville and Port Credit, died on Thursday last, April 25, at the age of 74 years.

August 20, 1903
The number of automobiles that pass here is increasing daily. There were 10 in one day, not long since.

Perhaps the reason for this is that there is a repair shop in Dixie. Nothing like being up-to-date.

February 25, 1904
Cooksville Public Library is growing very rapidly. Already over 50 members have joined the library, which is becoming very popular.

August 10, 1905
Sgt. Schiller attended the annual meeting of the Governor General's Body Guards, Sergeants' Mess, in Toronto, on Tues., and was elected to the Board of Management for 1905-1906.

March 28, 1907
The large iron smokestack on Walterhouse's saw mill on the back street of the village was blown down during Tuesday's fierce gale.

Those living in the neighbourhood were considerably startled by the noise it made in its fall.

November 7, 1907
The pupils of Cooksville Public School will hold a concert in the Town Hall on the evening of Feb. 21, 1908.

A grand musical and literary programme consisting of songs, recitations, comic dialogues, and music by mouth organ Quartette will be rendered.

Proceeds to be applied to the purchase of books for the School Library. Admission: adults, 20 cents; children not scholars of the school, 10 cents.

April 29, 1909
A travelling Medicine Co. advertises to give free entertainment here in the Township Hall Friday evening next.

August 26, 1909
More than ordinary attention is being given to the action of the automobilists, and it will not be surprising if a number of convictions follow the fast driving which is reported.

Jack Johnston, the famous pugilist, went along Dundas Street at a rate approaching 50 miles an hour. It is said that a Toronto gentleman made nearly as fast time in a recent journey through the village.

Last Saturday, in three hours, forty-seven automobiles crossed the Centre Road. Many of them were going at a higher rate of speed than the law permits.

There is no doubt that more stringent legislation will be asked for at the next session of the Legislature.

February 17, 1910
An Oyster Supper under the auspices of the Cooksville Lodge No. 238 AOUW was held on Monday evening in the Pharmacy Hall where a large number of members and their friends enjoyed a social and pleasant evening.

December 1, 1910
Mr Alfred Scott, of Burnhamthorpe, is this week taking possession of the general store business carried on for the past twenty years here by Mr George McClelland, who has removed to his new house on the Centre Road.

June 1, 1911
The first application of oil on Dundas Street has been made and looks very satisfactory.

Although the roads are very dry, the dust has been settled in the portion covered. Dundas Street, from Islington to Erindale, will all be oiled.

May 16, 1912
Cooksville can boast of a living centenarian who is yet hale and hearty, can eat three meals every day and regularly smoke his pipe, although he

says it makes him a little dizzy now. He was 100 years of age on the 27th day of April last. He is Mr James Allcock.

May 30, 1912
Mr Geo. Bowers, of the Cooksville House, has exchanged his auto for a new McLaughlin up-to-date touring car of 60 horse power.

It is a self-starter, electric head and rear lights, all generated within itself.

It can either be controlled to a snail's pace or cover 75 miles an hour, which satisfies George.

May 29, 1913
A scratch baseball team went up from here to Streetsville on Saturday, Victoria Day, and succeeded in doing up the team there by the score of 10 to 8. Some of those who went up were in a game for the first time. What do you think of that?

July 31, 1913
Cooksville is about the only unincorporated village that boasts a pool room and a lady barber.

There are a lot of good things about Cooksville that need no enumeration.

March 26, 1914
SPRING – It is here! How nice to see the boys playing marbles and the girls with their ropes once more. Everybody's in good humour once more.

Pa says there's no more coal to buy and he wears a smile from ear to ear. The other day it got back so far I thot his head would drop right off. Yes, and sap's runnin'. The bunch that were back in the bush the other day say the flowers are growing in the sunny places.

But it is strange to see the number of cameras around. Nothing can compare with the fun anyone can get out of one at such small expense. The month of roses (and weddings) is only 66 days off.

Can you tell me why we look forward to summer with such eagerness, for when those hot days do come, we want the winter back.

April 16, 1914
Mr S. E. Harris is putting in a new plate glass front, and fitting up his

299

The Brampton Conservator,
August 19, 1915

premises on Dundas Street for the purpose of opening up a new General Store.

June 22, 1916
A rather novel procession went through the village the other day, Mr Jos. Wolfe in his pony outfit driving a pig at the end of a long line. He experienced some difficulty in avoiding the motor cars but succeeded, by signal, in getting the right of way.

April 5, 1917
We believe several new cars have come to the village lately. Mr Jno. E. Bell Jr. has a new Chevrolet; and Messrs. Alex Thomas and Fred Death have new Grey Dorts. Evidently market garden prospects are apparently bright.

September 19, 1918
Miss Eva Wolfe, Cooksville, won first prize in the ladies driving contest at Weston Fair last Saturday.
    There was plenty of competition but Miss Wolfe knows how to handle a horse and won the ribbon easily.

August 26, 1920
The first School Fair for the County of Peel will be held at Cooksville on Sept. 13, 1920.

October 27, 1921
Maple leaves from this village will put the name of Cooksville before the eyes of thousands of Westerners next week, when a Hallowe'en display in one of Regina's leading store windows bearing the inscription 'from Cooksville, Ont.' will gladden the eyes of many former old and young Easterners, as well as those of Western birth.

The Brampton Conservator, May 18, 1922

April 27, 1922

The first Durant Car to adorn the streets as a locally owned one arrived here Saturday, W. J. Turner & Sons having the District agency for its sale.

On Monday morning, a demonstration was given of its hill climbing capabilities, and some real stunts were demonstrated. A stop was made in the centre of the steep Erindale hill, where the car was turned and started up on second gear, and before the top was reached, was hitting it off at 35 miles.

All the hills around here were tried and the performance was astounding. That a new Durant will have a big sale is assured.

W. J. Turner and Sons will soon start the erection of a splendid new Garage and Salesroom on their Dundas Street property.

Cooksville Motors, north side Dundas Street, east of Hurontario.
(Photo: Region of Peel Archives, Bleakley Collection 89.0009 M
N418-29)

Crofton Villa, Dundas Street, east of Hurontario. (Photo:
Mississauga Central Library, Cooksville School Collection F 149)

May 25, 1922
The new Ice Cream and Refreshment Stand built by M. Crofton has been opened, and is one of the finest in the district. It is a very attractive interior that greets the eye as the door is entered, the decorations and fixtures being of the latest type. Seats 36 people.

July 27, 1922
The Ontario Government's Auto Special, carrying 3 milch goats and the slogan on banners, 'Buy a Milking Goat,' visited town last Friday to present the virtues and values of goat's milk.

April 26, 1923
Victor Hepton has opened a Bicycle Shop on Ogden Street, in front of the Township Hall property.

November 26, 1925
Mrs R. Denison is starting a Fancy Goods and Notions Store at her residence, in Cooksville.

The Port Credit News,
December 18, 1931

The Port Credit News,
October 7, 1927

The Brampton Conservator,
August 19, 1915

Royal Bank, southwest corner Dundas and Hurontario Streets.
(Photo: Mississauga Central Library, Cooksville School Collection
F204)

March 25, 1926
The Cooksville barber, G. Hadlow, is moving his shop on April 1st to
the building adjacent to Fullwood's Bakery, and formerly a Barber Shop.

   These premises are being neatly renovated, and Mr Hadlow plans to
install 2 chairs and employ a second man.

June 24, 1926
Dr Ed. Hopkins' horse 'Jack Canuck' figured in the prize money in two
recent races, taking first at New Hamburg, and second at Tottenham.

June 24, 1927
Do you remember – When women did not powder, paint, smoke, play
poker, or do the Charleston? When the butcher gave away liver for the
cat, and treated the kids to bologna? When eggs were 3 dozen for a
quarter, round steak 3 pounds for 25 cents, and milk 5 cents a quart?

Progress

SOUND business prin-
ciples and a policy of
gradual expansion have
marked the steady growth of
this Bank for over fifty years.

   Today, one of the largest
and strongest banks in the
world, it serves every phase
of business and private
life at home, and is tak-
ing a leading part in the
expansion of trade in
foreign markets.

**The Royal Bank
of Canada**
COOKSVILLE, ONT.
W. G. DULMAGE
MANAGER

The Port Credit News,
June 24, 1927

June 24, 1927
One of the events in connection with the Diamond Jubilee in the village
of Cooksville, will be the opening of the new building of the Royal Bank
of Canada.

It is located on the corner of the junction of the Brampton and
Dundas Highways, It is built of stone, and makes a very handsome
appearance. There are Vaults and Safety Deposit Boxes located in the
new building.

W. G. Dulmage is the Manager of the Bank, and his Staff consists of:
Thomas Ault, Teller; Miss V. E. Cunningham, Ledgerkeeper; and K. J.
Baird, Junior.

July 14, 1928
House and lot on Dundas Street, at entrance to Fair Grounds, sold to
James Hartsock, who will use land to open a Fruit Market. Cooksville,
at present, has 3 Markets.

July 25, 1929
Miss Clara Ezard, Cooksville, won the Warden's Medal for obtaining the
highest marks in Peel County, at the recent High School Entrance
Examinations.

November 7, 1929
Clara Hartsock was chief ghost at the Hallowe'en Party at the
Continuation School.

February 13, 1930
Carnival Day for the youngsters of Cooksville Public and Continuation
Schools will have a particularly large mark for remembrance. Nearly 200
boys and girls from the five rooms took to the ice, many of them in
pretty, or striking, costumes.

April 3, 1930
Jim Allen, of Cooksville, won a Gold Medal at Kingston last week, and
the honour of being Champion Middleweight Wrestler of Ontario.

August 28, 1931
'THE SAUCY SUE' – The Saucy Sue is not a lake craft that slipped her
moorings and got away off up on Dundas Street. She is a bona fide craft

306

'The Saucy Sue'. (*The Port Credit News*, August 28, 1931)

The Port Credit Weekly, December 7, 1950

sailing on the high tide of business, and moored alongside Dundas Street to take on cargo and passengers.

It is surprising how many of the latter have been taking a cruise on the pleasant summer nights since 'The Saucy Sue' came to anchor, during the latter part of June.

'Bacon and a Bun,' with a cup of tea, on the upper deck in the shadow of the wheel house, is a delightful relaxation after a day in town or city. The skipper and the crew serve this and many other equally appetizing dishes.

Before 'The Saucy Sue' is laid up for the winter, get aboard and have a lunch, hear the music, dance, and form the habit in anticipation of next season.

March 22, 1933
There has been a great demand for the 4-cent bread which is being sold by McCord Bros. and William Copeland & Son, Cooksville.

March 28, 1934
Mr E. Korn to erect Service Station on Dundas Street.

June 24, 1936
Cooksville Business Men erected a 30-foot flag pole near the intersection of Centre Road and Dundas, in honour of the King's birthday.

August 19, 1936
There is no corner in Peel where as many automobiles cross, passing east and west and north and south, as the Cooksville Corner. Literally thousands pass every day. There is a stop sign on the Centre Road and it is partially observed, but there is danger every hour.

February 17, 1949
West of Korn's Garage, about a quarter of a mile, and across from the Cooksville Florist, West End Motors is being erected.

Frank Jugovich, the owner, is not sure when he will be open for business, but is working diligently to get the new structure completed. It will also consist of living quarters; the home is built on the east end of the building, and when we visited, the interior work was progressing rapidly.

* * *

From Roy's Mother's Cookbook:

Pumpkin Marmalade
(written by hand, c. 1920)

6 dippers pumpkin, cut fine
6 dippers sugar
6 oranges sliced, peel and all together

Let stand over night with sugar on like citron; put on to cook in the morning; boil hard till you think done; put in a little salt. When almost done, if you think 6 dippers of sugar is too much, put in less. I think it is.

Thoughts of Today

WHEN I WAS NINE and lived on Dundas Street near the four corners
of Cooksville, I would spend much time walking back and forth on the
sidewalk in front of the Bakery Shop a few doors east of our house,
looking in through the windows at all the delightful cakes and tarts and
Melton Mowbray pies put out on trays by Harry Fullwood, the baker.
Such delicious cooking smells came out through the shining glass
windows and surrounded you that, when you finally went inside the
shop, it was twice as hard to make up your mind which to buy. There
were red cocoanut-covered Metropolitans, butter tarts, and lemon tarts
with puff pastry – usually I picked out the lemon ones and, very
carefully, he would place them in a small brown paper bag.

I did not know then, as I do now, that Harry Fullwood was a Gold
Medallist who held the highest baking honours in England, granted him
in competition in London, and that he had even invented a new dainty
in food products called a Souffle, which caused big American bakery
men to come all the way from Boston to buy his patented recipe. I had
no idea then that I was eating, on our back porch on Dundas Street,
world champion lemon tarts, at two for a dime.

If you look for Fullwood's Model Bakery now, you will never find a
sign of it. It has long since passed away, like the village itself.

However, a short time ago I spent some pleasant moments walking
back and forth, peering in through the windows of another bakery shop.
It, also, was within sight of the four corners, standing just a short
distance south of where the old Cooksville Fair Grounds used to be; and
there before me were spread out trays of cakes and tarts of many
flavours and shapes – chocolate brownies, rounds of double shortbreads
joined together with jam coming out of round holes in their centres, and
butter tarts. Yes, the butter tarts looked somewhat like those of the
olden days, with all creamy fillings and lots of raisins, except that
Fullwood's always had little bits of cake on the tops of them.

I went straight in, and chose two each of the shortbreads with the
jam, the cookies, and the butter tarts; and when the lady in the shop
looked down at them where I had set them on a little styrofoam tray, she
said to me: 'If you buy three of the butter tarts it is better; they cost less
each.' And when I went and brought another she put it with the rest,
picked up the white tray and set it down inside a large brown paper bag,
right-side up on the bottom.

Canadian Imperial Bank of Commerce Building, northeast corner of
Dundas and Hurontario Streets (where George Bowers' Cooksville
Inn stood). (Photo: Verna Mae Weeks, 1996)

Cooksville Square, northwest corner of Dundas and Hurontario
Streets (where Edway Walterhouse's Revere House stood); in the
background, the southwest corner, south side of Dundas Street, is the
third Royal Bank Building (where Jacob Cook's home once stood).
(Photo: Verna Mae Weeks, 1996)

Store and restaurant, north side of Dundas, half block west of Hurontario Street. LEFT: former Smith's Dry Goods Store. RIGHT: Bombay Palace (where small roughcast house and Pardy Harness Shop stood). (Photo: Verna Mae Weeks, 1996)

Cooksville United Church, on Mimosa Row. (Photo: Verna Mae Weeks, 1996)

Huron Park, looking down from top of hill on Dundas Street (where Callanan's farm was). (Photo: Verna Mae Weeks, 1996)

Ball park, north side of Dundas, opposite Mason Heights Blvd. (where Cooksville Brick and Tile's championship softball teams played – all that remains today of the Cooksville Brick Yard). (Photo: Verna Mae Weeks, 1996)

As I left, I looked back and saw that many people were visiting this modern bakery, called Bun King, picking out their own choices themselves. There was no Mr Fullwood walking about in his big white apron and collecting them up for the customers, but the smells were the same – breads, pies, cakes, of all sizes and shapes – oatmeal date squares, and little gingerbread people dressed up with icing and sprinkles in Christmas-y colours, all over the place. It was a happy looking shop.

Bun King Bakery in plaza on Hurontario Street, south of King Street.
(Photo: Verna Mae Weeks, 1996)

On my way out, I held the door open for an elderly man with a grocery cart loaded down with shopping from the nearby Supermarket, and like myself, carrying his own big brown paper bag. As I headed up towards King Street, I felt, for a short while, that Cooksville had come alive, out of the past, and I was nine again.

Also by Verna Mae Weeks

My Villages of Mississauga, 1986
Lakeview, More Than Just Land (Vol. One), 1990
Lakeview, More Than Just Land (Vol. Two), 1990
Lorne Park, Dreams of Long Ago, 1993
Port Credit, A Glimpse of Other Days, 1995

Books are available by writing to the author –
6509 Glen Erin Drive, Apt. 910, Mississauga, Ontario L5N 2X9.